Elgar Introduction to Theories of Organizational Resilience

ELGAR INTRODUCTIONS TO MANAGEMENT AND
ORGANIZATION THEORY

Series Editors: Cary L. Cooper, *Alliance Manchester Business School, University of Manchester, UK* and Stewart R. Clegg, *School of Management, University of Technology Sydney, Australia*

Elgar Introductions to Management and Organization Theory are stimulating and thoughtful introductions to main theories in management, organizational behaviour and organization studies, expertly written by some of the world's leading scholars. Designed to be accessible yet rigorous, they offer concise and lucid surveys of the key theories in the field.

The aims of the series are two-fold: to pinpoint essential history, and aspects of a particular theory or set of theories, and to offer insights that stimulate critical thinking. The volumes serve as accessible introductions for undergraduate and graduate students coming to the subject for the first time. Importantly, they also develop well-informed, nuanced critiques of the field that will challenge and extend the understanding of advanced students, scholars and policy-makers.

Titles in the series include:

Elgar Introduction to Organizational Discourse Analysis
Marco Berti

Elgar Introduction to Theories of Organizational Resilience
Luca Giustiniano, Stewart R. Clegg, Miguel Pina e Cunha and Arménio Rego

Elgar Introduction to Theories of Organizational Resilience

Luca Giustiniano

Department of Business and Management, LUISS Guido Carli University, Italy

Stewart R. Clegg

University of Technology Sydney, Australia

Miguel Pina e Cunha

Nova School of Business and Economics, Universidade Nova de Lisboa, Portugal

Arménio Rego

Católica Porto Business School, Universidade Católica Portuguesa and Business Research Unit, ISCTE-IUL, Portugal

ELGAR INTRODUCTIONS TO MANAGEMENT AND
ORGANIZATION THEORY

 Edward Elgar
PUBLISHING

Cheltenham, UK • Northampton, MA, USA

Published by
Edward Elgar Publishing Limited
The Lypiatts
15 Lansdown Road
Cheltenham
Glos GL50 2JA
UK

Edward Elgar Publishing, Inc.
William Pratt House
9 Dewey Court
Northampton
Massachusetts 01060
USA

A catalogue record for this book
is available from the British Library

Library of Congress Control Number: 2018954428

This book is available electronically in the **Elgar**online
Business subject collection
DOI 10.4337/9781786437044

ISBN 978 1 78643 703 7 (cased)
ISBN 978 1 78643 704 4 (eBook)

Typeset by Servis Filmsetting Ltd, Stockport, Cheshire

Contents

Acknowledgements

This work was funded by National Funds through FCT – Fundação para a Ciência e Tecnologia under the project Ref. UID/ECO/00124/2013 and by POR Lisboa under the project LISBOA-01-0145-FEDER-007722. The authors are very grateful to Filipa Castanheira, Pedro Neves and Joana Story for their valued contributions to the ideas discussed in this book. The authors are also immensely grateful to Liisa Välikangas, Inês Peixoto and Patrick Reinmoeller for their comments and feedback on parts of the text. The authors would also like to express their gratitude to Martina K. Linnenluecke for kindly sharing with them the data she collected on similar research. Luca Giustiniano is personally grateful to Franca Cantoni for having introduced him to the world of resilience.

1. Introduction: the aim and structure of the book

> Failure is a predictor of success. This is, without question, one of life's great ironies. And it has deep roots into the evolution of life. And it is, without hesitation, simply true.
> (Geher, 2015)

> The challenge is to turn a negative experience into a productive one – that is, to counter adversity with resilience. Psychological resilience is the capacity to respond quickly and constructively to crises. It's a central dynamic in most survival stories, such as those of the shell-shocked individuals and organizations that rallied in the wake of 9/11 and Hurricane Katrina.
> (Margolis and Stoltz, 2010, p. 87)

RESILIENCE: A LARGELY (MIS-)USED TERM?

Organizational contexts are becoming growingly unstable and equivocal, increasingly as likely to host unforeseen and adverse events as to promote those that are uplifting. When crises and tragedies occur, whether the subject concerns an individual recovering from a trauma, an organization attempting to moderate the effect of a scandal, or a community returning to normality after a natural disaster or terrorist attack, they are globally broadcast by multiple media. In each case, the responses are frequently framed in terms of 'resilience'.

What, exactly, resilience denotes is less clear (for example, is it a 'quality' or a process? See Box 1.1 and Box 1.3 below). Resilience has become part of contemporary managerial jargon and, as such, it is often misinterpreted or misused.[1] When authorities and commentators are not quite sure what to say when they report on misadventure and some action or comment is called for, in these contexts, organizational resilience assumes the resonances of a portmanteau term. Under these circumstances being resilient requires a capacity to hold a wide range of meanings in the situations to which it is applied (Watson, 2005).

Apart from its use as cliché, resilience is a complex phenomenon, larger in scope and more powerful in its effects than many other similar terms, such as resistance, reaction or recovery. Generally speaking, resilience

BOX 1.1   RESILIENCE 'BASICS' FROM A NON-ACADEMIC PERSPECTIVE

For a non-academic perspective about resilience, you may consider the 'Resilience' entry on the *Psychology Today* website (https://www.psychologytoday.com/basics/resilience). Resilience is defined as follows:

> Resilience is that ineffable quality that allows some people to be knocked down by life and come back stronger than ever. Rather than letting failure overcome them and drain their resolve, they find a way to rise from the ashes. Psychologists have identified some of the factors that make someone resilient, among them a positive attitude, optimism, the ability to regulate emotions, and the ability to see failure as a form of helpful feedback. Even after misfortune, resilient people are blessed with such an outlook that they are able to change course and soldier on.

On 12 March 2018, texts and posts with suggestive titles (and subtitles) such as the following were found on the *Psychology Today* website:

- 'Super survival of the fittest' ('Ordinary people aren't powerless in the face of tragedy and suffering; many bounce back with resilience. But some do more. They bounce forward and succeed in unimagined ways'; by David B. Feldman and Lee Daniel Kravetz, 9 June 2016).
- 'The Art of Resilience' ('Research on resilience breaks down the myth that a troubled childhood leaves us emotionally crippled as an adult'; by Hara Estroff Marano, 9 June 2016).
- 'Resilience: The Capacity to Rebuild and Grow from Adversity' ('Children learn to succeed by overcoming obstacles'; by Marilyn Price-Mitchell, 14 July 2015).
- 'Challenging Success-via-Failure' ('The Tortoise and the Hype: Yes, failing has its upside; but it's not necessarily the one we valorize'; by Carlin Flora, 26 June 2015).
- 'Failure as the Single Best Marker of Human Success' ('Glorious dandelion fields betray stories of failures. The same is true with us'; by Glenn Geher, 5 September 2014).
- 'On the Benefits of Failure' ('Failure is nothing to be ashamed of!'; by Nigel Barber, 14 February 2013).

The *Psychology Today* website also includes links to several resilience blogs with headings such as *A Widow's Guide to Healing*, *Finding Meaning in Life's Struggles*, *It's OK That You're Not OK*, *Resilient Leadership*, *The Resilient Brain* and *What Doesn't Kill Us*.

connotes capacities to absorb external shocks and to learn from them, while simultaneously preparing for and responding to external jolts, whether as organizations, teams or individuals. Resilience is claimed to be necessary to protect actors and agencies from shocks, crises, scandals and business fiascos that generate fear and create dissonance. Resilient people and organizations get knocked down and get up again, ready to learn from events and to be ready for future challenges: the ultimate connotation of resilience.

In abstract terms, resilience seems to be expressed by Nietzsche's (1889 [1968]) famous aphorism: 'What does not destroy me, makes me stronger'. As remarked by Clair and Dufresne (2007), resilience can also refer to the Mahayana Buddhism expression, 'changing poison [that is, unhappiness and unfortunate circumstances] into medicine' (happiness and improvement). The expression, coined by the scholar Nagarjuna (Jones, 2014), living from the second to the third century, means that whenever we experience loss, failure or suffering, we have the capacity to transform suffering into joy and good fortune.

In contemporary managerial use, 'resilience' is a word with more than a little totemism implicit in it. If not exactly worshipped or deified, it is certainly lauded as something that leaders and managers are expected to nurture and cultivate. In the context of organizations, being resilient suggests that these high priests of resilience, leaders and managers, can turn toxicity and damage from a crisis into 'substantial learning and improved, rather than damaged, performance' (Clair and Dufresne, 2007, p. 63).[2] In practice, resilience entails not only resisting stressors but also learning from them. With this learning, we shall argue, the totemic magic that often attaches to the cult of leadership can be demystified by cultivating means to be resilient, leading to a more enlightened and less enchanted view of the matter.

Taylor (2017) reports several examples of leadership that is not enchanted with its own myths. James Quincey, immediately after having become President and Chief Executive Officer (CEO) of Coca-Cola Co. (on 1 May 2017):

> called upon rank-and-file managers to get beyond the fear of failure that had dogged the company since the 'New Coke' fiasco so many years ago. 'New Coke' was the unofficial name for the reformulated 'new taste of Coca-Cola', which became 'Coke II' in 1992, and was finally discontinued in July 2002. 'If we're not making mistakes,' Quincey insisted, 'we're not trying hard enough.' (p. 3)

The same spirit of not being disenchanted by failure appears to animate successful companies such as Netflix and Amazon, whose CEOs defend the ultimate success of their businesses as being able to learn from failures (Taylor, 2017).

In a paradoxical contrast with the idea of 'failure as a predictor of success', continued success may threaten the pain from which future plenitude can arise, phoenix-like in its resilience. Non-resilient (vulnerable) individuals, teams and organizations enjoying a streak of constant success may be doomed to fail as a result of hubris (see, for example, Box 5.4 in Chapter 5). Successful ventures can easily trigger the hubris of leaders. They may develop overoptimism and overconfidence. They might also push their organizations towards aggressive growth strategies or undertake overpriced acquisitions, triggering leadership failures eventually destroying the organization (Kroll et al., 2000). 'Success is toxic', Nokia's Chairman Risto Siilasmaa explained; failure – or the fear of failure – may be critical for success (*The Economist*, 2018).

If resilience must not be deified, then neither should it be reified. Peremptory statements such as 'Risk is inevitable. Resilience is everything' (Thomson, 2017), the title of an article published in *Forbes* magazine, must be regarded with caution. Much as most studies do, this article emphasizes the 'bright side' of resilience. However, some recent contributions also chart its potentially 'dark side', when 'too much of a good thing can be a bad thing' (Chamorro-Premuzic and Lusk, 2017; Williams et al., 2017). An extreme concern for resilience may induce people to become overly persistent in seeking to achieve unattainable goals. An extreme focus on resilience may make people overly tolerant of adversity, and of unpleasant or counterproductive circumstances such as putting up with boring or demoralizing jobs, toxic bosses or dangerous working conditions. Adam Grant epitomized this idea in his commencement speech at Utah State University, in May 2017 (Box 1.2).

THE STRUCTURE OF THE BOOK

We wrote this book on the basis of a systematic academic literature review (see the Appendix) with which we sought to delineate the diversity, contradictions and conflicts related to the heterogeneity of the disciplinary fields, metaphors and analogies used in discussing resilience. The book explores and illuminates such contradictions, rather than refuting them, in order to provide readers with more solid and perhaps more sceptical grounds for decisions. In articulating organizational resilience, rather than merely reporting what the extant literature has already produced, this book aims to present concepts, offering insights that stimulate critical thinking. We propose two innovative perspectives, namely, a multi-level diffusion model, and a dialectical interpretation of resilience.

Chapter 2 discusses the origins and applications of thinking about

BOX 1.2 IS RESILIENCE LIKE A VITAMIN?

A great philosopher named Aristotle thought virtues were like Vitamin D. Too little of a virtue is bad, but so is too much. He believed that every virtue lies between vices of deficiency and excess. Too little humor is dry; too much is silly. Too little pride makes us meek; too much breeds narcissism. Too much self-restraint leaves you doing homework while your friends are tailgating [i.e., partying in car parks at concerts and sporting events]. Too little self-restraint means you'll really regret eating that fourth Scotsman Dog . . . You need resilience to stay generous on the days when you lose faith in humanity. You need resilience to stay true to yourself on the days when others lose faith in you. And you need resilience to persevere on the days when you lose faith in yourself. But if you're too obsessed with any of these virtues, you might undermine your own resilience. Virtues can be a little bit like vitamins. Vitamins are essential for health. But what if you get more than your body needs? If you take too much Vitamin C, it won't hurt you. If you overdose on Vitamin D, though, it can do serious harm: you could wind up with kidney problems.

This is an excerpt from Adam Grant's commencement speech at Utah State University, May 2017. Do you agree with Grant that to be resilient, one must not be 'too virtuous'? Why? Can you identify any virtue or psychological strength for which more is always better?

resilience in various fields and in various forms of human agglomeration. Resilience can appear in two differentiated ways: as an adaptive or as a reactive response to external jolts and stressors. Chapters 3 and 4 introduce, respectively, individual and collective resilience, on the basis that resilience can be found, understood and nurtured at different levels of aggregation (from individuals to collectivities, from citizens to communities, from employees to teams, from teams to organizations). These chapters elaborate the differences between resilience and other related constructs, emphasizing shared antecedents, processes and effects (see also Luthar, 2006).

Chapter 5 clarifies what characterizes individual, team and organizational resilience, and describes how resilience might be built and nurtured. This chapter also discusses the interplay of resilience at individual, team and organization levels, demonstrating that interdependence between these different levels appears to be a constitutive property of overall organizational resilience. The multi-level model proposed shows how resilience can be spread within organizational settings and beyond, and how, at the same time, collective resilience can make individuals more resilient. Chapter 6 presents a dialectical interpretation emphasizing synthesis between proactive and reactive resilience. Contrasting forces constitute resilience (that is, adaptation versus anticipation, solidity versus adaptability, control versus innovation, and so on): innovative syntheses can occur between contradictory elements. Finally, Chapter 7 paves the way for future research.

Overall, with this book, we aim to reach the following goals:

- To illuminate the meaning of resilience.
- To distinguish it from other concepts with which it shares similarities.
- To articulate a cross-level diffusion model of organizational resilience and its enabling interactive components.
- To present a dialectical understanding of the resilience process, one in which resilience is the synthesis of reaction and adaptation.

As we will discuss, resilience will be presented not as the product of the application of any sort of recipe but rather as the ongoing pursuit of opposite processes of zooming in and out, seeing the macroscopic and the microscopic, being supportive and demanding, caring as much about the future as the present. Resilience is not a steady trait, is not a superpower; instead, it entails a constant process (see Box 1.3 and Box 1.4) of trimming and perfecting by which individuals and organizations (as well as other human collectivities) aim to perfect themselves while knowing that at some points they will fail. Failures are critical for further improving systems.

Resilience does not accept failure passively. While to err is human, being complacent about (preventable) error is unwise. Therefore, resilience uses small errors to prevent big ones; when unavoidable errors do occur, it regards them as events from which to learn, on the principle that we learn from exposure to poisons by building resistance to them. As the phrase attributed to Paracelsus explains, 'the dose makes the poison' (*sola dosis facit venenum*), a central adage of toxicology. Not only toxicology but also business: OutSystems, a global enterprise software company, espouses the following rule (OutSystems, 2013):

> Fail Fast, Fail Cheap. At OutSystems errors are acceptable. How are you going to learn if you don't make mistakes? Just make sure that you learn from those mistakes and that those mistakes do not end up in a major crisis. Fail fast and fail cheaply, but don't be afraid of trying. Be proactive.

Individuals, teams, organizations and communities seeking resilience must be aware that they need to experience small doses of venom to build

BOX 1.3 THE AMERICAN PSYCHOLOGICAL ASSOCIATION (APA) GUIDE FOR RESILIENCE

'The Road to Resilience'

On the American Psychological Association (APA) website, you may find *The Road to Resilience* guide (http://www.apa.org/helpcenter/road-resilience.aspx) where relevant materials are available. Resilience is defined as follows: 'Resilience is the process of adapting well in the face of adversity, trauma, tragedy, threats or significant sources of stress – such as family and relationship problems, serious health problems or workplace and financial stressors. It means "bouncing back" from difficult experiences'.

We suggest that you read the text '10 ways to build resilience' (http://www.apa.org/helpcenter/road-resilience.aspx). The ten ways are as follows: (1) 'Make connections'; (2) 'Avoid seeing crises as insurmountable problems'; (3) 'Accept that change is a part of living'; (4) 'Move toward your goals'; (5) 'Take decisive actions'; (6) 'Look for opportunities for self-discovery'; (7) 'Nurture a positive view of yourself'; (8) 'Keep things in perspective'; (9) 'Maintain a hopeful outlook'; (10) 'Take care of yourself'. Several other texts in the *The Road to Resilience* guide are interesting, especially for non-scholarly audiences.

Resilience – A Process or a Quality?

Note that while *Psychology Today* defines resilience as a quality (Box 1.1), the APA defines it as a process. We suggest that you reflect on the difference between resilience as a process or a quality, thinking about the implications of each definition. Even if we assume that resilience is a quality, a question arises: is it a stable quality or a developable one?

Reflect about the consequences of each assumption. Think about why Caza and Milton (2012, p.895) define resilience at work as 'a positive developmental trajectory characterized by demonstrated competence in the face of, and professional growth after experiences of adversity in the workplace'. What do you think they mean by 'trajectory'? Is it possible to experience both upward and downward trajectories? What factors may influence such trajectories?

protection to its poison. Therefore, to gain resilience organizations must to some extent make themselves vulnerable.

Dear reader, you may be alarmed at the prospect of being advised to undergo a little poisoning. That one never knows what the dose should be that builds resilience is one of the challenges involved in its construction:

BOX 1.4   'RESILIENCE IS A MUSCLE WE CAN HELP KIDS BUILD'

In 2015, when Sheryl Sandberg (Chief Operating Officer of Facebook) and her husband were on vacation he died suddenly from a cardiac arrhythmia. She shared her traumatic experience (Sandberg, 2017) in the *New York Times*, in a beautiful text that we consider worth reading. If you don't have access to the article, read the following excerpts (p. A23):

> Flying home to tell my 7-year-old daughter and 10-year-old son that their father had died was the worst experience of my life. During that unimaginable trip, I turned for advice to a friend who counsels grieving children. She said that the most important thing was to tell my kids over and over how much I loved them and that they were not alone. In the fog of those early and brutal weeks and months, I tried to use the guidance she had given me. My biggest fear was that my children's happiness would be destroyed by our devastating loss. I needed to know what, if anything, I could do to get them through this.

She also explained how she had dealt with her children's feelings:

> One afternoon, I sat down with my kids to write out 'family rules' to remind us of the coping mechanisms we would need. We wrote together that it's OK to be sad and to take a break from any activity to cry. It's OK to be happy and laugh. It's OK to be angry and jealous of friends and cousins who still have fathers. It's OK to say to anyone that we do not want to talk about it now. And it's always OK to ask for help. The poster we made that day – with the rules written by my kids in colored markers – still hangs in our hall so we can look at it every day. It reminds us that our feelings matter and that we are not alone.

For the purposes of this book, her 'conclusion' is worth considering, not only by parents but by all of us:

> As parents, teachers and caregivers, we all want to raise resilient kids – to develop their strength so they can overcome obstacles big and small. Resilience leads to better health, greater happiness and more success. The good news is that resilience isn't a fixed personality trait; we're not born with a set amount of it. Resilience is a muscle we can help kids build.

You may also read an article published in *Time* magazine (Luscombe, 2017) about the tragic event and how Sandberg made the decision to help others to find a way through grief (including through writing *Option B: Facing Adversity, Building Resilience, and Finding Joy,* co-authored by Adam Grant; Sandberg and Grant,

2017). Take notice of how Sandberg recovered through sharing her feelings with friends and family (and the public in general; see her Facebook post on https:// www.facebook.com/sheryl/posts/10155617891025177:0), asking for help and advice, and receiving unconditional support from her boss, Mark Zuckerberg.

- Too much poison, and the organization intoxicates itself (for example, by assuming too much risk).
- Too little poison, and the organization will perish in contact with danger (for example, due to lack of preparation to deal with risks).

TOOLS[3]

The text of this book is splashed here and there by boxes, which are used to invite you, our reader, to reflect on yourself and the surrounding reality. Four types of boxes, marked with small icons, are included: (1) tools or measures; (2) illustrations and examples; (3) questions used as 'food for thought'; and (4) 'for practice' exercises.

Tools, or measures, are intended to help you measure some characteristics related to resilience.

Illustrations aim to connect the abstract concepts with some reality that puts them in context.

Questions for reflection (or 'food for thought') are aimed at asking questions that might be funny and rewarding for you to explore on your own.

'For practice' exercises are indications that might be useful for translating the ideas discussed in the book to the reader's reality.

We hope these additions to the standard book layout will render exploring this book more interesting. We trust that you will enjoy the experience!

NOTES

1. During the writing of this book, probably under the effect of hallucinations and other obsessive symptoms that academic writing can generate, one of the authors noticed that (skin) resilience was also reported as one of the effects that his body wash was promising.
2. Clair and Dufresne (2007) label as 'hyper-resilience' the situation in which 'the crisis becomes a catalyst for positive transformation' (p. 99).
3. Source of the images: https://stock.adobe.com/images/100-education-school-graduation-icons-set-on-white-background/111625234 and https://stock.adobe.com/images/education-icons/47584640.

2. Resilience in management and organization studies

> Being adaptable, resilient, flexible, and above all ready is the new normal. 'Every successful business model works until it doesn't,' notes one CEO [Chief Executive Officer].
> (Saïd Business School and Heidrick & Struggles, 2015, p. 5)

POSITIONING ORGANIZATIONAL RESILIENCE

Many contemporary organizations deal with high levels of environmental uncertainty, complexity and equivocality (D'Aveni, 1995; Carroll, 1998; Van Hove et al., 2015). Organizations struggle with not only strong competitive pressures but also increasing uncertainty related to socio-political and economic trends within the frame of a risk society (Beck, 1999; McFarlane and Norris, 2006; Asano, 2012; Kaplan and Mikes, 2012; BCI, 2015; Fiksel et al., 2015; WEF, 2015).

Oil exploration is inherently risky, notably in marine environments. The case of the oil giant BP, whose Deepwater Horizon rig located in the Gulf of Mexico exploded in 2010, is a case in point. The explosion killed 11 workers, causing an outflow of crude oil that continued for 87 days, creating incalculable damage to the surrounding wildlife, and massively affecting fishing and tourism activities in the whole area of the Gulf of Mexico. The damage did not stop there. To assess the magnitude of the harmful event, we have to consider that BP had spent significant efforts and resources over the years in trying to become an environmentally responsible company and, accordingly, a reputable brand. In 2000, the organization launched 'Beyond Petroleum', its $200 million global public relations and advertising campaign. In seven years, its brand awareness leapfrogged from 4 to 67 per cent by 2007 (French, 2016). After 2010, the brand associations changed dramatically in people's consciousness of the company.

More recently, Johnson & Johnson (J&J) has been sued by thousands of women (4800 as of 2 July 2017; Hsu, 2017) over J&J baby powder. The first talc suit was heard in 2013. The plaintiffs have claimed that talcum particles in the product caused them to have ovarian cancer. According to the *New York Times* (Hsu, 2017, p. B1), 'The tally of damages from verdicts against Johnson & Johnson is already in the hundreds of millions of dollars. And the harm to the company is not just financial: Its reputation could suffer if baby powder, one of its longest-standing products, is seen by the public as unsafe'.

Likewise, in September 2015, the United States (US) Environment Protection Agency claimed that Volkswagen was responsible for installing 'defeat devices' in its diesel vehicles. The devices were able to switch to cars to a lower-emission regime while being tested, but in fact releasing nitrogen oxide emissions up to 40 times higher than the federal limit in regular on-the-road functioning (Ewing, 2017; see also Jung and Park, 2017). The impact on the brand has been dramatic. A survey (AutoList, 2016) suggested that public willingness to buy a Volkswagen 'had fallen by 28 per cent, while perception of the brand's environmental consciousness had tumbled almost 50 per cent. A quarter of those surveyed considered the scandal as bad as – or even worse than – the BP Deepwater Horizon catastrophe' (French, 2016).

Risks can unfold in their harmfulness and create a backlash sometime after the events in question occurred. In February 2018, Oxfam ('an international confederation of 20 NGOs [non-governmental organizations] working with partners in over 90 countries to end the injustices that cause poverty', Oxfam.org) had to face the allegation that, in lieu of helping the local population, a staff member had paid women for sex in the aftermath of the Haiti earthquake in 2011. The scandal exposed Oxfam – seven years later – to the potential loss of £34 million from the United Kingdom (UK) government (Booth, 2018).

These cases – BP, J&J, Volkswagen and Oxfam – demonstrate that organizational survival is constantly under potential challenge from risks past and present (Van der Vegt et al., 2015). When organizations and their members are confronted with crises (Kobasa and Puccetti, 1983; Pearson and Clair, 1998; Beasley et al., 2003; Fredrickson et al., 2003; Boin, 2004; Maddi and Khoshaba, 2005; Roux-Dufort, 2007; Furniss et al., 2011; Carmeli et al., 2013; Kahn et al., 2013; Mitchell, 2013; Xavier et al., 2014; Kossek and Perrigino, 2016), economic distress (Klehe et al., 2012; Endo et al., 2015), and 'ugly' surprises (Weick and Sutcliffe, 2001 [2007]; Hadida, 2009; Sutcliffe and Vogus, 2008; Buchanan and Denyer, 2013; Van der Vegt et al., 2015; Cunha et al., 2018a), the value of resilience increases. To survive and prosper, organizations must transform stressors, jolts and shocks into new and resilient solutions (Ashmos and Huber, 1987).

As an example, some companies, such as Toyota, have developed sufficient resilience to be able to cope with the disruptions caused by Japan's frequent earthquakes (Asano, 2012; Schreffler, 2012). The risk of

Table 2.1   *Emblematic recent events rendering the role and importance of resilience more visible to management and organization studies*

	Business and society	The environment	Politics
September 11 attacks (2001)	√	√	√
Space Shuttle *Columbia* Disaster (2003)	√		√
The 2004 Madrid train bombings ('11-M')	√		√
Hurricane Katrina (2005)	√	√	√
BP Deepwater Horizon spill (2010)	√	√	
Fukushima Daiichi nuclear disaster (2011)	√	√	√
The 2011 Norway attacks ('22 July')	√		√
Global financial crisis (2008–2012)	√		√
Volkswagen emissions scandal (2015)	√	√	√
Charlie Hebdo shooting (2015)	√		√
Nice attack (2016)	√		√
Summer wildfires in Portugal (2017)	√	√	√
Oxfam scandal (2018)	√		√
Genoa bridge collapse (2018)	√		√

events such as unplanned information technology and telecommunications outages, cyber-attacks and data breaches, as well as adverse weather and other natural events, can cause a loss of productivity due to supply chain disruption (BCI, 2015). Evidence suggests that some of these risks will only tend to increase in the future (Whiteman and Yumashev, 2018).

In the face of such stories concerning disruptive events, promoting resilience has become a major strategic concern for many organizations, in terms of not only their survival, but also their recovery and emergence as even stronger after setbacks (Wildavsky, 1988; Tugade and Fredrickson, 2004, 2007; Mitroff, 2005; Moenkemeyer et al., 2012; Välikangas and Romme, 2013). A number of highly visible events turned resilience into a relevant process in management of organization studies, as depicted in Table 2.1. These events have important business, environmental and political dimensions.

The global financial crisis also contributed to populate the theme, incorporating it in the political discourse as a response to adversity that should be shared rather than centralized in governments (e.g., Cunha and Tsoukas, 2015). Czech Prime Minister Bohuslav Sobotka, when delivering the opening address at the Defence and Security Conference Prague on Friday 9 June 2017, stated:[1] 'We need to strengthen the resilience of EU member states to traditional and new threats'. In June 2017, the Australian Prime Minister Malcolm Turnbull announced[2] the creation of a Cyber

Resilience Taskforce, 'to drive fast action on Australia's capability and response to cyber security and cybercrime threats and incidents'. See, also, how the role of the Minister for Government Resilience and Efficiency in the UK is defined:[3]

> The Minister for Government Resilience and Efficiency supports the Minister for the Cabinet Office in delivering Cabinet Office policy. Responsibilities include: efficiency and controls; functions (Infrastructure and Projects Authority, Civil Service HR [Human Resources], the Government Digital Service, commercial and Crown Commercial Service, Government Property and commercial models); shared services; Civil Service workforce issues; Single Departmental Plans; cyber; resilience.

RESILIENCE, RESILIENCY AND THEIR ORGANIZATIONAL IMPLICATIONS

Resilience is the ability of a substance or object to spring back into shape; it denotes elasticity under pressure. As a scientific term, 'resilience' arose initially in engineering and physics. Etymologically, 'resilience' derives from the Latin verb *salire* (climb or jump), in particular from its extension, *resilire*, which means to jump back or recoil. The importance of *resilire* has been stated at the individual level (e.g., Luthar and Zigler, 1991) and later generalized to higher levels of analysis (e.g., Klein and Kozlowski, 2000; Waite and Richardson, 2004). These levels of analysis include organizations and networks (e.g., Van Der Vegt et al., 2015), as well as industry, communities (Norris et al., 2008; Brodsky et al., 2011; Bach, 2015) and nations.

In the latter case, our Irish readers will be pleased, no doubt, to read that Ireland has been named as 'The world's most resilient country' (Lynch, 2010). Differently, *The Economist* (2011) characterized 'Pakistan as a supreme danger, a fantastically diverse nation and a tough, resilient country' (for a different perspective, see Box 4.5 in Chapter 4, ranking countries based on their enterprises' resilience to disruptive events). These are relatively recent examples. Historically, the Volga Tatars (Box 4.6 in Chapter 4) have been studied as a case of resilience over centuries; see also Box 2.1.

Linnenluecke (2017) discusses the genealogy of organizational resilience and raises potential research questions. She positions resilience as 'an increasingly common theme in academic research, business practices, public policy and popular press [while] its conceptualization and operationalization have been quite varied across studies' (p. 5). 'Resilience', therefore, is a word with a large variety of uses and a complex range of applications. For Annarelli and Nonino (2016):

BOX 2.1 ON *SISU* AND RESILIENCE (BY LIISA
VÄLIKANGAS)

Sisu, a word implying particular resilience, is said to characterize Finns. *Sisu* means to fight on, even against impossible odds: 'When your knife is broken, fight with your sheath'. *Sisu* is offered as an explanation of the Finnish ability to survive and even thrive in a harsh, northern climate. Frequently used in the context of sports, *sisu* is evoked for example to explain Finnish successes in long-distance running.

The term is originally derived from our inner organs: guts. Today it symbolizes determination: the rise from poverty to prosperity that Finland accomplished during the last 100 years. In business, *sisu* may have contributed to Nokia's recent re-emergence as a globally leading telecommunications network company. Delaying the onslaught of the behemoth Soviet forces in the Winter War 1939–1940 required great *sisu*.

Sisu means never giving up. Being *sisukas*, full of *sisu*, is about resourcefulness. When one avenue is blocked, a clever person with *sisu* finds another way. No problem managing alone: your neighbours may be far away in a sparsely populated country, so trusting one's own competence and judgement may be the only option. Nobody but oneself to rely on may make a person a bit selfish. It is said that *sisu* is good for coping with hardship but offers little for overcoming the seductive consequences of success. A joke has it that the Finns manage anything but continued success. Perhaps *sisu* reflects a shared human condition: hardship builds resilience against the future but success can fool us all to become comfortable in the current, potentially fleeting circumstances. Amidst all the economic comforts the cultivation of *sisu* may be needed more than ever.

Source: Liisa Välikangas, Aalto University and Hanken School of Economics. See also Välikangas (2010).

[T]he research stream on the organizational and operational management of resilience is distant from its infancy, but it can still be considered to be in a developing phase . . . the academic literature has reached a shared consensus on the definition of resilience, foundations, and characteristics . . . Nevertheless, the literature is still far from reaching consensus on the implementation of resilience, i.e. how to reach operational resilience and how to create and maintain resilient processes. (p. 1)

In the *Academy of Management Annals* (Kossek and Perrigino, 2016), the occupational implications of the adaptive characteristics of resilience can be found. The topic of resilience has been addressed in a vast number of contributions (e.g., Weick, 1993; Collins and Porras, 1994; Comfort et al., 2001; Weick and Sutcliffe, 2001 [2007]; Coutu, 2002; Sutcliffe and Vogus, 2003; Hirschhorn et al., 2004; Reinmoeller and van Baardwijk, 2005; Cunha and Cunha, 2006; Folke, 2006; Gittell et al., 2006; Lengnick-Hall, 2008; Somers, 2009; Beermann, 2011; Bhamra et al., 2011; Lengnick-Hall et al., 2011; Välikangas and Romme, 2013; Edgeman, 2014; Edgeman and Williams, 2014; Fiksel et al., 2015), with a number of proposed research agendas (e.g., Mallak, 1997; Vogus and Sutcliffe, 2007; Sutcliffe and Vogus, 2008; Zhang and Liu, 2012; Kossek and Perrigino, 2016; Linnenleucke, 2017; Williams et al., 2017).

Although the analysis of resilience in organizations is gaining momentum, contributions are generally characterized by a high level of specialization, in terms of level of analysis (for example, individuals versus organization), the partiality of perspective (for example, strategic resilience versus disaster recovery), the nature of resilience itself (for example, as a form of reaction versus proaction) or the outcomes it generates (for example, adaptation versus learning). Integrative works are necessary.

Resilience in Practice

As an innate capacity of some materials to bounce back quickly after stress, to endure greater stresses, and to be less malformed by a given amount of stress (Campbell, 2008), definitions of resilience are commonly applied to the object world of nature. However, socially, most global risks are systemic in nature, and a system – unlike an object – may show resilience not by returning to its previous state exactly, but by finding different ways to carry on after stress (see Box 2.2, and Box 4.1 in Chapter 4). A merely mechanical interpretation of resilience leaves important questions unanswered (e.g., Sutcliffe and Vogus, 2008; Tillement et al., 2009; Meneghel et al., 2016; Linnenluecke, 2017).

BOX 2.2   (UNINTENTIONAL) EXPRESSIONS OF
          RESILIENCE BY PUBLIC FIGURES

Michael Jordan, basketball legend: 'Obstacles don't have to stop you. If you run into a wall, don't turn around and give up. Figure out how to climb it, go through it, or work around it' (https://www.brainyquote.com/quotes/michael_jordan_165967).
    Nelson Mandela, politician: 'I never lose. I either win or I learn' (https://www.inc.com/jim-schleckser/nelson-mandela-s-secret-to-winning.html).
    Muhammad Ali, boxing legend: 'Only a man who knows what it is like to be defeated can reach down to the bottom of his soul and come up with the extra ounce of power it takes to win when the match is even' (https://www.brainyquote.com/quotes/muhammad_ali_122278).
    Alessandro 'Alex' Zanardi, former F1/CART pilot, Paralympic cycling gold medallist: 'I once thought I'd rather die than have no legs [amputated as a consequence of a car crash] but now I see I was wrong' (https://www.theguardian.com/sport/2007/jul/29/motorsports.features).

Holling (1996, p. 41) notes that engineering resilience is defined by 'operating near to an equilibrium far from instability', while ecological systems learn at different levels of aggregation. So 'management and institutional regimes can . . . preserve or expand resilience of systems as well to provide developmental opportunity' (Holling, 1996, p. 41). Most global risks are systemic in nature and a system – unlike an object – may show resilience by finding different ways to operate. For instance, resilience in ecology is 'the persistence of systems and . . . their ability to absorb change and disturbance and still maintain the same relationships between populations or state variables' (Holling, 1973, p. 14).

The concept of 'absorptive capacity' and the stress on learning (Zahra and George, 2002) have been associated with organizational resilience in management and organization theory from the outset (Sun and Anderson, 2010; Andersen, 2016). Similarly, organizational improvisation (e.g., Cunha et al., 1999; Furu, 2013; Hadida et al., 2015) contributes to tackle situations that cannot be completely predicted *ex ante* but require flexibility and extemporaneity in their agency (e.g., Gibbert and Välikangas, 2004). In all such cases, resilience refers to a developmental 'process' (e.g., Williams et al., 2017). Its study has gained momentum with a consistent growth in scholarly attention (Linnenluecke, 2017).

Over the last decades, there have been several important academic contributions to the understanding of resilience (Table 2.2). From these contributions, we will extract a dialectical interpretation of (human and social) resilience. The dialectical interpretation that this book expounds in Chapter 6 is consistent with the idea that, distinct from the field of natural science (e.g., Garmezy, 1973; Holling, 1973), resilience in business and management research entails a learning process grounded, as in Nietzsche, in dialectics. Resilient individuals, teams, organizations and even societies thrive on the alternation between adaptive and proactive resilience as possible reactions to rigidity (Staw et al., 1981) and vulnerability (Kahn, 1998; Barrett, 2012; Kahn et al., 2013).

Resilience is therefore not only a matter of learning but also of 'learning to learn' (Andersen, 2016), 'resisting the bias against doing new things, scanning the horizon for growth opportunities, and pushing yourself to acquire radically different capabilities – while still performing your job. That requires a willingness to experiment and become a novice again and again: an extremely discomforting notion for most of us' (p. 99).

Organizational Resilience as a Process

As pointed out by Luthar et al. (2000), the identification of resilience as a process distinguishes it from a personal trait ('resiliency'), or a static

Table 2.2   Representative studies on resilience

Year	Authors	Journal/book/chapter	Contribution
1973	Garmezy	In Dean, S.R. (ed.), *Schizophrenia: The First Ten Dean Award Lectures* (Book chapter)	Resilience in clinical psychology
1973	Holling	*Annual Review of Ecology and Systematics*	Resilience in ecological sciences
1981	Staw et al.	*Administrative Science Quarterly*	Threat-rigidity effects in organizational behaviour
1982	Meyer	*Administrative Science Quarterly*	Resiliency and environmental jolts
1984	Perrow	*Normal Accidents* (Book)	Resilience, accidents and high-risk systems
1988	Wildavsky	*Searching for Safety* (Book)	Resilience, risks and technology
1993	Weick	*Administrative Science Quarterly*	Sources of organizational resilience and sensemaking
2001 [2007]	Weick and Sutcliffe	*Managing the Unexpected* (Book)	Organizational resilience as anticipation and adaption to surprises
2001	Masten	*American Psychologist*	Resilience processes in human development
2002	Coutu	*Harvard Business Review*	Bricolage and resilience in practice
2003	Hamel and Välikangas	*Harvard Business Review*	Strategic resilience
2005	Kleindorfer and Saad	*Production and Operations Management*	Resilience and disruption risks in supply chains
2007	Luthans et al.	*Personnel Psychology*	Development and operationalization of Psychological Capital (PsyCap)

2007	Vogus and Sutcliffe	*ISIC. IEEE International Conference on Systems, Man and Cybernetics*	Theory systematization and research agenda
2011a	Seligman	*Harvard Business Review*	The 'building' of resilience
2012	Caza and Milton	In Cameron and Spreitzer (eds), *The Oxford Handbook of Positive Organizational Scholarship* (Book chapter)	Developing resilience at work
2015	Luthans et al.	*Psychological Capital and Beyond* (Book)	Developing PsyCap (including resilience) at work
2016	Kossek and Perrigino	*Academy of Management Annals*	Review of resilience using a grounded integrated occupational approach
2017	Linnenluecke	*International Journal of Management Reviews*	Systematic literature review of resilience in business and management research
2017	Williams et al.	*Academy of Management Annals*	Interaction between crisis and resilience in dynamic processes

Note: This list provides a necessarily non-exhaustive and arbitrary guide for the further exploration of the theme.

property of collective entities (Norman et al., 2005; Peterson et al., 2008). In this sense, the process of resilience refers to the achievement and maintenance of positive adaptation, despite experiencing adversities (e.g., Rak and Patterson, 1996; Dooley, 1997). The discussion is supported by three major assumptions.

First, organizational resilience embeds both the material characteristics depicted by the natural sciences and the learning features proposed by psychology (e.g., Lengnick-Hall et al., 2011). Second, distinguishing adaptive resilience from proactive resilience is consistent with the two types of 'organizational responses' identified in the seminal paper by Meyer (1982): the absorption of the impact by first-order change and single-loop learning (referred to here as 'adaptive resilience')[4] and the adoption of new practices or configuration through second-order change and double-loop learning (referred to here as 'proactive resilience'). Third, organizations are relational systems (Kahn, 1998; Dutton, 2003; Kahn et al., 2013). Therefore, as a process, resilience characterizes specific types of interactions that show contradictory elements of adaptive and proactive resilience. In this sense, resilience is perceived not as a state of being, a disposition or a structural property, so much as a processual practice (Feldman and Orlikowski, 2011) of becoming (Tsoukas and Chia, 2002).

CAN RESILIENCE BE CULTIVATED?

The literature has so far made evident that cultivating resilience should constitute a major strategic concern for organizations not only to survive but also to emerge stronger after setbacks (Mitroff, 2005; Välikangas and Romme, 2013). Accordingly, 'design for resilience' includes both micro or individual-level and macro or design-level features (Giustiniano and Cantoni, 2018), as well as the combination of these 'organizational elements' (e.g., Grandori and Furnari, 2008). The building of resilience can follow various trajectories, at both the individual and the collective level. The stronger a destabilization of routines, the greater needs to be the efficacy of recovery and learning; in fact, in facing any form of hostility, the more severe is the shock, the greater the confidence individuals (and collectives) will need to develop.

Resilience also arises from failure and occurs when individuals are able to transform traumas into future strengths, when (post-)traumatic stress disorders turn into post-traumatic growth (see, for example, Box 2.7 below). In principle, individuals can resolve vicious circles themselves. More frequently, human beings get out of vicious circles via the intervention of others (Maitlis, 2018). The dynamics of such responses can be understood at both the individual and the collective level via the impact of optimism and the cultivation of positive mentalities and significant sensemaking efforts.

In their study of the San Diego Zoo Global (SDZG), Asch and Mulligan (2016) explore these dynamics: they propose that the design of 'resilience at work' can be secured via the combination of emotional intelligence, wellness, time management, strong communications and the promotion of mindfulness, the latter being a way to help individuals to maintain relaxed yet focused attention. In the Asch–Mulligan model, honest communication, based on transparency and recognition of vulnerability, is the 'glue' that combines all the components together at any level of aggregation.

THE INDIVIDUAL BIOLOGY OF RESILIENCE

Social support and positive social relationships are important predictors of resilience (Caza and Milton, 2012; Ozbay et al., 2007; Ozbay et al., 2008). One possible mediator of this relationship is oxytocin[5] (Campbell, 2010; Tops et al., 2014), a hormone that acts as a neurotransmitter in the brain and plays a very important role in human bonding. Positive social relationships increase oxytocin levels, and oxytocin, in turn, facilitates human affiliative behaviours and increases interpersonal trust, thus instigating prosocial and bonding behaviours and giving rise to upward spirals (Campbell, 2010; Heinrichs et al., 2009; Sanchez et al., 2009). Research suggests that oxytocin reduces stress responses, and protects against the damaging consequences of stress on health (Heinrichs et al., 2009; Tops et al., 2014).

This explains why social support, social capital, social networking and high-quality relationships have emerged as significant predictors of resilience, at both the individual and the collective levels. 'Social glue' helps the individuals and the organizations to proactively act against 'disasters' and to react more resiliently to them. This has important implications for leadership. Leaders may operate as cultivators of resilience, nourishing it, if they act 'humanely' as shields (Sutton, 2010; Box 2.3). As Sutton (2010, p. 109) suggests, good managers protect their people and, when they:

> can't protect people – for example, from layoffs, pay cuts, or tough assignments – the best ones convey compassion, do small things to allay fears, and find ways to blunt negative consequences. Operating in this way helps bolster your people's performance and well-being. And a nice by-product is that they will have your back, too.

BOX 2.3   TO SPREAD RESILIENCE, 'BE HUMAN'

In seeking answers to the question 'Why do so many managers forget they're human beings?', Hougaard et al. (2018) conducted research that involved more than 1000 leaders via surveys, assessments and interviews. Out of the evidence they collected, they point out a remarkable quote by Javier Pladevall, CEO of Audi Volkswagen, Spain: 'Leadership today . . . is about unlearning management and relearning being human.' According to the study, this quest for humanization of leadership, and therefore of organizations, is widely shared and it is becoming more and more important as the new generations of workers – the so-called Millennials – are involved. That is related to the fact that Millennials seem to be 'not satisfied with only a paycheck, bonus, and benefits. They want meaning, happiness, and connectedness, too.'

The claim appears to be paradoxical: in the age of machine learning and artificial intelligence, there is a growing demand for – if not a true exigency of – 'human leadership' and humanized organizing. In fact, the paradox is just in the patina of situations. As human beings, no matter the level of automation with which we interact and by which we connect, we still relate to meaning, happiness and human connectedness. Additionally, the level of oxytocin that affects human behaviours is still influenced by the positiveness of human interactions and desire to contribute positively to others' lives. In turn, human leadership enables forms of intrinsic motivation, which have upsides for loyalty, engagement and performance.

As synthetized by Hougaard et al. (2018), human leadership encompasses elements such as the following:

1. Being *personal* – e.g. 'For all decisions being made, that has impact on employees, he asks himself: If my child or parent or good friend worked here, would they appreciate this decision? In this way, he makes any managerial decision a personal question.' (Bob Chapman, CEO of Barry Wehmiller, a global manufacturing company, and co-author of *Everybody Matters* [Chapman and Sisodia, 2015]).
2. Being *self-aware* – e.g. 'You cannot manage other people unless you manage yourself first.' (Peter Drucker, management guru).
3. Being *selfless* – e.g. 'Selflessness is the foundation of good leadership. Leadership is not about you, but about the people and the organization you lead. With selflessness, you take yourself out of the equation and consider the long-term benefits of others. Selflessness does not mean you become a doormat for others and refuse to stand up for yourself. Selflessness comes out of self-confidence and self-care.' (Dominic Barton, global managing director of McKinsey & Company).
4. Being *compassionate* – e.g. do your best to bring happiness to others.

By following these tips, leaders can be 'humans before managers'. Human leaders contribute to the resilience of the surrounding social environment.

If you are a leader, how do you act in this regard? Are you self-aware? Are you sure that other people would say so? Are you compassionate? Or do you protect yourself by neglecting others' feelings? Would you feel comfortable in sharing with your children and other family members what you are doing? Submit yourself to a 360° feedback assessment – and then answer these questions again.

While the magnitude of the effects of positive psychology has mainly been tested via positive interactions with and amongst humans, interactions with some non-human beings appear to be helpful too. In fact, one implication of research on oxytocin and stress responses is that humans should develop more positive social relationships to experience higher levels of oxytocin and resilience. Should they also develop more positive relationships with dogs? Empirical evidence suggests that human–animal interaction may contribute to humans' resilience (see Box 2.4). For example, Mueller and Callina (2014) suggested that attachment to an animal associates with positive youth development for military-connected youth, as well as with adaptive coping strategies for youth with a deployed family member. Harlinger and Blazina (2016) suggested that dog–human interactions may help humans to develop resilience (see also Cunha et al., 2018c; Sibley et al., 2018; Yarborough et al., 2017).

INDIVIDUAL AND COLLECTIVE RESILIENCE: 'WHAT DOES NOT DESTROY US . . .'

As anticipated in Chapter 1, a 'maxim and arrow' with which we explore resilience is one of Friedrich Nietzsche's (1889 [1968]) most famous aphorisms: 'Out of life's school of war: What does not destroy me, makes me stronger'. Although the maxim is part of a wider and more elaborated discourse on the eschatology of beings and humanity (Ausmus, 1978), it has been read in modern terms as a threefold property of human behaviour. First, life is a process of learning from struggle (dialectics). Second, 'what does not destroy me . . .' implies that individuals can recover after crises (adaptive resilience). Third, '[it] makes me stronger' relates to becoming more alert, aware and responsive in case of future similar events (proactive resilience).

In popular culture, the sentiment was paraphrased as 'that which does not kill us makes us stronger' in the rhetoric of US President Richard Nixon (Aitken, 1996). Nietzsche's maxim is ego-centred, focusing on

BOX 2.4   TO BE MORE RESILIENT, BUY A DOG?

A study published in *Science* (Nagasawa et al., 2015) revealed that modern dogs and their owners secrete oxytocin when they interact with each other. The human–dog interactions elicit an oxytocin positive feedback loop similar to that observed between mothers and their infants. According to David Grimm, the online news editor of *Science*, this explains why and how 'dogs stole our hearts' (Grimm, 2015).

This evidence is consistent with literature suggesting that dogs (as well as other pets) have calming effects in humans, contribute to emotional and social well-being (Figure 2.1), provide comfort, reduce feelings of loneliness during adversity,

Source: Photo: Staff Sergeant Mary Junell. Retrieved from https://commons. wikimedia.org/wiki/File:Man%E2%80%99s_best_friend_helps_NC_Guardsman_with_ PTSD_140111-Z-GT365-027.jpg. The image is in the public domain in the United States.

Figure 2.1   Rosco, a post-traumatic stress disorder companion animal, helping Syriac, a two-time Iraq war veteran, to deal with post-traumatic disorder and to help him recover

and provide the opportunity to nurture others (Kingwell et al., 2001; McConnell et al., 2011; Sable, 1995; von Begen and Bressler, 2015). Cary Cooper (in Rigby, 2007, p. 20), then Professor of Organizational Psychology and Health at Lancaster University Management School, argued that 'inviting pets into the workplace could reduce stress, act as a perk and make the company a more fun place to be'. Pets definitely humanize co-workers: 'People step out of the corporate roles they play with animals. You no longer think "Fred's my manager", you think "Fred loves his dog".'

This evidence is consistent with the lay idea that dogs are our best friends (McConnell et al., 2011; von Begen and Bressler, 2015). It has been said that US presidents' 'best friends often have four legs' (Kingson, 2016), helping to explain why many leaders and 'even tech billionaires love their pets' (Stone, 2016) and why some companies have pet-friendly policies (Cole, 2014; Kokalitcheva, 2016; von Begen and Bressler, 2015; Cunha et al., 2018c). Dogs have been awarded dozens of medals for saving human lives in risky contexts (Helton et al., 2009). Should they also be rewarded for their contributions to humans' resilience?

the self rather than us. Shifting the focus of the maxim away from specific individuals to aggregated social entities refocuses the strength of resilience as a property of groups, organizations and entire collectivities. Similarly to other studies, we refer to 'groups' for addressing generic intra-organizational formations of employees such as formal teams, departments and hierarchical groups of any kind (e.g., Pinto, 2014). Collective resilience is not the mere sum of the resilience of the members of that collective. A group of individually resilient team members may be unable to make the team recover from an adversity. Each individual may continue to flourish, and individual resilience may even help team members to bounce back from team disaster, but this does not prevent team failure and extinction. Likewise, modestly resilient individuals may strengthen their individual resilience when working in a supportive, flourishing and resilient team.

In contemporary managerial discourse, the centrality of resilience is mostly related to responses to the social, political, environmental and economic turmoil to which organizations have been exposed in recent decades; in particular, the experience of 'jolts' (Meyer, 1982) of various kinds. High levels of uncertainty, complexity and equivocality distinguish the environments with which many contemporary organizations deal (D'Aveni, 1995; Carroll, 1998; Van Hove et al., 2015). Firms and various types of private and public institutions are obliged to struggle not only with strong competitive pressures but also with increasing uncertainty related to socio-political, economic and environmental trends (see Table 2.1).

Increasingly, organizations are inscribed within the frame of a global risk society (Beck, 1999; McFarlane and Norris, 2006; Asano, 2012; Kaplan and Mikes, 2012; BCI, 2015; Fiksel et al., 2015; WEF, 2015; Giustiniano and Cantoni, 2018). The global risks are many: the uncertainty (e.g., Vaughan, 1996) and speed of global markets, as well as human-made disasters such as nuclear power plant accidents, oil spills (e.g., Goldberg and Harzog, 1996; Lee et al., 2011), climate change (Howard-Grenville et al., 2014; Winston, 2014; Linnenluecke and Griffiths, 2015), terrorist attacks (e.g., Bell, 2002; Kendra and Wachtendorf, 2003; Bonanno et al., 2006; Gittell et al., 2006; Ressler, 2006), global financial crises (Garmezy, 1991; Clegg, 2010; Carvalho and Areal, 2016), as well as natural disasters such as hurricanes and floods (Pelling and Uitto, 2001; Goodman and Mann, 2008; McManus et al., 2008; Nakanishi et al., 2014; Butts et al., 2012; Schreffler, 2012; Powley, 2013; Smith, 2013; Stevenson et al., 2014; UN, 2015; UNISDR, 2015; Simpson et al., 2015; Williams and Shepherd, 2016). Organizational survival and long-term sustainability are increasingly challenged by such risks (Endo et al., 2015; Van der Vegt et al., 2015).

Organizations that survive and prosper in the context of a risk society develop the ability to fulfil their missions and deploy their core functions by finding and implementing organizational macro and micro structures in a fast and timely manner, in a way that enables them to transform jolts and shocks into new solutions and possibilities (Ashmos and Huber, 1987). In short, they express resilience. Organizational resilience ultimately is a manifestation of a socially constructed process, embedding minimal constraints, deviations and constructions, allowing individuals and their forms of professional and social relations to be adaptive and flexible as action unfolds (e.g., Cunha et al., 2002).

In short, resilience, as a multi-level construct, spans at least three levels of aggregation (e.g., Drazin et al., 1999; Hackman, 2003; Sutcliffe and Vogus, 2003): intrasubjective (individual), intersubjective (team) and collective (organization). At different levels of aggregation, resilience generates sustainable creative ideas for problem-solution (e.g., Luthar and Cicchetti, 2000; Luthar et al., 2000). Resilience conserves adaptive capacity (Gratton and Ghoshal, 2003; Zolli and Healy, 2012). As a way of overcoming challenges, studying resilience at multiple levels is paramount. Understanding the mechanisms of organizational resilience (Sutcliffe and Vogus, 2003, 2008) can enable decision-makers to understand how cultivating or inhibiting it occurs, and allow them to use this knowledge as a source of competitive advantage (e.g., Pfeffer, 1994; Spreitzer and Porath, 2012).

There's No Success Like Failure, and Failure's No Success At All[6]

Resilience is not necessarily found in those with a clear streak of remarkable successes; in fact, unexpected results can come out of teams and individuals that are generally considered ordinary, if not 'underdogs' (see Box 2.5).

BOX 2.5   THE SILENT RESILIENCE OF THE UNDERDOGS – PART I: PHILADELPHIA EAGLES AND JEREMY LIN

The Resilience That Didn't Stop Them

On 3 February 2018, just one day before the final game of the 2017 National Football League (NFL) season in the US, the defending Super Bowl champion and American Football Conference (AFC) champion New England Patriots, a.k.a. 'the perennial Super Bowl contenders' (Jhabvala, 2018), were foreseen to be the winners of the Super Bowl LII (the 52nd Super Bowl overall). The opponents, the Philadelphia Eagles, were considered as 'underdogs' by the press, as Coach Doug Pederson admitted:

> We've been the underdogs. I think that's the mentality of our football team. I think that's the mentality of our city, and I'm OK with that, I'm fine that . . . I've been an underdog my whole career, my whole life. Everything I've done, I either haven't been good enough or something negative has been written or said, and I just blow it off. I have confidence in these guys and this team. (Jhabvala, 2018)

Against all predictions, the day after, the Eagles defeated the Patriots 41–33, and won their first Super Bowl. Their quarterback Nick Foles – 'who until this year defined the term journeyman' (Armour, 2018) – was named Super Bowl MVP (Most Valuable Player). As the Eagles' linebacker Chris Long said, 'We were a team of – I hate to use the word, but, destiny . . . Too much went wrong, and we couldn't be stopped' (Armour, 2018). Although the Eagles were considered the underdogs for the final, all the injuries and the critical situations they had to face during 2017 surely deserved the label of 'built for adversity' (Jhabvala, 2018). In the words of Nick Foles, 'We just went out there and played football . . . We've played this game since we were little kids, we dreamed about this moment' (Armour, 2018).

The Flattering and Terrifying Feelings of a 'Linsane' Basketball Player

Another story of resilience coming from an 'underdog' in the game is that of Jeremy Shu-How Lin, a US National Basketball Association (NBA) player who in 2012 led the formerly struggling New York Knicks to an incredible turnaround of seven straight wins. The streak was so incredible that he appeared on the cover of *Time* under the label of the global craze he generated: 'Linsanity' (27 February 2012). Before 2012, the professional career of Lin was characterized by ups and downs. In fact, despite earning the title of Northern California Player of the Year at high school, Lin received no athletic scholarship offers. He attended Harvard University, he played for the Ivy League and was nominated All-Conference player three times. As he was undrafted out of college, in 2010 Lin was able to reach only a partially guaranteed contract deal (Golden State Warriors), playing very rarely and ending up assigned three times to the NBA Development League (D-League). After having been waived by his team and the Houston Rockets, Lin joined the New York Knicks in the 2011/12 season. Also in New York, he was rarely employed and sent some time in the D-League. As summarized by Rodriguez (2016): 'Lin didn't look the part of the typical NBA superstar and certainly didn't have the pedigree. Some NBA draftniks were fans, but nobody saw this stretch coming'.

In February 2012, sustaining a dramatic number of injuries and because of lockout, the Knicks had to give Lin a chance. From that moment, Lin led an incredible winning streak and was promoted to the line-up. In December 2011, he commented on the decision of the Knicks to play him with the awareness that he is 'competing for a backup spot, and people see me as the 12th to 15th guy on the roster. It's a numbers game' (Thompson, 2011). Despite aware of being far from a first choice in the line-up, 'the same traits [he] showed in Golden State quickly emerged. He was the first to arrive every day, and the last to leave. He sought and devoured game tapes. When he requested his own clips, Lin asked to see his turnovers and missed jumpers, not his assists' (Beck, 2012).

As Rodriguez (2016) later said:

Linsanity was at a fever pitch heading into February 23, 201[2]. In Jeremy Lin's first nine games of the 2011–12 season, he'd scored a combined 32 points. And then, for whatever reason, something clicked . . . The [Miami] Heat were built to end all of the nonsense ['Linsanity' – Lin's way of playing]. They had terrifying athleticism and length on the perimeter, and bigs that could trap nearly out to half court and still recover back to their man. Lin didn't have a chance.

Lin commented upon the attention that the eventual NBA champions dedicated to him this way:

It's flattering – and terrifying . . . It's flattering because it's like, Okay, they actually care. They actually know who I am and I'm on their scouting report, which never would have happened before. And then it's terrifying because they're really good . . . and it's so different for me to all of a sudden become the focal point of a team's defense. That's just uncharted territory for me. I felt like they were all like hawks circling me and staring. It was a learning experience. (Leitch, 2012)

That night, 'Linsanity' ended.

Paradoxically, while failures, shocks and other jolts are necessary ingredients for testing and nurturing resilience, successful experiences and important achievements cannot prevent individuals and organizations from failures (see Box 2.6). Successful organizations might trigger the

BOX 2.6   WHEN SUCCESS (AND THE LACK OF IT) EXACERBATES VULNERABILITY

From Flying High to Falling into Deep Holes

On 1 June 2016, an article in the *Financial Times Europe* reported that Martin Senn, the former CEO of Zurich Insurance, had committed suicide six months after he had quit the company (Atkins, 2016). According to the author, this suicide and those of other executives in the last few years had 'focused attention on the stresses placed on senior managers in the Alpine economy, their ability to cope with a sudden job loss, and whether Swiss society creates particular pressures'. Possible explanations for the phenomenon were provided (Atkins, 2016, p. 12):

- Thomas Heinsius, head doctor at Winterthur's Policlinic for integrated psychiatry, stated: 'If you are high in a hierarchy and have a dominant psychology, and you define your life and values as such, it can be very damaging for your psychological wellbeing if you lose your position'.
- Rolf Butz, director of the Zurich branch of the Swiss professional employees association, stated: 'You become depressed if your psychological repertoire is not sufficiently equipped to deal with the new challenge.' He added, 'Top people who lose their jobs often fall into a deep hole', and that 'It is difficult to define their life beyond their profession, their function, status.'

According to Atkins (2016, p. 12):

> the emotional challenges might be more acute in Switzerland, where the business elite moves in small circles and the loss of job can lead to exclusion from social networks ... Some in Switzerland's business community also point out there is less of a culture of 'acceptable failure' than in the US – the idea that you can recover after a setback – which means the stakes are even higher for chief executives. Those involved in big corporate failures are often never heard of again.

From Brilliance to Suicide

So many times, sadly, we read, see or hear of news reports of famous, successful people ending up in trouble, trapped into depressive spirals, enslaved by drugs or alcohol, or – in the most unfortunate cases – committing suicide, such as the case above. These phenomena have several psychological explanations and can be summarized by saying that 'the same qualities that drive a person to brilliance may drive that person to suicide', as Andrew Salomon writes. In fact, 'highly successful people tend to be perfectionistic, constantly striving to meet impossible standards. And celebrities tend to be hungry for love, for the adoration of audiences. No perfectionist has ever met his own benchmarks, and no one so famished for admiration has ever received enough of it' (Salomon, 2014).

> In some other cases, business success or popularity clash with the original, genetic idea that gave rise to success: for example, indie labels in the music industry. As studied by Cunha et al. (forthcoming-a), when exposed to sudden success, individuals somatize the 'collision of competing logics'. Craving 'music as art' and being successful in achieving 'music as business' can create somatization that operates at a micro level, making the individual (that is, the founder of an indie label or band) less resilient. A similar reasoning applies to bands when one component (generally the person out in front) senses that their individual potential as an entertainer or performer is higher than that of the group. In this case, the band in question frequently unravels, demonstrating the vulnerability of the team when confronted by an ego out of control. Sometimes, as in the case of Mick Jagger of the Rolling Stones, when attempts at being solo fail, the ego becomes reabsorbed in the band.

hubris of their leaders and eventually result in leadership failure and the ruin of the organization. Kroll et al. (2000) note that Napoleon's Russian campaign of 1812, in which he lost his army before later losing his empire, is a notable example. It remains a history lesson still to be learnt by many contemporary leaders that resolutely push their organizations towards unsound and overpriced mergers and acquisitions, tolerate misconduct under the illusion of being 'almighty in the business', and pursue aggressive growth strategies with the assumption that they are 'too big to fail'. Unfortunately, hubris is so problematic that it prevents leaders from learning how dangerous hubris is. Recent corporate scandals epitomize the danger. As the *New York Times* stated (Eichenwald, 2006, p. A1) about Enron, 'one of the great frauds in American business history': testimonies and documents admitted during the trial 'painted a broad and disturbing portrait of a corporate culture poisoned by hubris, leading ultimately to a recklessness that placed the business's survival at risk'.

Resilience operates at different levels of human aggregation (and analysis), potentially but not necessarily flowing across levels. It may involve individuals, teams, organizations and communities as they respond to some significant occurrence. They may develop intra-level self-contained capabilities or inter-level capabilities, with resilience at one level spilling over (or not, as discussed above) to other levels.

The Nurturing (or Destructive) Effects of Interactions

Whether resilience is an intra-level or inter-level competency, its cultivation is critically dependent on the role of interactions. Some interactions help to build resilience, whereas others inhibit resilience (Carmeli and Gittell, 2009; Furniss et al., 2011; Caza and Milton, 2012; Kahn et al., 2013). It is entirely possible that people who are individually resilient will be working in non-resilient teams (and that non-resilient individuals will be working in resilient teams), and that resilient teams might emerge in non-resilient organizations (and that non-resilient teams will work in resilient organizations). However, it is plausible that resilience at one level will tend to lead to resilience at other levels, such as when a positive practice is transferred to a higher level (Kohlrieser et al., 2012; Norman et al., 2005; Story et al., 2013). A resilient and/or hopeful leader can act as a source of energy helping a team confront and triumph over hostile environments or traumatic changes.

In order to understand the resilience process within and across levels, it is important to consider that social resilience concerns 'the relationships that help us find resources when we need them' (McGonigal, 2012, p. 38). Positive relationships or high-quality connections (to be discussed later) within a team create opportunities to expand behavioural repertoires and to confront challenges in a mindful manner (Caza and Milton, 2012; Stephens et al., 2012; Stephens et al., 2013; see Chapters 5 and 6). Organizationally, resilience has been associated with social capital, that is, relationships that can be activated as resources (Gittell and Douglass, 2012) and that allow responses to challenges that are purposeful and mindful rather than a resort to rigid, standard routines; such behaviours characterize how non-resilient systems respond to threats (Weick, 1993). Thus, resilience thrives on relationships and positive interactions. In practice, it is the presence of these interactions that allows a system to express the capacity to adapt in the face of challenges that are unexpected or that transcend the ordinary.

The interdependence between levels of aggregation appears to be a constitutive property of organizational resilience. Egeland et al. (1993, p. 518) note that facing challenging conditions translates into 'a hierarchical integration of behavioral systems whereby earlier structures are incorporated into later structures in increasingly complex forms'. However, the process is not cumulative: resilience at a higher level is not the sum of resilience resources at a lower level. As discussed above, a team with resilient individuals is not necessarily a resilient team (on this point, see the case of Jeremy Lin reported in Box 2.5, versus the case of Obdulio Varela reported in Chapter 5, Box 5.4).

ADAPTIVE AND PROACTIVE RESILIENCE AS CONCEPTUAL TEMPLATES

Resilience thus refers to the maintenance of positive adjustments in significantly evolving contexts (Sutcliffe and Vogus, 2003). Representationally, it

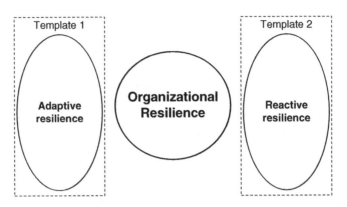

Figure 2.2   The foundational templates of resilience

is 'a dynamic process encompassing positive adaptation within the context of significant adversity' (Luthar et al., 2000, p. 543). Two major conceptual templates have been identified: adaptive resilience and proactive resilience. By 'templates' we refer to 'interpretations ... based on different but internally coherent sets of a priori theoretical premises' (Langley, 1999, p. 698). Such conceptual templates are not consolidated by empirical data but by theoretically coherent convergence within a nomological network (see the Appendix). Next, we discuss the two templates. Later, in Chapter 6, we will articulate them in an integrative model informed by a dialectical perspective. In terms of the dialectics of resilience, Figure 2.2 graphically depicts the two templates.

The idea of resilience as a process highlights the dynamics through which individuals and collective forms create or retain resources (cognitive, emotional, structural or relational) necessary to cope successfully with and learn from the unexpected (Sutcliffe and Vogus, 2003). Furthermore, while resilience as a construct is unique, it shares some characteristics with other well-known organizational processes. Such similarities can be classified according to the adaptive or proactive nature of resilience (see Table 2.3, and Chapter 6).

Successfully resiling from challenging conditions 'initiates a positive feedback loop to an organization's capabilities such that they are strengthened and further resilient in the face of novel events' (Sutcliffe and Vogus, 2008, p. 499). Our model reacts to the challenges for future research posed by Sutcliffe and Vogus (2008) by clarifying how learning can be 'both an input and an output' of organizational resilience. We extend the bivalence input/output of resilience as proposed by Sutcliffe and Vogus (2008), positing resilience as the antonym of vulnerability (Weick, 1993) in a synthetic

Table 2.3 Resilience and related constructs

Concept	Definition	Where it diverges from resilience	How it contributes to resilience	What it has in common with resilience
Proactive resilience				
Agility Representative works: Doz and Kosonen (2008a, 2008b), Martin and Carlile (2000)	The capacity to purposefully change and move nimbly in and out of different domains.	Organizations can develop fast strategies without much resilience. Agility is mainly related to speed. Rapid organizations may not be resilient.	The concepts are different, but agile organizations, in principle, 'constantly' adjust courses of action (Doz and Kosonen, 2008b, p. 95).	*Agility can be an antecedent of resilience, sharing outcomes in common* Resilience is a construct that implies exposure to adversity and the manifestation of positive adjustment outcomes (Luthar and Cicchetti, 2000; Välikangas and Romme, 2013).
Anticipation (prevention) Representative works: Carroll (1998), Wildavsky (1988)	Mode of anticipative control aimed at predicting and preventing potential dangers before damage is done.	While anticipation aims at preventing potential dangers before damage is done, resilience involves coping with unanticipated dangers after they have emerged (i.e., fixing orientation versus learning orientation).	Resilient entities are more likely to prevent (future) damages.	*Antecedents* Resilience is 'a unique blend of cognitive, behavioral, and contextual properties that increase a firm's ability to understand its current situation and to develop customized responses that reflect that understanding' (Lengnick-Hall and Beck, 2005, p. 750).
Flexibility Representative works:	'Real-time adjustment of actions in response to actual events' (Eisenhardt et al., 2010, p. 1264).	Organizations can be flexible because they can change rapidly. This is not indicative of resilience. For example, employing virtual	Resilience is intended to create flexibility, helping collectives or individuals to adapt flexibly to new realities.	*Outcome* The ability to respond while avoiding engagement in regressive behaviour (Horne, 1997).

Table 2.3 (continued)

Concept	Definition	Where it diverges from resilience	How it contributes to resilience	What it has in common with resilience
Bahrami and Evans (2011), Eisenhardt et al. (2010)		freelancers rather than full-time staff increases flexibility (Johns and Gratton, 2013) but it does not necessarily increase resilience. It could instead endanger resilience.		
Improvisation Representative work: Miner et al. (2001)	The capacity to respond in the absence of planning with the available rather than with the optimal resources.	Improvisation may be a one-off process, responding to an event without building the organization's resilience.	Continued, trained and cultivated improvisation skills may be a critical component of resilience.	*Antecedents* Bricolage has been associated both with improvisation (Cunha et al., 1999) and with resilience (Coutu, 2002).
Robustness Representative work: Miller (1993)	'Taking hits with minimal damage to functional capability' (Bahrami and Evans, 2005, p. 15).	Systems may progressively become more robust without gaining resilience. They may actually develop a simpler and more robust organizational architecture (Miller, 1993). They may be hard to bend but, submitted to the required amounts of pressure, they may break rather than express resilience.	Resilience may be viewed as a combination of robustness and flexibility (Hollnagel, 2012, p. 234).	*Outcomes* The 'capacity to be robust under conditions of enormous stress and change' (Coutu, 2002, p. 52).
Manoeuvrability Representative work: Nissen and Burton (2011)	'Manoeuvrability . . . concerns the quickness of a controlled system's planned change from one trajectory to another' (Nissen and Burton, 2011, p. 423).	While manoeuvrability expresses the capacity of reacting in a timely manner, resilience embeds learning properties that can increase the organizational capability to tackle futures stressors.	Both resilience and manoeuvrability refer to the capacity of reacting to external jolts by searching for a new state of equilibrium which differs from the previously existing one.	*Outcomes* To be able to return to a stable state after disruption (Bhamra et al., 2011).

Adaptive resilience

	Definition			
Adaptability Representative work: Chakravarthy (1982)	The capacity to re-establish a state of fit with a changing environment.	Organizations may regain adaptation without expressing resilience, for example via restructuring and downsizing.	Not all forms of adaptability express resilience, but resilience is intended to facilitate the ongoing adaptation of organizations.	*Outcomes* Organizational resilience is defined as a dynamic process encompassing positive adaptation within the context of significant adversity (Zhang and Liu, 2012). Adaptive efforts may also result in higher (hyper) resilience (Clair and Dufresne, 2007).
Coping Representative work: Lazarus and Folkman (1984)	Coping is defined as 'constantly changing cognitive and behavioral efforts to manage specific external and/or internal demands that are appraised as taxing or exceeding the resources of the person' (Lazarus and Folkman, 1984, p.141).	While coping 'refers to processes of adaptation' and 'coping can be viewed as efforts', resilience 'can be viewed as the successful outcome of these actions' (Compas et al., 2001, p.89).	'Coping and resilience often go hand-in-hand when describing how to maintain and return to normalcy after crisis (Bonanno, 2004; Bonanno et al., 2006); (Powley, 2013, p.45).	*Outcomes* Resilience builds on the foundation of the resilience of members of that organization (Riolli and Savicki, 2003).
Hardiness Representative works: Kobasa (1979), Kobasa and Puccetti (1983), Maddi and Khoshaba (2005)	Adaptive behaviors of resilient individuals. Capacity for toughness and durability, involving control, commitment, and challenge (Maddi, 2013; Maddi and Khoshaba, 2005).	While resilience is a process leading to the achievement and maintenance of 'positive adaptation' despite experiencing adversities, hardiness is a capacity that nourishes (and is nourished by) resilience.	Hardiness facilitates resilience under stress and is the 'basis for' or 'pathway to' resilience (Maddi, 2013). However, hardiness may also be an outcome of resilience, as well as a moderator of relationships between resilience and other variables.	*Antecedents* Resilience is the ability to 'rebound from adversity strengthened and more resourceful' (Sutcliffe and Vogus, 2003, p.97).

Table 2.3 (continued)

Concept	Definition	Where it diverges from resilience	How it contributes to resilience	What it has in common with resilience
Recovery Representative work: Tax and Brown (1998)	A system recovers when it returns to its baseline conditions. Recovery refers to the 'process of regaining something that has been lost and of returning to a former state' (Sonnentag et al., 2012, p. 867).	Resilient systems may evolve to a new condition rather than return to some previous condition. An effective recovery system does not necessarily mean that a system is resilient. While a recovered individual returns to their prior level of competence, the resilient one emerges from the adverse circumstances 'with growth and strengthened capabilities for dealing with future challenges' (Caza and Milton, 2012, p. 898).	Resilience aims to help the system in recovering and learning in the process of recovery.	*Outcomes* Resilience is a dynamic property of systems and is linked to a system's capacity of response (Gallopi'n, 2006).
Redundancy Representative work: Powley (2009)	The ability of a system to persist even when some parts of it are compromised. An organization can increase redundancy by creating backups, and resilient systems may actually have redundancies.	But backups may be of little use when conditions change dramatically, which means that the presence of backups does not necessarily lead to greater resilience.	Redundancy may help the organization in preserving a culture of learning. 'Relational redundancy' activates relational networks that enable resilience (Powley, 2009). Some redundancy is necessary for building resilience.	*Antecedents* The resilience of a system is determined by a set of dynamic capabilities and resources that form a system's adaptive capacity (Norris et al. 2008).
Post-traumatic growth (PTG) Representative works:	'The experience of positive change that occurs as a result of the struggle	PTG differs from resilience in both: (1) the magnitude of change or growth (greater and	Both post-traumatic growth and resilience involve improvement after	*Outcomes* Resilience is one of the 'four positive psychological

Maitlis (2012), Tedeschi and Calhoun (2004)	with highly challenging life crises' (Tedeschi and Calhoun, 2004, p. 1).	'transformational' on PTG); and (2) the source of the change or growth (achieved mainly through cognitive processing and disclosure on PTG) (Caza and Milton, 2012).	adverse circumstances, rather than merely returning to the baseline.	resources' that compose an individual's psychological capital; it has a 'positive impact on attitudes, behaviors and performance' (Luthans and Youssef, 2007; Avey et al., 2011).
Healing Representative work: Powley (2013)	'Organizational healing refers to the work of repairing practices, routines, and structures in the face of disruption and strengthening organizational functioning through social relationships' (Powley, 2013, p. 42).	Resilience is only a constituent of healing, this construct involving both resilience and 'growth and strengthening from crisis' (Powley, 2013).	Resilience is a constituent of healing. Healing is unviable without resilience.	*Outcomes* Resilience is viewed as the quality that enables the individual, community or organization to cope with, adapt to and recover from a disaster event (Horne, 1997; Buckle et al., 2000; Pelling and Uitto, 2001; Riolli and Savicki, 2003).

Organizational resilience (both proactive and adaptive)

Grit Representative work: Duckworth et al. (2007)	'Perseverance and passion for long-term goals' (Duckworth et al., 2007, p. 1087).	Resilience is only one component of grit.	Resilience is one component of grit. Gritty people are resilient, perseverant and passionate toward long-term goals.	*Antecedents and outcomes* Process differs: grit applies at the individual level; learning is undermined in grit.
Thriving Representative work: Spreitzer et al. (2005)	'Psychological state in which individuals experience both a sense of vitality and a sense of learning at work' (Spreitzer et al., 2005, p. 538).	While resilience presupposes the agent faces adverse circumstances before experiencing vitality and learning, thriving can occur with or without adversity.	Both resilience and thriving refer to the capacity for adaptability and positive adjustment (Sutcliffe and Vogus, 2003; Spreitzer et al., 2005).	*Antecedents and outcomes* Process differs: thriving can flourish in ignorance of possible threatening events.

interpretation based on dialectics. We articulate such reasoning in what follows.

Adaptive Resilience

Adaptive resilience represents a reactive view of process, as in Bridges' (1995, p. 5) definition: 'the ability to bend and not to break'. In this case, resilience is an expression of absorptive capacity, the ability to appreciate, transform and utilize knowledge for adaptive purposes (Zahra and George, 2002) that eventually changes the organization (or other agents). The concept of adaptive resilience is close to the definition used in physics, where resilience is the ability of a material to absorb energy when it is deformed elastically and to release that energy upon unloading (Campbell, 2008). The concept is not static per se. In fact, it can be seen as a 'dynamic process' where the life of an organization is seen as a chain of infinite resilience processes, and the final level of functioning can be defined as the sum of all resilience processes. In this vein, resilience is a dynamic capability that refers to successful adaptation, despite adversity. Although each resilience process might seem to be a return to homeostasis, multiple resilience processes over time lead to an increase in the level of functioning.

Adaptive resilience embeds responses to crisis and post-traumatic growth (see Box 2.7), perhaps the most visible form of resilience, as it puts an entity to the test. Adaptive resilience matters because it ultimately constitutes the test of a unit's capacity for resilience. The literature on resilience after crises epitomizes this approach. It is possible, however, that once the organization responds, resilience will evanesce, leading to little or no organizational learning, other than first-order learning not inscribed in organizational knowledge systems.

Adaptive Resilience and Related Constructs

Adaptive resilience differs from adaptability, coping, hardiness, recovery and redundancy (see Table 2.3). Adaptability typically is taken to mean the capacity to fit a changing environment (Chakravarthy, 1982; Waugh et al., 2008). Organizations may regain adaptation without expressing resilience, for example via restructuring. Resilience also differs from recovery. A system recovers when it returns to some baseline condition, but resilient systems may evolve to a new condition rather than return to a previous state. Resilience is conceptually different from coping, the process of managing (external or internal) demands that exceed existing resources (Lazarus and Folkman, 1984; Pargament, 1997; Tugade et al.,

BOX 2.7   A PARAGON OF POST-TRAUMATIC GROWTH

Rhonda Cornum, former US Army, a flight surgeon, with a doctorate in biochemistry and nutrition from Cornell University, was captured in Iraq on 27 February 1991. The *New York Times* described the events in the following way (Sciolino, 1992, p. A1):

> On a cold night during her weeklong captivity in Iraq in the Persian Gulf war, Maj. Rhonda Cornum was loaded into a pickup truck with another American prisoner of war, a young male sergeant, and taken from an underground bunker to a small prison. During the 30-minute drive, an Iraqi guard kissed her repeatedly, pulled a blanket over their heads so that they would not be seen, unzipped her flight suit and fondled her breasts. Major Cornum . . . had broken both arms, smashed her knee and had a bullet in her right shoulder as a result of the downing of her Army helicopter. She screamed in pain when the Iraqi tried to pull her flight suit down over her untreated and swollen arms. Before the ordeal was over, she told a Presidential commission on women in the military this month, she was 'violated manually – vaginally and rectally'.

Released eight days later, she became a war hero. She participated in many initiatives aimed to study and develop resilience. Martin Seligman (2011b, p. 160) described her as a 'poster child for post-traumatic growth'. Her traumatic experience was reframed by herself as follows (Seligman, 2011b, p. 160):

- 'I felt much better prepared to be a military physician and surgeon than previously. The concerns of my patients were no longer academic'.
- 'I felt far better equipped to be a leader and commander. That is the standard by which other experiences are now based, and so I feel much less anxiety or fear when faced with challenges'.
- 'I became a better, more attentive parent and spouse. I made the efforts to remember birthdays, to visit grandparents, and so on. No doubt, coming that close to losing them made me appreciate them more'.

She became the director of Comprehensive Soldier Fitness (Cornum et al., 2011), a programme including three components: a test for psychological fitness, self-improvement courses available following the test, and a Master Resilience Trainer Course (Figure 2.3) for drill sergeants. The programme was designed to 'increase psychological strength and positive performance and to reduce the incidence of maladaptive responses of the entire US Army' (Cornum et al., 2011, p. 4).

Figure 2.3   *Rhonda Cornum, speaking at the opening session of
a Master Resilience Trainer Course in Grafenwoehr, 13
September 2010*

2004; Caverley, 2005). For example, Compas et al. (2001, p. 89) considered
that while coping 'refers to processes of adaptation' and 'coping can be
viewed as efforts', resilience can be seen 'as the successful outcome of
these actions'. Moreover, although coping may help individuals to build or
foster resilience, some coping strategies may be maladaptive and damage
resilience capabilities (Cicotto et al., 2014).

Resilience is also different from hardiness, in that hardiness facilitates
resilience under stress and is the 'basis for' or 'pathway to' resilience
(Maddi, 2013). Hardiness represents the capacity for toughness and
durability, involving control, commitment and challenge (Maddi and
Khoshaba, 2005; Maddi, 2013):

> Cognitively hardy individuals (1) believe that they can control or influence
> events, (2) have a commitment to activities and their interpersonal relationships
> and to self, in that they recognize their own distinctive values, goals and priori-
> ties in life, and (3) view change as a challenge rather than as a threat. (Beasley et
> al., 2003, p. 79, based on Kobasa, 1979)

Finally, adaptive resilience is different from redundancy, typically seen as 'the time-tested way to improve the ability of a system to persist even when compromised' (Zolli and Healy, 2012, p. 13). An organization can increase its redundancy by creating backups and buffering zones, and these may characterize resilient systems (e.g., McGonigal, 2012). Backups and buffering do not necessarily lead to superior resilience: their presence may be of little use when conditions change dramatically. Conceptually, adaptive resilience incorporates the absorption of shocks and its respective transformation into a source of growth. From an organizational perspective, the issue is not whether organizations will need to respond to crises but whether they will be able to respond to crises with the necessary efficacy.

Proactive Resilience

A second important conceptual template corresponds to proactive resilience: the cultivated preparedness to cope with surprises, and the ability to view negative incidents as sources for organizational, team and individual opportunities and growth (Clair and Dufresne, 2007; Hamel and Välikangas, 2003; Story et al., 2013; Välikangas and Romme, 2013; see also Grant and Ashford, 2008). Proactive resilience can be viewed as an act of anticipation and active waiting (Sull, 2005; Waugh et al., 2008) in order to develop an organization's readiness for change (Armenakis et al., 1993). It is premised on preparedness.

Proactive resilience refers to survival in the face of threats, to the ability to view challenges and the preparation for them as sources of opportunity and growth. Consequently, it leads potentially to transformation in response to environmental shifts, even before these shifts happen (Hadida, 2009; Gilbert et al., 2012). However, the stimulus for resilient preparation is a shock, actual or potential, rather than an environmental possibility that can be neutralized by planning or anticipation. Resilience concerns absorption, not neutralization. The distinction between proactive and adaptive resilience, seen from the perspective of dynamic processes, helps us to understand that the latter embeds the mechanisms of the former, while adding some cognitive features and learning effects that are typical of living systems (Gilbert et al., 2012), including both organizational learning and the implementation of 'lessons learned' (e.g., Buchanan and Denyer, 2013).

Vulnerability, the failure of resilience (Weick, 1993; Whiteman and Cooper, 2011), results from occasions when sensemaking capacity is exceeded by feedback (Egeland et al., 1993). When this imbalance occurs, sensemaking agents, at any level of aggregation, are unable to face up to the challenges confronting them, and may become progressively more rigid and unable to express adaptive capacity (e.g., Gallopi'n, 2006; Finkel,

2011). Vulnerability is a dangerous condition because it progressively decouples agencies from their environment, increasing their rigidity in the face of threats.

Proactive resilience complements adaptive resilience. An organization develops resilience, proactively, by incorporating previous experiences in its collective behavioural repertoire. By this means, action is used as a source of reflection facilitating learning that will increase preparation for subsequent action. The proactive component of resilience results in a form of second-order, double-loop learning, leading the organization to reflect on its actions and to incorporate this learning in its operations.

Proactive Resilience and Related Constructs

Proactive resilience differs from other structural organizational features, such as agility, anticipation, flexibility, improvisation, robustness and manoeuvrability (see Table 2.3). Agility has been conceptualized as the capacity to rapidly express and execute new dynamic moves. Organizations can develop fast strategies via time management, time compression and other temporal management practices (Doz and Kosonen, 2008a, 2008b) without expressing resilience. Anticipation (or prevention) is a 'mode of control' characterized by efforts aimed at predicting and preventing potential dangers before damage is done (Wildavsky, 1988, p. 77); while resilience involves coping with unanticipated dangers after they have become manifest, and learning to bounce back (see also Boin, 2004; Carroll, 1998). Anticipation represents a fixing orientation, while resilience represents one that is able to learn (Carroll, 1998).

Resilience also differs from flexibility. Flexibility refers to the organization's capacity to change rapidly and without major impediments (McCann, 2004; Bahrami and Evans, 2005, 2011; Ward et al., 2015). Again, organizations can be flexible, for example, because they adopt modular types of structures or move to a position in the market where the products and services that are delivered inherently generate more value (Edwards et al., 2004; Nenni and Giustiniano, 2013; Ward et al., 2015). Nonetheless, such flexibility does not make an organization resilient: as in natural science, being able to bend does not entail being able to reach the previous shape, state or equilibrium (Crichton et al., 2009).

Resilience is also conceptually different from improvisation. Improvisation refers to the capacity to respond in the absence of planning with the available rather than with the optimal resources (Cunha et al., 1999; Hadida et al., 2015). Improvisations can be isolated, episodic responses to events without contributing to building resilience. Further, resilience also differs from robustness, the hardening of the characteristics of a system. Robust systems may be hard to bend but fragile under pressure and therefore unresilient (Miller, 1993). Further, although the idea of resilience seems to overlap with the concept of manoeuvrability (Nissen and Burton, 2011), within the more general framework of dynamic fit (Burton and Obel, 2004, 2013; Nissen, 2014), resilience's distinctive traits refer to organizations as systems exposed to multiple stressors (Du et al., 2010) rather than single stressors.

Resilience shares similarities with post-traumatic growth ('a positive psychological change experienced as a result of the struggle with highly challenging life circumstances'; Caza and Milton, 2012, p. 898), although the terms are conceptually distinct. In fact, both post-traumatic growth and resilience involve improvement after adverse circumstances (Maitlis, 2012), rather than merely returning to baseline functioning (such as in recovery). However, the magnitudes and sources of change or growth after facing adversity differ (Tedeschi and Calhoun, 2004).

Finally, resilience differs from healing (Powley, 2013). While at an individual level healing is the process of the restoration of health, organizational healing 'refers to the work of repairing practices, routines, and structures in the face of disruption and strengthening organizational functioning through social relationships' (Powley, 2013, p. 42). Healing involves not just resilience but also 'growth and strengthening from crisis', in such a way that 'neither resilience nor growth alone is sufficient to build healing' (Powley, 2013, p. 44), both being required. Thus, an organization may be resilient without experiencing healing.

Conceptually, proactive resilience differs from the above constructs by incorporating the absorption of shocks through anticipation. Exposure to controlled shocks may offer organizations a capacity to absorb them and to incorporate learning in their respective functioning (Sutcliffe and Vogus, 2003).

Articulating Adaptive and Proactive Resilience: Related Constructs

The two constructs of grit and thriving seem to overlap with some aspects of both adaptive and proactive resilience, while they differ from it in terms of the mechanisms involved. Thriving is a 'psychological state in which individuals experience both a sense of vitality and a sense of learning at work' (Spreitzer et al., 2005, p. 538). While resilience presupposes the existence of significant adversity before individuals experience vitality and learning, thriving does not (Caza and Milton, 2012). What is referred to as 'grit' (see Box 2.8) shares similarities with resilience, although the two concepts differ (Duckworth et al., 2007). Duckworth (in Perkins-Gough, 2013, pp. 14–16) argues that there is a relation between grit and resilience that:

BOX 2.8   LEARNING ABOUT GRIT FROM ANGELA DUCKWORTH'S WEBPAGE

The webpage of Angela Duckworth (https://angeladuckworth.com/qa/) provides relevant materials about the recently fashionable concept of grit. There you may find answers to questions such as the following:

- 'What is grit?'
- 'Is there anything I can do to build my grit?'
- 'If I'm gritty about one thing, will I be gritty about other things?'
- 'Is grit the same as self-control or conscientiousness?'
- 'Can you be too gritty?'
- 'Are women grittier than men? Or are men grittier than women?'
- 'Is grit more important than honesty and kindness?'
- 'Isn't grit, like everything else, in your genes? So why write a book about how to grow grit?'

You may also find materials about the measurement of grit and its validation in different countries. Several scholarly papers are also available. You may also watch Angela Duckworth's TED Talk on 'Grit: The power of passion and perseverance', at https://www.ted.com/talks/angela_lee_duckworth_grit_the_power_of_passion_ and_perseverance.

To have a better understanding of the perseverance toward long-term goals (that is, grit), explore the life of Maria da Conceição, the founder of Maria Cristina Foundation (http://mariacristinafoundation.org/maria-conceicao/). Her mother became sick when Maria da Conceição was two years old. An African immigrant, Maria Cristina, who worked as a cleaner, agreed to look after Maria until her mother got better, but she never did get better. Maria Cristina raised Maria da Conceição as one of her own, despite already having six mouths to feed. Over the years, Maria da Conceição developed great gratitude toward her adoptive mother, and life circumstances led her to reciprocate towards others. In 2005, Maria da Conceição visited a slum and a hospital in Dhaka while on a 24-hour break as a part of her job with the Emirates airline. The desperate struggle the slum-dwellers face daily made a deep impression on Maria, who cancelled her next holiday plans and instead spent two weeks in the slums, starting what grew to become the Maria Cristina Foundation.

Difficulties to fund the foundation led Maria da Conceição to take desperate measures to get attention, raise awareness and make public appeals for help to support 'her children'. Although she had never been an athlete, she embarked upon dozens of extreme sport activities. As at March 2018, her main achievements included: six full Ironman races on six continents in 56 days (2017); eight times Guinness World Record holder (2018); seven marathons on seven continents in ten days (2015); seven ultra-marathons, in six weeks, on seven continents (2014); 13 full marathons (2014); first and only Portuguese woman to climb Mount Everest (2013); last degree to North Pole (2011); last degree to South Pole (2018). In 2011,

Maria da Conceição entitled her Ted Talk 'Turning caterpillars into butterflies' (https://www.youtube.com/watch?v=75DjsB2EK4Y). Considering her life and her purpose, reflect on the following questions:

- How important for Maria's grit and resilience has been the affection she received from her adoptive family?
- Why may a meaningful purpose be a strong energizer of resilience?
- Why are social support and love (see Barsade and O'Neil, 2014; van Dierendonck and Patterson, 2015) important as nourishers of resilience?
- One of Maria's children aims to be Prime Minister and change the conditions for children in Bangladesh. This seems to represent a positive upward spiral. How can organizational leaders behave as nourishers of similar positive upward spirals?

because part of what it means to be gritty is to be resilient in the face of failure or adversity. But that's not the only trait you need to be gritty . . . So grit is not just having resilience in the face of failure, but also having deep commitments that you remain loyal to over many years.

Grit, much as most of the previously mentioned concepts, partly overlaps with resilience. These related concepts are either involved in the creation of resilience or are the result of it, confirming the idea that organizational resilience is a multifaceted construct covering different levels of analysis.

RESILIENCE AS A SYNTHESIS: A PRELIMINARY VIEW

Taken singularly, 'adaptive' and 'proactive' resilience seem to represent two opposite ways of facing challenges, revealing the ambivalent nature of resilience to be betwixt and between 'sponge and titanium' (Giustiniano and Cantoni, 2018). Resilience in organizations needs to capture the qualities that enable the individual, team or organization to cope with, adapt to and recover from jolts, crises and disasters (Horne, 1997; Buckle et al., 2000; Pelling and Uitto, 2001; Riolli and Savicki, 2003; Ponomarov and Holcomb, 2009); therefore, the dialectical interplay of proactive and adaptive resilience is necessary. Reaction without future anticipation lacks proactive resilience: it is 'learning but forgetting'. Proactive resilience in the absence of adaptive resilience corresponds to contemplative reflection without corresponding action. The synthesis between the two templates articulates action and reflection, which eventually fosters the cultivation of ongoing reflective practice (see Chapter 6).

In contradistinction to natural science (e.g., Garmezy, 1973; Holling, 1973), as will be made clearer in Chapter 5, we stress the idea of organizational resilience as having dialectical rather than mechanical foundations, foundations prepared in Nietzsche's famous aphorism. To this extent, the enriched version of Figure 2.2 that will be described in Chapter 6 (Figure 6.1) will show how the 'sublated' achievement of Template 3 overcomes the alternative of pursuing either adaptation (action) or reaction (reflection).

We propose dialectics as an interpretive lens, one that will integrate research on organizational resilience via the decoupling of adaptive and learning mechanisms. Additionally, Chapter 6 will achieve the synthetic articulation of perspectives (Clegg and Cunha, 2017). Dialectics has been an important conceptual framework in organizational theory for some considerable time (e.g., Benson, 1977), in which organizations are represented as constituted by opposing tensions. The tension between a thesis and an antithesis may result in a form of synthesis (Harvey, 2014), or it may exist as an ongoing state benefiting from the creative energy that the tension generates (Cunha et al., 2002).

RESILIENCE AND THE QUEST FOR CROSS-LEVEL INTERACTIONS

The literature shows that organizational knowledge, whether gained adaptively or produced proactively, which resides at one level does not automatically diffuse to higher or lower levels. For example, pockets of experts in an organization may be able to see a surprise coming, one that may not be perceived or considered relevant by other experts elsewhere in the organization (Cunha et al., 2006). How these experts interact with others will be decisive in terms of the action taken or not taken. Organizational researchers have explored such processes in the now classical case of the *Challenger* launch decision (Vaughan, 1996; Starbuck and Farjoun, 2005; see Box 6.2 in Chapter 6). Experts at Thiokol were aware of the risks but were not able to influence NASA's top decision-makers. Similarly, at NASA, Rodney Rocha was unable to get his concerns about operational safety heard (Wildavsky, 1988), creating a major problem resulting in the Space Shuttle Columbia disaster (Edmondson, 2012).

The failure to address problems results from a number of possible causes. These include, first, attempts to reduce uncertainty (Tsoukas, 2005) that progressively decouple the organization from undesired uncertainty-generating processes. Second, a focus premised on the assumption that, rather than the need to reinvent, improvements of existing processes are sufficient (Starbuck and Milliken, 1988). Third, seeking protection from the environment as a source of danger, rather than embracing environmental change as an inevitable source of change and surprise (Rak and Patterson, 1996; Plowman et al., 2007). Fourth, cognitive biases, groupthink, and ignoring relevant information that contradicts the preferred course of action. All of these processes are defensive and do not increase resilience.

Resilience also operates at different levels of analysis, flowing potentially but not necessarily across levels. It may involve individuals, teams, and organizations as they respond to some significant occurrence. These units may develop intra-level self-contained capabilities, or inter-level capabilities with resilience at one level spilling over to other levels. Whether resilience is an intra-level or inter-level competency is critically dependent on the role of interactions. Some interactions help to build, whereas others inhibit resilience (Carmeli and Gittell, 2009; Caza and Milton, 2012; Khan et al., 2017). It is then possible that resilient individuals work in non-resilient teams (and that non-resilient individuals work in resilient teams); that resilient teams emerge in non-resilient organizations (and that non-resilient teams work in resilient organizations); and that resilient organizations make a difference in the context of non-resilient communities (and that non-resilient organizations do not disturb resilient communities). It is also plausible that resilience at one level leads to resilience at other levels, such as when a positive practice is transferred to a higher level (for example, a resilient and hopeful leader acts as a source of energy helping the team to face hostile environments or traumatic changes; Norman et al., 2005; Kohlrieser et al., 2012; Story et al., 2013).

In order to understand the resilience process within and across levels, it is important to consider that 'social resilience is about the relationships that help us find resources when we need them' (McGonigal, 2012, p. 38). Positive relationships (or 'high quality connections') within a team create opportunities to expand the behavioural repertoire and to confront challenges mindfully (Caza and Milton, 2012; Stephens et al., 2012; Stephens et al., 2013; see Box 2.9). As anticipated, resilience has been associated with the idea of relationships as resources (social capital; see Gittell and Douglass, 2012) that allow the organization to face challenges in a purposeful, mindful way, avoiding the trap of repeating acquired and standard behaviours that rigid, non-resilient systems express when threatened (Weick, 1993).

Thus, resilience thrives on relationships and positive interactions. In fact, it is the presence of these interactions that allows a system to express the capacity to adapt in the face of challenges that are unexpected or that transcend the ordinary. The triggering of resilience requires, therefore, the activation of specific endeavours and intentions at all the organizational levels.

BOX 2.9 CRITICAL INFRASTRUCTURE SECURITY AND RESILIENCE MONTH

Physical and logistic infrastructures are critical for the well-being of local populations, for the conduct of regular lives and the operation of businesses. That is why some public agencies promote initiatives that aim at attracting the communitarian attention towards the defence and preservation of such infrastructure. One case of deliberate attraction of such attention is represented by the Critical Infrastructure Security and Resilience Month initiative promoted by the US Department of Homeland Security. In its words (see https://www.dhs.gov/cisr-month):

> We know critical infrastructure as the power we use in our homes and businesses, the water we drink, the transportation systems that get us from place to place, the first responders and hospitals in our communities, the farms that grow and raise our food, the stores we shop in, and the Internet and communication systems we rely on to stay in touch with friends and family. The security and resilience of this critical infrastructure is vital not only to public confidence, but also to the Nation's safety, prosperity, and well-being.
>
> Critical Infrastructure Security and Resilience Month, observed in the month of November, builds awareness and appreciation of the importance of critical infrastructure and reaffirms the nationwide commitment to keep our critical infrastructure and our communities safe and secure. Securing the nation's infrastructure is a national priority that requires planning and coordination across the entire community.

The initiative attempts to develop 'critical partnerships between the private sector and the public sector in order to mitigate risk and enhance the security and resilience of public gathering sites and special events'. Storytelling plays an important role, as one of the aims is to 'share stories and information [with] customers, constituents, partners, residents, and employees through newsletters, websites, emails, blog posts, and tweets.'

Taking place at different levels of aggregation, resilience is the concerted effort to make sense and adjust the organization via generative, engaged interactions, taken as reservoirs of ideas and assistance that can be activated as needed (Lengnick-Hall, 2008). Similarly to other organizational constructs (e.g., Spreitzer, 2007; Fisher, 2010; Brown, 2015), resilience bridges levels of analysis and disciplinary boundaries.

How resilience at one level may propagate throughout the system (or fail to do so), positively influencing other levels (or failing to do so) so that it is systematically cultivated, requires further research. An example of the dynamics of propagation is reported in the case of the trading room of Lower Manhattan at the time of 9/11 (Beunza and Stark, 2003; see Chapter 6, and Box 4.1 in Chapter 4). While the trading room itself was damaged during the terrorist attack on the Twin Towers, the organization using it was able not only to recreate itself (relocation, restart of the activities: reactive resilience) but also to innovate the business in conditions of radical uncertainty (active resilience) (Kendra and Wachtendorf, 2003). Other financial firms operating in the World Trade Center area followed a similar pattern (see Box 4.1 in Chapter 4).

With organizations increasingly exposed to threats of various kinds, the understanding and pursuit of resilience is become of growing significance for management studies. Resilience can characterize individuals, teams, organizations and societies as they are able to adaptively absorb external shocks and to reactively learn from them, while simultaneously preparing for and responding to external jolts. Resilience represents the capacity to bounce back from failures, setbacks and adversities in the face of natural and human-generated adverse events.

NOTES

1. https://www.vlada.cz/en/clenove-vlady/premier/speeches/prime-minister-we-need-to-streng then-the-resilience-of-eu-member-states-to-traditional-and-new-threats-157474/.
2. https://www.pmc.gov.au/cyber-security/cyber-resilience-taskforce.
3. https://www.gov.uk/government/ministers/minister-for-government-resilience-and-efficien cy.
4. Meyer (1982) originally labelled this as 'resiliency'. We follow Luthar et al. (2000), distinguishing between 'resilience' and 'resiliency': the first related to process, while the latter is a personal trait (Waugh et al., 2011).
5. The word derives from the Greek, meaning 'quick birth' (Keeler et al., 2015).
6. Title adapted from Bob Dylan's (1965) 'Love minus zero/No limit'.

3. Resilience in individuals

Nurturing personal resilience is a skill CEOs [chief executive officers] must develop over time, and those CEOs we spoke to used words such as energy, courage, and strength to describe their coping mechanisms for the physical, emotional, and intellectual demands of the job.
(Saïd Business School and Heidrick & Struggles, 2015, p. 21)

DISCOVERING INDIVIDUAL RESILIENCE

Human being is a complex combination of intertwined agency and events that makes humans and their social constructions fascinating and unpredictable. In fact, as events unfold, failures and mistakes in constituting their significance enable us to learn how to identify pitfalls and what to avoid next time, how to 'transform poison into medicine' (Clair and Dufresne, 2007).

In nature, traumatic events trigger the generation of biological antibodies and, by analogy, the formation of similar psychological defensive mechanisms. So, when the young Elisabeth contracts measles, her body suffers for as long as it will take to build the necessary defences lasting her whole life. Similarly, when Julius finds out that his wife has cancer, he will be more prepared and ready if the fates decree that a similar tragedy afflicts siblings, children or other relatives and friends. He will be more familiar with the symptoms as well as possible cures, and more aware of available assistance.

Now think about Anna, who has a very bad and nasty boss as her first manager. Will she replicate the same uncivil behaviour that her superordinate displays to her if she has the chance to manage other individuals? Or, being conscious of what it entails, will she behave in a polite and civil manner towards her subordinates? Is she able, now, to keep calm, to sleep well and to perform her tasks appropriately? Or is she losing control and projecting her rage on to colleagues and family members at home?

At the individual level, resilience has been defined differently over time and across disciplines (Caza and Milton, 2012). However, as illustrated by the examples of Elisabeth and Julius, two consistent aspects emerge from almost all definitions. First, resilience requires the presence of some negative stressor and an individual being exposed to significant threats (Luthar et al., 2000). Second, resilient individuals perform a positive adaptation in the face of stressful or threatening events. So if Anna is able to nurture her resilience, she will be able to be a better boss than her current one and keep psychologically healthy.

In Chapter 2 we learned that resilience, in both its adaptive and proactive forms, is conceptually and practically linked to related constructs. In this chapter we will discuss how these related constructs articulate with individual resilience (which is a component of psychological capital; Box 3.1) to isolate its antecedents and consequences, an exercise that will be completed later in Chapter 4.

BOX 3.1   RESILIENCE AS A COMPONENT OF PSYCHOLOGICAL CAPITAL (PSYCAP)

Psychological capital (PsyCap) is an individual's positive psychological state of development, characterized by:

> (1) having confidence (efficacy) to take on and put in the necessary effort to succeed at challenging tasks; (2) making a positive attribution (optimism) about succeeding now and in the future; (3) persevering toward goals and, when necessary, redirecting paths to goals (hope) in order to succeed; and (4) when beset by problems and adversity, sustaining and bouncing back and even beyond (resilience) to attain success (Luthans et al., 2015, p.2)

This definition makes clear that resilience is a component of PsyCap, the other components being self-efficacy (or self-confidence), hope (willpower and way-power), and optimism. The inclusion of these four strengths in the same construct makes sense in two ways. First, the four components influence each other. For example, resilience allows employees to re-establish self-efficacy after experiencing a failure in pursuing work goals. Hopeful employees are more resilient in that they are more perseverant in pursuing goals in spite of failures and setbacks. Second, the underlying mechanism common to the four components is a positive agentic motivation toward employees' performance and success (Luthans et al., 2015; Bandura, 2008).

Readers interested in a better understanding of the topic may read Luthans et al. (2015), Luthans and Youssef-Morgan (2017) and Newman et al. (2014). The literature about PsyCap may be very helpful to understand the antecedents and consequences of resilience.

ANTECEDENTS OF INDIVIDUAL RESILIENCE

Coutu (2002) argues that three conditions qualify resilient individuals (and in general also organizations): (1) the acceptance of reality; (2) the propensity to make meaning from an adverse situation; (3) the ability to make do with whatever is at hand (for example, bricolage; Weick, 1993). These three qualities characterize individuals who do not falter when facing hard times, despite suffering. Abraham Lincoln represents an iconic case (Box 3.2). Rhonda Cornum, discussed in Box 2.7 in Chapter 2, is another paragon of a resilient individual who became stronger after having a 'near-death' traumatic experience. Resilience was also a precious other-directed psychological resource that Sheryl Sandberg (the Chief Operating Officer of Facebook) exhibited with a concern for her children after her husband, aged 47, died suddenly (see Adam Grant, in Buchanan, 2017; see Box 1.4 in Chapter 1).

A question arises: how do those three 'conditions' of accepting reality, making meaning from adversity and the ability to be a bricoleur emerge? What explains why some individuals are more resilient, or develop more resilience, than others? Table 3.1 provides several examples of possible antecedents of resilience (see also Box 3.3). Some relate to the individual, others to the context. Unsurprisingly, those two kinds of antecedents interact. For example, contextual factors are interpreted and dealt with differently by different individuals. Further, while a self-effective and hopeful employee is more likely to react resiliently toward a toxic leader, for other employees such a leader may be a risk factor. Note that Table 3.1 includes extra-work factors, which makes sense because employees are holistic beings. For example, while a functional family may be a source of resilient assets, a dysfunctional one may aggravate the consequences from a dysfunctional workplace, a toxic leader, or a problematic downsizing leading to unemployment (Masten and Monn, 2015).

As a process, resilience is considered to be 'a developmental trajectory characterized by demonstrated competence in the face of, and professional growth after, experiences of adversity in the workplace. Each enables an individual to handle future challenges' (Caza and Milton, 2012, p. 896). Resilience is open to development. It is not 'an inherent characteristic of personality' and can be developed at any time during the lifespan (Gillespie et al., 2007, p. 124). If a process of development of resilience unfolds, it cannot be independent of the context in which the individual is immersed. Contexts characterized by trust and social support amidst adversity will be more resilience-friendly than contexts rife with cynicism, distrust and social toxicity. Such an approach differs from perspectives that afford resilience a stable trait. While the developmental view considers that an

BOX 3.2   THE ONE ALL OF THEM WANT TO BE MORE LIKE?

Abraham Lincoln (16th President of the United States from March 1861 until his assassination in April 1865; see Figure 3.1) is 'regularly named the greatest President in surveys of historians' (Baker, 2015, p. A11). He was described as 'the one President all of them want to be more like' (Baker, 2015). The *Washington Post* surveyed 162 members of the American Political Science Association's Presidents & Executive Politics section, Abraham Lincoln having been rated the greatest

Source: Photo: Alexander Gardner (1821–1882). Retrieved from https://commons. wikimedia.org/wiki/File:Abraham_Lincoln_half_length_seated,_April_10,_1865.jpg. This work is in the public domain: http://www.loc.gov/pictures/resource/cph.3a11367/.

Figure 3.1   Abraham Lincoln (5 February 1865 or 10 April 1865)

President (Rottinghaus and Vaughn, 2015). In an article in the *New York Times* magazine 'Lincoln's School of Management', Nancy F. Koehn (a historian at Harvard Business School, who studied Lincoln for more than a decade) wrote: 'The legacy of Abraham Lincoln hangs over every American president. To free a people, to preserve the Union, "to bind up the nation's wounds": Lincoln's presidency, at a moment of great moral passion in the country's history, is a study in high-caliber leadership' (Koehn, 2013, p. BU1). Howard Schultz, CEO of Starbucks, pointed out that 'Lincoln's presidency is a big, well-lit classroom for business leaders seeking to build successful, enduring organizations' (in Koehn, 2013, p. BU1).

Resilience, according to Koehn (see also Goodwin, 2005), is one of the most distinctive strengths of Lincoln: 'despite all of his mental suffering, Lincoln never gave way to his darkest fears. His resilience and commitment to preserve the Union helped sustain him.' The ability to experience negative emotions without giving in to them is vital for entrepreneurs and business leaders. Ari Bloom, a strategic adviser to consumer-related companies, put it this way: 'Nothing prepares you for the emotional ups and downs that come with starting a business. There *will* be obstacles, big and small, that come at you every day, from personnel issues to supplier delays, to late payments or even hurricanes.' Throughout, entrepreneurs must maintain their professional composure while staying true to their vision and their integrity, he said. 'Lincoln is striking because he did all this under extremely difficult circumstances,' Mr Bloom said:

> Some of his ability to navigate such difficult terrain was about emotional intelligence and the deep faith he nurtured about his vision. But some of it was also about how he gathered advice and information from a wide range of people, including those who did not agree with him. This is important in building a business because you have to listen to customers, employees, suppliers and investors, including those who are critical of what you are doing.

individual may show different states of resilience in different moments, the trait perspective assumes that one is or is not resilient across situations.

In this book we espouse a processual perspective. However, we also consider that various dispositions can make some individuals more resilient than others, including personal traits such as optimism, confidence (Bonanno et al., 2006) or faith (Pargament, 1997). In short, some individual characteristics may make some people more prone to develop resilience than others. Some individuals may be more proficient than others in developing social capital and being involved in rich social networks (Pressman et al., 2005) that make them more liable to bounce back from adversity. And some contextual conditions may affect the individuals' capacity to be resilient. For a child abandoned by parents, the social support offered by friends, teachers or members of the community is important. For an employee targeted by a bullying boss, family, friends and co-workers' social support is significant in building resilience. Naturally, having a bullying

Table 3.1   Illustrative antecedents of individual grit

	Assets and resources	Risk factors
Personal characteristics and behaviours	Positive self-perceptions Positive affect Faith Motivation to learn and develop Positive outlook in life Emotional stability Self-regulation Sense of humour Insight Independence Initiative Creativity Personal identity Self-esteem Morality Optimism Self-efficacy Hope (willpower and waypower) Psychological hardiness (commitment, control and challenge)	Alcoholism Drug abuse Poor health Stress Burnout
Context (including leadership)	Care-giving adults Effective parenting Collective efficacy in the community Pro-social and rule-abiding peers Social support Relationship quality and virtuousness within the team Ethical and trustworthy team/organizational culture Reciprocal trust in team Mentorship Meaningful work Hopeful leaders Developmental leadership Transformational leadership	Undereducation Dysfunctional family Failed social institutions Unemployment Exposure to trauma* Experiencing violence Toxic team climate Toxic leadership

Note: * For example, traumas experienced during childhood, such as: (1) personal abuse: physical, verbal and sexual; (2) physical and emotional neglect; (3) family members', especially parents', alcoholism; a mother who is a victim of domestic violence; a family member in jail or diagnosed with a mental illness; the disappearance of a parent through divorce, death or abandonment. See https://acestoohigh.com/got-your-ace-score/.

Sources: Abstracted from Caza and Milton (2012), Cohn et al. (2009), King et al. (2016), Luthans et al. (2006b), Luthans et al. (2007), Meneghel et al. (2016), Norman et al. (2005), Sommer et al. (2016), Stephens et al. (2013) and Tugade et al. (2004).

BOX 3.3   INTERVENTIONS TO FOSTER RESILIENCE

Literature has shown that resilience, as well as the other components of PsyCap, may be fostered in workplaces via several interventions. Consider looking at the following papers for more detail: Luthans et al. (2006a), Luthans et al. (2010), Luthans et al. (2008), Peterson et al. (2008) and Verleysen et al. (2015).

If you are a leader, answer the following question: How may I promote my employees' resilience? If you are not a leader, think about how you may help your co-workers to develop their resilience.

boss may be both a risk factor and a trigger for developing resilience. Resilience is thus a paradoxical strength: risk factors may destroy but where they do not destroy it resilience may be energized.

Related Constructs as Antecedents of Individual Resilience

As anticipated in Chapter 2 and represented in Table 3.1, many constructs can be related to resilience. We discuss some of them next. It is important to note from the beginning that a construct may be both an antecedent and a consequence of resilience. For example, experiencing positive emotions may help in dealing with adversity, but being resilient in the face of adversities can be a source of positive emotions. Something similar by way of being an antecedent may happen with the following constructs.

Hardiness is the individual capacity for toughness and durability, involving control, commitment and challenge (Kobasa, 1979; Kobasa and Puccetti, 1983; Maddi and Khoshaba, 2005; Maddi, 2013). When individuals are exposed to stress, hardiness facilitates resilience, representing a 'basis for' or a 'pathway' to resilience (Maddi, 2013). So, hardiness is an antecedent of resilience as it nourishes the ability of individuals to 'rebound from adversity strengthened and more resourceful' (Sutcliffe and Vogus, 2003, p. 97). Hence hardiness expresses a 'positive adaptation' that nourishes adaptive resilience, and it is nourished by it in return.

Anticipation of events is a proactive way to predict and prevent potential dangers before damage is done (Carroll, 1998; Wildavsky, 1988). The individual adopting an anticipative attitude seeks to prevent potential danger arising from risky events before the damage is done. Being resilient is based also on 'cognitive behaviors' (Lengnick-Hall and Beck, 2005,

p. 750) such as anticipation, which is necessary though not sufficient for the unfolding of resilience. Resilience also involves coping with dangers that emerge after the event and were not anticipated. Several studies show that in the face of a lack of anticipation, organizations may unravel in the face of the unexpected (Weick, 1993), or even trigger disastrous events in systems that are designed to prevent them (organizational zemblanity; e.g., Giustiniano et al., 2016a; Giustiniano et al., 2016b).

Within the framework of resilience, improvisation is complementary to the construct of anticipation. Individual improvisation has been defined as dealing with the unexpected: responding 'in the moment', adapting effectively to sudden changes (Balachandra et al., 2005), adapting planning to the circumstances ('psychology'; Gardner and Rogoff, 1990), creative and spontaneous managing of an unexpected event (Magni et al., 2009). Not all unplanned actions can be considered to be improvised, as improvisation entails deliberate new design, conceptually excluding random change. Improvisation requires several components (Cunha et al., 2017): (1) the convergence of design and performance (extemporaneity); (2) the creation of some degree of novel action (novelty); and (3) the deliberateness of the design that is created during its own enactment (intentionality). Further, it often involves (4) working with an improvisational referent (Miner et al., 2001), such as a prior version of an action pattern, a previous plan, or an internal or external benchmark. Individual improvisation takes place in organizations when 'employees adjust their work in real time to emerging information or are stretched beyond their routines to deliver a novel solution to a problem' (Hadida et al., 2015, p. 447). Weick (1993) recognizes improvisation and bricolage as a source of resilience that may start from a single individual and affect the whole organization.

MEASURING INDIVIDUAL RESILIENCE

Individual resilience can be measured in several ways. Some measures include only resilience, while others consider resilience as a component of a wider construct. An example of the former is the Resilience Scale (Wagnild and Young, 1993), one of the best-known and most frequently used measures of resilience. It includes 25 items. A global score, or two scores representing two dimensions (personal competence; acceptance of self and life), may be computed. A short version of this scale, containing 14 items (Wagnild, 2009a, 2009b), has been validated in Brazil (Damásio et al., 2011) and Japan (Nishi et al., 2013). The Ego-Resiliency Scale may be found in Block and Kremen (1996). The Brief Resilience Scale (BRS), which assesses the ability to bounce back or recover from stress, may be

BOX 3.4   MEASURE YOUR INDIVIDUAL RESILIENCE

The Tachikawa Resilience Scale has been validated by Nishi et al. (2013). Some sample items are presented next. To what extent do you agree with each statement? Use the following seven-point scale to answer, from 1, strongly disagree to 7, strongly agree:

- Even during hardships, I think I will be able to manage.
- I accept things as they are when there are no alternatives.
- I am good at changing my way of thinking.
- During hardships, I think things could be even worse so I should feel lucky.
- Even if I am angry with someone who caused serious problems for me, my anger does not last long.

Using the complete scale of ten items, the mean score obtained by Nishi et al. (2013) in two samples was 45.1 and 38.4. Refer to the work of Nishi et al. (2013) and calculate your score. Is your score lower, higher or around those two scores? Compare your score with scores of other individuals. If you are a trainer or an instructor, you may calculate the average of all individuals in the classroom and then invite them to compare their individual score with the average score.

   You may also self-assess your 'Resilience Core' and interpret your score at http://www.trueresilience.net/briefresiliencescale.aspx. Other self-assessments may be found at: (1) http://www.resilience-project.eu/uploads/media/self_evaluation_en.pdf; (2) https://acestoohigh.com/got-your-ace-score/; and (3) http://www.peaklearning.com/about_aq-profile.php.

found in Smith et al. (2008). The Tachikawa Resilience Scale, validated by Nishi et al. (2013), includes ten items (see Box 3.4).

   The PsyCap Questionnaire (PCQ) (Luthans et al., 2015) measures not only resilience but also self-efficacy, hope and optimism. Two PCQ versions have been adopted: PCQ-24 includes 24 items, while PCQ-12 includes 12. PCQ is a self-reported measure, like the other measures of resilience mentioned above. Recently, a measure of implicit PsyCap was developed (Harms et al., 2017). Implicit measures may help to deal with some limitations of self-reported measures. For example, individuals may have biased perceptions of their own psychological strengths. Other authors (Rego et al., 2017c) have suggested the use of other-reports to measure PsyCap, including resilience. Other-reports may be more relevant than self-reports to measure the impact of leaders' PsyCap on their employees, because leadership is a relational process (Uhl-Bien, 2006) and what likely matters most for the impact of leaders on their team members is what the leaders convey to them, and not simply what the leaders feel and believe.

CONSEQUENCES OF INDIVIDUAL RESILIENCE

Studies of individual resilience indicate that resilience is related to problem-solving capabilities, favourable perceptions, positive reinforcement and strong faith (Zolli and Healy, 2012). Resilience also relates to workplace performance (Caverley, 2005; Coutu, 2002; Luthans et al., 2010; Waite and Richardson, 2004), as well as to a number of other coping processes, such as employability (Chen and Lim, 2012). Coping is defined as 'constantly changing cognitive and behavioral efforts to manage specific external and/ or internal demands that are appraised as taxing or exceeding the resources of the person' (Lazarus and Folkman, 1984, p. 141). Hence, when exposed to pressure, individuals tend to adapt in an effort to tackle the challenging events; while coping refers to such individual reaction, adaptive resilience 'can be viewed as the successful outcome of these actions' (Compas et al., 2001, p. 89). In facing adversity, 'coping and resilience often go hand-in-hand when describing how to maintain and return to normalcy after crisis (Bonanno, 2004; Bonanno et al., 2006)' (Powley, 2013, p. 45).

When exposed to critical and traumatic situations, individuals may not only cope with them but also grow, that is, they reassess these situations via learning to be better prepared for the future. In fact, post-traumatic growth (PTG) is 'the experience of positive change that occurs as a result of the struggle with highly challenging life crises' (Tedeschi and Calhoun, 2004, p. 1; see Box 3.5, and Box 2.7 in Chapter 2). Both post-traumatic growth and resilience involve improvement after the experience of adverse circumstances, rather than merely returning to a baseline. Nonetheless, PTG differs from resilience in both: (1) the magnitude of change or growth, which is expected to be greater and 'transformational' in PTG; and (2) the source of the change or growth, which is achieved mainly through cognitive processing and disclosure of PTG (Caza and Milton, 2012).

Coping with stressful or traumatic situations and trying to move beyond them exposes the individual to distress and potential breakdowns. Healing, rather than prolonging trauma, is an action that involves 'repairing practices, routines and structures . . . in the face of disruption' (Powley, 2013, p. 42). Healing requires both resilience and 'growth and strengthening from crisis' (Powley, 2013). Hence, despite being a necessary but not sufficient condition, adaptive resilience is vital for healing: without individual resilience, healing may not be viable.

BOX 3.5   USING HARDSHIP TO GROW

Explore the life of Nelson Mandela. Mandela is applauded as one of the most important leaders of the twentieth century. In your exploration, you will learn that he was imprisoned because of his ideals. It seems possible to say that he used the very adverse circumstance of being arrested to grow as an individual and as a politician. What lessons can be drawn from this case?

Read Cascio and Luthans (2014), who describe the 'metamorphosis' that emerged at Robben Island, where Mandela was imprisoned (Cascio and Luthans, 2014). They summarize the events as follows (p. 51):

> Nelson Mandela and other political prisoners from South Africa were imprisoned on notorious Robben Island from the mid-1960s until the end of the apartheid regime in 1991. The stark conditions and abusive treatment of these prisoners has been widely publicized. However, upon reflection and in retrospect, over the years, a type of metamorphosis occurred. Primarily drawing from first-hand accounts of the former prisoners and guards, it seems that Robben Island morphed from the traditional oppressive prison paradigm to one where the positively oriented prisoners disrupted the institution with a resulting climate of learning and transformation that eventually led to freedom and the end of apartheid.

Do you consider that similar metamorphoses may happen in 'normal' organizations? Mandela, the resilient prisoner, became a leader, not only of the other prisoners, but also of guards. Do you consider that an analogous process may occur in 'normal' organizations? If so, under what conditions?

Explore also the life of Pepe Mujica, a former President of Uruguay (2010–2015). He was qualified as the 'world's poorest President' (Yam, 2015) thanks to his very modest lifestyle and to his decision to donate 90 per cent of his salary to charity. The rock band Aerosmith offered him an autographed guitar as a gift, which he put up for auction to raise money to build housing. His donations left him with roughly $800 a month of his salary (Romero, 2013) ($1250, according to Cappelli, 2011). He told *El Mundo*: 'I do fine with that amount; I have to do fine because there are many Uruguayans who live with much less' (Cappelli, 2011).

As a consequence of striving for political ideals (including through violence) at an early age, Mujica 'spent 14 years in prison, including more than a decade in solitary confinement, often in a hole in the ground. During that time, he would go more than a year without bathing, and his companions, he said, were a tiny frog and rats with whom he shared crumbs of bread' (Romero, 2013, p. A1). When in 2014 *The Economist* asked him if it has been very difficult for him to recover from his experiences in jail, and the answer was:

> There's a rule: it affected less those with the greatest political commitment. There are reserves of resilience. But I'll tell you something. I went seven years without being allowed to read a book. I didn't know it but a lot of what

came later was the fruit of how much I thought, thought and rewound. It's a strange thing, it seems as if man sometimes learns more from pain than from good times. I wouldn't be who I am today, I wouldn't have developed the political persona that I have today if I hadn't lived such tough years. For this reason I never get tired of saying to young people that those who are defeated are those who cease to fight, it's always worthwhile to start over in all aspects of life, not just in politics. I believe that life is a marvelous adventure. And it's worthwhile to start again 20 times over. If I hadn't lived those dark, horrible years (pauses). But they gave me a lot. For example, I do not hate. Do you know what a luxury it is not to hate?

Pause and reflect upon the following questions: Where did Mujica find his reserves of resilience? Is his capacity to forgive a source or a consequence of resilience? How do you interpret the statement that 'It's a strange thing, it seems as if man sometimes learns more from pain than from good times'?

INDIVIDUAL RESILIENCE AND COMPLEMENTARY PROCESSES

As suggested previously, grit and thriving have many things in common with both adaptive and proactive resilience, representing both antecedents and outcomes. At the individual level, thriving is a 'psychological state' that sees the contemporary presence of 'vitality and a sense of learning at work' (Spreitzer et al., 2005, p. 538). While both resilience and thriving entail the capacity for adaptability and positive adjustment (Sutcliffe and Vogus, 2003; Spreitzer et al., 2005), thriving can also be experienced in the absence of adverse circumstances, which are instead required for triggering resilience (Caza and Milton, 2012). Further, the 'sense of learning' characterizing thriving does not necessarily translate into actual learning, which is vital for resilience.

Grit entails 'perseverance and passion for long-term goals' (Duckworth et al., 2007, p. 1087). Gritty individuals not only display resilience in the face of failure or adversity but also express deep commitment and loyalty to long-term goals over the years (Duckworth, 2016). Angela Lee Duckworth, who has been conducting ground-breaking studies on grit, in an interview with *Educational Leadership,* answered as follows when asked, 'How are grit and resilience related? Is there a difference between the two?' (in Perkins-Gough, 2013, p. 14):

The word *resilience* is used differently by different people. And to add to the confusion, the ways people use it often have a lot of overlap. To give you an example, Martin Seligman, my advisor and now my colleague here at Penn, has a program called the 'Penn Resiliency Program.' It's all about one specific definition of resilience, which is optimism – appraising situations without distorting them, thinking about changes that are possible to make in your life. But I've heard other people use resilience to mean bouncing back from adversity, cognitive or otherwise. And some people use *resilient* specifically to refer to kids who come from at-risk environments who thrive nevertheless. What all those definitions of resilience have in common is the idea of a positive response to failure or adversity. Grit is related because part of what it means to be gritty is to be resilient in the face of failure or adversity. But that's not the only trait you need to be gritty.

The other trait that makes people gritty is having consistent interests (that is, passion). To understand both components of grit, the reader may carry out the self-assessment reported in Box 3.6. Duckworth stated in the mentioned interview: 'So grit is not just having resilience in the face of failure, but also having deep commitments that you remain loyal to over many years' (in Perkins-Gough, 2013, p. 16). In short, gritty people are resilient and hardworking, but they also 'know in a very, very deep way what it is they want' (that is, they are energized by a purpose) (Brooks, 2016; see

---

BOX 3.6   HOW TO MEASURE GRIT

The following eight items, proposed by Duckworth and Quinn (2009, p. 167), represent the short grit scale (the full scale is in Duckworth et al., 2007). Two dimensions are included: consistency of interest (that is, passion) and perseverance of effort:

1. I often set a goal but later choose to pursue (follow) a different one.
2. I have been obsessed with a certain idea or project for a short time but later lost interest.
3. I have difficulty maintaining (keeping) my focus on projects that take more than a few months to complete.
4. New ideas and projects sometimes distract me from previous ones.
5. I finish whatever I begin.
6. Setbacks (delays and obstacles) don't discourage me. I bounce back from disappointments faster than most people.
7. I am diligent (hard working and careful).
8. I am a hard worker.

You may obtain your score directly through answering ten questions available on Angela Duckworth's webpage: https://angeladuckworth.com/grit-scale/.

BOX 3.7   STRESS AS A RESILIENCE BUSTER

Excessive levels of stress put resilience in jeopardy. Marston and Marston (2018) presented multiple signs of distress that may reduce resilience. Here are some:

- Back pain.
- Headaches.
- Sleepless nights.
- Comforting habits (such as drinking and excessive eating).

Becoming familiar with these signals can be helpful in tackling stress and constructing resilience before the toll is too high. Are you experiencing any of the signs? What are the causes? Develop a plan to handle the issue.

Duckworth, 2016). Gritty people can express enduring persistence because of the example they get from others including their leaders (Rego et al., 2018).

As with thriving, grit thus partly overlaps with resilience. Grit is both an antecedent, being involved in the creation of resilience, as well as a consequence of resilient processes. Similarly to thriving, grit underlines the importance of learning as well as the necessity to adjust to externally adverse events instead of succumbing to stress (Box 3.7). Following the same reasoning, resilience also differs from the exploitation of individual emotional intelligence (e.g., Cartwright and Pappas, 2008) and work–life balance (e.g., Özbilgin et al., 2011).

DESILIENCE: THE REVERSE SIDE OF RESILIENCE

As the Latin expression *resilire* constitutes the root for 'resilience' (Chapter 2), its opposite *desilire* ('leap or jump down', 'dismount') is also relevant for the life of individuals and their forms of collective life (e.g., Chamorro-Premuzic and Lusk, 2017). In fact, individuals can trigger processes (that is, spirals of insecurity) that operate in such a way that they become less resilient or less likely to be resilient, via the self-creation of stressors or the exaggeration of the extant ones. As explained by Konnikova (2016), a contributor to the *New Yorker*:

BOX 3.8   TOO MUCH PRESSURE ON A STAR

André Gomes, a football player, arrived at FC Barcelona in July 2016, with the aura of stardom. His first months at the club were successful but his performance declined over time and criticisms emerged. On multiple occasions he was booed by the Camp Nou crowd (Salahpour, 2018). As a consequence, he confessed in an interview to *Panenka* magazine (March 2018[1]) that he was not enjoying his football and was struggling with the pressure (see Lowe, 2018):

> I don't feel good on the pitch . . . I am not enjoying what I am doing. The first six months were pretty good but then things changed. Maybe it's not the right word to use but it has turned into a kind of hell because I have started to feel more pressure. With [some] pressure I feel fine but with the pressure [I put] on myself I don't. The feeling that I have during games is bad.

These negative feelings spilled over to outside the field:

> On more than one occasion I didn't want to leave my house because [of the way] people look at you . . . You have a fear of going on the street out of embarrassment. I close myself off. I don't talk to anybody. Thinking too much has hurt me. I think about the bad things and what I have to do. My teammates help me a lot but things don't work out the way they want them to work out. In training, I am generally relaxed although there can be days when I feel a little low on confidence and it's noticeable.

Reflect on the following questions: Considering that 'players and coaches are [generally] careful not to show any insecurity or weakness', as FC Barcelona manager Ernesto Valverde pointed out, why did André show his vulnerability? Ernesto Valverde defended him, saying that 'André has lots of qualities' and that having shown insecurity or weakness had been a 'brave' thing to do. Is this relevant for rebuilding André Gomes's resilience? Do you consider that André Gomes's confession is a sign of resilience, or of lack of it? Why? What can leaders in other organizations learn from the case?

'We can become less resilient, or less likely to be resilient,' Bonanno [a clinical psychologist at Columbia University's Teachers College] says. 'We can create or exaggerate stressors very easily in our own minds. That's the danger of the human condition.' Human beings are capable of worry and rumination: we can take a minor thing, blow it up in our heads, run through it over and over, and drive ourselves crazy until we feel like that minor thing is the biggest thing that ever happened. In a sense, it's a self-fulfilling prophecy. Frame adversity as a challenge, and you become more flexible and able to deal with it, move on, learn from it, and grow. Focus on it, frame it as a threat, and a potentially traumatic event becomes an enduring problem; you become more inflexible, and more likely to be negatively affected.

Desilient individuals tend to magnify the probability or the impact of negative events, getting trapped in a spiral of cognitive misrepresentation of the reality they face (see Box 3.8).

NOTE

1. http://www.panenka.org/miradas/pensar-demasiado-me-dano/.

4. Resilience in collectives

> Not every windstorm, earth-tremor, or rush of water is a catastrophe.
> A catastrophe is known by its works; that is to say, by the occurrence of
> disaster . . . It is the collapse of the cultural protections that constitutes the
> disaster proper.
> (Carr, 1932, p. 211)

> First, managers . . . should be alert to the risks that face their firms and the
> ways they can mitigate these risks. Second, managers must be proactive in
> their risk management. Rather than reacting to specific disruptions, manag-
> ers should become forward looking to identify methods of shielding their
> firms from risk . . . Third, developing the capability to reconfigure the firm's
> resources in the face of disruption is a much-needed capability . . . Fourth,
> managers should invest in risk averting infrastructure.
> (Parker and Ameen, 2018)

SURVIVING IN EXTREME CONDITIONS – HOW SENSEMAKING NURTURES RESILIENCE: *EL MILAGRO DE LOS ANDES*

We shall next consider an extreme case of resilience in practice, one that involved innovating taboo-breaching norms. *El Milagro de los Andes* (the 'Miracle of the Andes') is the name associated with the incredible survival of 16 of the 45 passengers on a chartered Uruguayan Air Force plane (Flight 571) that crashed in the Andes (Chile) on 13 October 1972. Most of the passengers died in the crash or rapidly succumbed to cold and injuries, while an avalanche that destroyed their shelter later killed eight. Exposed to scarcity of food, polar temperatures, avalanches and absence of means of communication, 16 people were able to survive for ten weeks and were eventually rescued on 23 December 1972.

It was a Uruguayan rugby team that had chartered the flight, with the passengers comprising the team, their friends, family and associates. The case has been nominated by Karl Weick as an example of a resilient team, in parallel with the analysis of the Mann Gulch disaster (Weick, 1993). Weick sees the case as one of those in which a group of people created spontaneous forms of organizing, with subgroups taking care of the emerging priorities: 'demand shifted from caring for the wounded, in which two medical students took the lead, to acquiring food and water, where the [rugby] team became leader' (p. 648). In this case, a clear occurrence of situational leadership and interweaving of spontaneous and pre-existing organizational structures is illustrated.

The case reports the processes of resilience of a group of people (some of them already teammates) who were able to survive by 'infringing taboos and de-tabooing infringements'. Being exposed to unbearable conditions in terms of hygiene and starvation, and with few chances to return home, the group articulated that they 'would not be rescued and could sustain life only if people consumed the flesh of the dead' (Weick, 1993, p. 648). The dramatic situation depicted represents an extreme case (Siggelkow, 2007) in which a group of individuals, all of whom were Roman Catholic, gave sense to the practice of necrotic cannibalism.

In the field of organization studies, sensemaking refers to processes through which people give meaning to experience (Weick, 1979). As noted by Weick (1988), in crisis conditions, sensemaking is more difficult and individuals might be exposed to dilemmas because 'people think by acting' and 'action that is instrumental to understanding the crisis often intensifies the crisis' (p. 305). The resilience of the survivors of the 'Miracle of the Andes' goes well beyond the four potential sources of organizational resilience identified by Weick (1993): improvisation, virtual role systems, attitude of wisdom, and norms of respectful interaction. In fact, the survival of the group relates to some 'sensemaking of the unthinkable', namely sins and taboos.

As in many other similar accidents, the survivors of Flight 571 had only a meagre amount of food at their disposal. The food was parsimoniously stored and divided to last as long as possible. Water was obtained from artificially melting the snow, which at the altitude of 3600 m (11 800 ft) was at that time of the year abundant in the Andes. Unfortunately, the extreme conditions restricted population by natural vegetation and animals.

With the prospect of starvation as soon as the food stock dwindled, the group collectively made the decision to eat flesh from the frozen bodies of their dead comrades. The exceptionality of the decision was increased by two additional factors: (1) most of the passengers were close friends or classmates; (2) all of them were Roman Catholic. In retrospect, survivors were exposed to a dilemma: to die, or to eat pieces of close acquaintances in order to live, and, in case of survival, to live the rest of their lives in sin (or with guilt). The situation exemplifies the sensemaking dilemma, described by Weick (1998) as '[something which] is interpreted from the perspective that people enact the environments which constrain them' (p. 305). One of the survivors, Nando Parrado, described the condition as follows:

At high altitude, the body's caloric needs are astronomical . . . we were starving in earnest, with no hope of finding food, but our hunger soon grew so voracious that we searched anyway . . . again and again we scoured the fuselage in search of crumbs and morsels. We tried to eat strips of leather torn from pieces of luggage, though we knew that the chemicals they'd been treated with would do us more harm than good. We ripped open seat cushions hoping to find straw, but found only inedible upholstery foam . . . Again and again I came to the same conclusion: unless we wanted to eat the clothes we were wearing, there was nothing here but aluminium, plastic, ice, and rock. (Parrado, 2007, p. 170)

The existence of a 'group' as an organized community within the same institution (Catholic religion), seen as organization 'outside organizations' (Ahrne and Brunsson, 2011; Holt and den Hond, 2013; Meyer and Höllerer, 2014), helped individuals to make sense of necrotic cannibalism. In fact, as reconstructed by Read (1974), some survivors enacted the practice of necrotic cannibalism as equivalent to the ritual of Holy Communion, while some others justified it in the light of the verse of John (15:13): 'no man hath greater love than this: that he lay down his life for his friends'. The initial, individual, sensemaking exercise soon spread in the group of survivors, reaching those who were reluctant to accept the idea. It is exemplary in the sense that one of the surviving passengers, Liliana, despite being constrained by her strong religious convictions, was eventually convinced by her husband and other survivors. The 'conditions' in which the practice was enacted suggest the respect that survivors paid to the dead bodies of their friends, buried under the snow. Only two volunteers were taking flesh from the bodies of the unlucky travellers. Furthermore, frozen meat did not taste of anything. According to the survivors, that made things easier.

The practice of cannibalism is not (just) a sin from a Catholic perspective: 'All unrighteousness is sin: and there is a sin not to death' (I John 5:17). If it was just that, we, as *ex post* rationalizers of the case, might argue that the Catholic religion contains its inner mechanisms (repentance, confession, reconciliation) for forgiving whatever is constituted as sin. In fact, the stronger the individual faith, the higher the sense of relief from the sins. But necrotic cannibalism was indeed something even bigger than a sin; it was a taboo. Taboos divide the sacred from the profane. Herodotus describes one of the first taboos in the Western world as the practice of making 'a meal of their dead fathers' (as reported in Schoemaker and Tetlock, 2012, p. 8), indicating that 'the sanctity of human life cuts across diverse culture' (Schoemaker and Tetlock, 2012, p. 6), as does respect for corpses.

From another angle, given that institutional logics are the 'the organizing principles that shape the behavior of field participants . . . [referring] to a set of belief systems and associated practices . . . [that] define the content and meaning of institutions' (Reay and Hinings, 2009, p. 631), the case shows how the practice of necrotic cannibalism was enacted within a coherent institutional logic of prizing life itself (Jackall, 1988; Thornton and Ocasio, 1999).

The protagonists of the 'Miracle of the Andes' were able to infringe a taboo by a sensegiving practice that enacted the development of new meanings attached to a profane practice otherwise believed unthinkable. In short, through collective support and shared, incremental sensemaking, they were able to consecrate a profane practice, de-tabooing the unthinkable in order to survive. In doing that, the group challenged their most solid values and expressed resilience.

DISCOVERING COLLECTIVE RESILIENCE

The 'miracle' described above shows that resilience can develop, not only at the individual level but also collectively, the focus of this chapter. While Chapter 3 investigated the distinctive features of individual resilience and related constructs, this chapter focuses on collective resilience (see Box 4.1). Following Brodsky et al. (2011), when dealing with resilience, 'a focus on the individual is not enough' (p. 233). So, in this chapter we will deal with the specificities of collective expressions of resilience, which takes place even in the absence of, or with only a minor role of, a resilient individual.

Resilience is thus a multi-level construct, connecting the individual, the team, the organization and its environment (even including a country as a whole, some suggest; see Box 4.6 below). To some extent, resilience preserves the same characteristics independently from the level of aggregation considered. Typically, resilience is the general quality that enables the individual, community or organization to cope with, adapt to and recover from a disastrous event (Horne, 1997; Buckle et al., 2000; Pelling and Uitto, 2001; Riolli and Savicki, 2003). Nonetheless, while potentially related, collective and personal resilience are not synonymous (Alliger et al., 2015).

Organizational resilience incorporates the collective personal resilience of individuals, 'but goes beyond it' (Flint-Taylor and Cooper, 2017). In fact, as individuals engage in collective forms of action (teams, organizations, communities), these acquire additional features that strengthen their response to pressures, stressors and adversities. The resilience of a collective is not the sum of the individuals' resilience: it can be greater or lesser. For example, team members may be resilient precisely to deal with the low resilience of the team as a whole. The economic decline of a community (as a result of the obsolescence of the specific sector in which the local

BOX 4.1   USING AN 'ASTOUNDING RECOVERY' AFTER 9/11
           TO LEARN ABOUT BUILDING COLLECTIVE
           RESILIENCE

Read the following excerpt from Freeman et al. (2004, p. 69):

> Despite devastating losses in the September 11th attacks, Sandler O'Neill, an investment bank formerly based in the World Trade Center, emerged stronger than ever within one year. The combination of moral work and the pull of opportunity released extraordinary physical and psychological resources that fuelled this astounding recovery. The case shows that in an organization that permits advancement through moral work, people feel exceptionally energetic and psychologically available.

Moral work takes place in organizations that promote their agents (managers and employees) to be active interpreters and promoters of moral value. Suppose you are the Chief Executive Officer (CEO) of your company. To foster a resilient organization, you want to develop a social context characterized by mutual support and care. Specifically, you want employees to support and care about others who are in trouble and experience pain for professional, personal and family reasons. What should you do? Is it enough that you 'walk the talk' regardless how managers at lower levels behave? Will every manager imitate your caring and shielding behaviours? If not, what can you do? What happens when you have to adopt tough decisions toward people you kindly helped some time ago? Can you be both tough and caring? Gain familiarity with the notion of 'tough love' (Blatt, 2009; Meyer, 2017) and reflect upon these questions again. In which conditions is 'tough love' a euphemism for 'bullying' (Leong and Crossman, 2016)?

economy had been based) may coexist with the resilient capacity of its inhabitants to face such adversity. Flint-Taylor and Cooper (2017, p. 129) perfectly capture the relation between individual and team resilience:

> Consider a scenario where your team recruits a new member to replace someone who has left. This is a situation that we are all likely to be familiar with. Arguably if team resilience were simply made up of the personal resilience of team members, then it would increase or decrease in a straightforward way depending on whether the new team member was more or less resilient than the person who left. However, what if this team member exhibited behaviour that undermines other team members and challenges the morale of the team? In this scenario, there would be a negative impact on team resilience above and beyond the change in individual-level resilience, especially if the team's manager fails to act quickly to address the issue.

Moreover, many resilience processes operate only at a collective level (Brodsky et al., 2011), via the creation of a culture supporting the sense of community, the collective reframing of stressors via sensemaking (e.g., Weick, 1993) and the development of shared values. Collective resilience can be seen therefore as a 'a *unique blend* of cognitive, behavioral, and contextual properties that increase a firm's [as well as other collectivities'] ability to understand its current situation and to develop customized responses that reflect that understanding' (Lengnick-Hall and Beck, 2005, p. 750).

Considered as a multilevel construct, resilience spans at least three levels of aggregation (e.g., Drazin et al., 1999; Hackman, 2003; Sutcliffe and Vogus, 2003): intrasubjective (individual), intersubjective (team) and collective (organization, and other collectivities, such as communities). According to some studies, collective resilience builds on the foundation of individual resilience that its members display (Riolli and Savicki, 2003). From such a perspective, agents that are rich in resilience are argued to be better prepared to act as creative problem solvers (e.g., Luthar and Cicchetti, 2000; Luthar et al., 2000), and to possess adaptive capacity (Gratton and Ghoshal, 2003; Zolli and Healy, 2012). Nonetheless, some features of resilience can be observed and best appreciated only at an interpersonal level, considering the collective entities in and through which individuals operate. A sports team that returns to a winning track after a losing streak of games, a listed company surviving a big scandal, a community rebuilding a semblance of normalcy after a major natural disaster, or a family overcoming a personal loss: such experiences, it is suggested, lead to a collective feeling of being more united than previously.

RESILIENCE AT THE TEAM LEVEL

The primary form of collectivity in which individuals group are teams, defined as social entities in which members share – implicitly or explicitly – a common identity and pursue some collective goal, interdependently (see Figure 4.1). A family, for instance, might be a team, unless it was a house divided by rivalrous behaviours, divorce or some other breach of trust. A group of marathon runners who represent a country in the Olympics might not be a team: if they were working together to position one team member in a winning position, they would be; if they were competing against each other individually, they would not. Conversely, a group of diplomats who campaign, in a coordinated and interdependent way, in different countries, in favour of their candidate for the Secretary-General of the United Nations, may be considered to be a temporary team.

*Figure 4.1   Teams in a resilience training exercise: Fairchild Air Force
Base Airmen raft down the Spokane River during a Base
Chapel resilience trip, 16 April 2016*

Team resilience can be defined as 'a dynamic, psychosocial process which
protects a group of individuals from the potential negative effect of
stressors they collectively encounter. It comprises of processes whereby
team members use their individual and collective resources to positively
adapt when experiencing adversity' (Morgan et al., 2013, p. 552). Although
team-level resilience has received only modest research attention (Alliger et
al., 2015), resilient teams are crucial to current management practices for a
number of reasons. It has been argued that:

> teams are ubiquitous in the working world; most teams will face challenges that
> can drain resources, adversely affect performance, and diminish team cohesion
> and team member well-being; in challenging environments, reliable and sustain-
> able team performance and well-being is only possible when the team is resilient;
> a group of resilient individuals does not make a resilient team; teams can be
> prepared in ways that augment their resilience. (p. 177)

Resilient teams develop the capacity to see failure and imperfection as
sources of learning and progress rather than fault or error (Edmondson,

2012). They develop an appreciation for imperfection (Weick, 1979, 1995) that increases their collective mindfulness and consequent alertness to opportunities for improvement. Resilient teams are potentially better able to adapt and bounce back from failures, setbacks, threats and other adverse circumstances. They are more cohesive and more willing to support other members to maintain their positivity, and to adopt more prosocial behaviours, thus improving their performance (Clapp-Smith et al., 2009; West et al., 2009; Walumbwa et al., 2011). Groups that are able to embrace a 'broader perspective' while struggling with stressors tend to adapt positively rather than trying to dodge challenging situations. They develop and leverage a learning orientation (Bennett et al., 2010; Morgan et al., 2013; Sutcliffe and Vogus, 2003; West et al., 2009). In advocating the need for further research on reliance at a group level, Bennett et al. (2010) posited that 'resilience may be viewed as much as a social factor (existing in teams or groups) as an individual trait' (p. 225).

Components of Team Resilience

Team resilience is characterized by some psychosocial factors, such as caring relationships and effective team working (Gittell et al., 2006; Lengnick-Hall et al., 2011; Morgan et al., 2013; Norris et al., 2008). Edmondson (1999, 2008, 2012) proposed that a combination of psychological safety and accountability are critical ingredients for the emergence of resilience at the group level. Sharma and Sharma (2016) see team resilience capacity as being affected by ten components. Such components can be grouped into four factors (see also Box 4.2):

1. Group structure (for example, reflections on a shared vision during stressors, open and honest communication, shared leadership) represents the enabling structure that defines the relations between team members over time.
2. Mastery approaches towards adversities (for example, focus on learning and improvement as a group during setbacks, intensive preparation to face stressors, learning from challenging situations) represent the team members' shared attitudes and behaviours that promote team learning and improvement.
3. Social capital (for example, deep bonds between team members, perceived social support, 'no-blame' culture when experiencing failures) reflects social networks, social norms and trustful relationships that enable team members to work together in pursuing shared goals.
4. Collective efficacy (for example, remaining together during crises, and gaining belief and confidence from the actions of some team members

BOX 4.2   HOW TO MEASURE TEAM RESILIENCE

Shikha Sharma and Sanjeev Kumar Sharma (Sharma and Sharma, 2016) developed and validated a questionnaire for measuring Team Resilience. The questionnaire includes ten components (grouped into four factors). We present some of the items below, grouped into the ten components. You may assess your team resilience by using a five-point Likert scale (from 1, 'strongly disagree' to 5, 'strongly agree'). You are invited to refer to the original paper (Sharma and Sharma, 2016, pp. 45–46) for the complete list of items (http://journals.sagepub.com/doi/pdf/10.1177/0972262916628952). To calculate the score for each component, sum the scores of all items measuring that component, and divide the sum by the number of items.

Team Learning Orientation

1. Mistakes are openly discussed in the team in order to learn from them.
2. Differences between real and expected performance are critically and constructively analysed in my team.
3. The lessons learned are made available to all the team members.
4. Actions are taken in the team to continuously improve the performance.
5. Even when an error is caught in time, team members are still told about it, so it does not happen again.
6. The same mistakes are made over and over again in the team.
7. Team members are encouraged to ask 'why', regardless of their rank.
   . . .

Team Flexibility

1. Team members adjust their approach(es) to overcome obstacles.
2. Team members easily handle a variety of tasks.

Network Ties

1. Teammates maintain close social relationships with each other.
2. Team members effectively communicate with one another.
   . . .

Shared Language

1. Team members try to use common terms for work.
2. Team members use understandable communication patterns during discussions/meetings.
   . . .

Trust

1. I believe my team members trust each other.
2. I have little faith that my teammates will consider my needs when making decisions.
   . . .

Team Competition

1. My team is larger than it needs to be.
2. My team is just the right size to accomplish its purpose.
3. Members of my team are too dissimilar to work together well.
   . . .

Task Design

1. We do a whole, identifiable piece of work.
2. My team does such a small part of the overall task that it is hard to point specifically to our special contribution.
3. My team's work is inherently meaningful.
   . . .

Group Norms

1. Standards for members' behaviour in my team are vague and unclear.
2. It is clear what is – and what is not – acceptable member behaviour in my team.
   . . .

Perceived Efficacy of Team Members

1. I have confidence that my team members can perform tasks that are assigned to them.
2. The members of my team are capable of doing their share of work whenever asked.
   . . .

Perceived Efficacy for Collective Team Action

1. My team is capable of helping a team member solve their problem.
2. My team can work together in order to accomplish a goal.
3. I believe in my team's ability to do things together.
   . . .

during adversities) represents the team's shared belief that team members, as a whole, are able to organize and carry out the activities required for the team to be effective and successful.

Resilient teams do not protect people from mistakes, but protect people while recognizing that mistakes are made. They do not adopt an attitude of blame, or institutionalize and reproduce a blaming culture, when experiencing failures: they strive to create a 'no-blame culture'. Such teams are characterized by high levels of interpersonal trust, a shared belief that they can be successful amidst adversity while learning from mistakes and failures and working together in the pursuit of relevant team goals.

Confronting mistakes constructively is particularly relevant for cultivating resilience. The learned capacity to analyse mistakes but not adversely deal with those who made them results in increased confidence in tackling problems and developing a learning attitude that embeds resilience in team functioning. Resilient teams cultivate rich relationships among team members (Pentland, 2012) by avoiding attributing mistakes to individuals (Deming, 1982). Attenuating the disadvantages of hierarchy in unstable environments (Anderson and Brown, 2010) develops this capacity. Leaders can nurture this type of capacity by combining grit and humility (Rego et al., 2017a; Rego et al., 2017b; Rego et al., 2018) and promoting psychological safety (Edmondson and Lei, 2014; Frazier et al., 2017; Hu et al., 2017).

Sports teams are a frequent point of reference for managerial discussions of resilience in teamwork. It is not only managers who attempt to be inspirational or motivational who make use of these metaphors, but also team members (Gibson and Zellmer-Bruhn, 2001). Sport is a common trope of everyday life, so it is hardly surprising that it plays a role in managerial discourse. Hence, understanding how resilience can be measured and tested in sports teams is useful for more general management practice (Morgan et al., 2013; Decroos et al., 2017). Building on Morgan et al. (2013), Decroos et al. (2017) developed and validated an inventory for the Characteristics of Resilience in Sports Teams (CREST) model. The CREST model has been argued to be reliable over time both at the 'between-players' and the 'between-teams' level. The research was conducted in four related studies, sampling 1225 athletes from Belgium and the United Kingdom. The findings of the studies provided evidence for a two-factor measure of resilience in sports teams, encompassing: (1) the team's ability to display resilient characteristics; as well as (2) the vulnerabilities being displayed under pressure. While CREST was employed as a state-like measure of team-level resilience, Decroos et al. (2017) suggest that the model can be also used in a process-oriented perspective on resilience by examining the functioning of sports teams before and after adverse events (Box 4.3).

BOX 4.3   MEASURING RESILIENCE IN SPORTS TEAMS

The Characteristics of Resilience in Sports Teams (CREST) model (Decroos et al., 2017) includes two main dimensions: (1) demonstrating resilient characteristics; and (2) vulnerabilities shown under pressure. If you are a member of a team sport, you may assess its resilience through focusing on the pressure felt by the team in the past month and reflecting on the extent to which you agree (that is, from 1, 'completely disagree' to 7, 'completely agree') with the following statements:
   In the past month, when my team was under pressure (selected items) . . .

1. The team was able to focus on what was important.
2. Teammates started to communicate negatively with each other.
3. Team members fought for each other.
4. The team lost its confidence.
5. I felt that I could count on other members of the team.
6. The level of collective effort in the team dropped.
7. Effective communication kept players' minds focused on the task at hand.
8. Team members started to mistrust one another.
9. Members of the team were committed to contributing to the collective belief of the team.
10. Team members fought hard to not let each other down.
   . . .

To compute the score on demonstrating resilient characteristics, refer to Decroos et al. (2017). Team resilience is higher when the score on 'demonstrating resilient characteristics' is higher and the score on 'vulnerabilities' is lower.

RESILIENCE AT THE ORGANIZATIONAL LEVEL

As an organizational attribute, resilience results from understanding that, on the one hand, organizational members have to be able to face challenges that often emerge unexpectedly (Weick and Sutcliffe, 2001 [2007]), while on the other hand, they have to transform themselves to be able to navigate and prepare the organization for fundamental organizational shifts (Garud et al., 2006). Preparing for future jolts without considering present dangers is as limiting as responding to present threats without trying to anticipate and to accommodate predictable shifts.

Organizational resilience (see Box 4.4 for how to measure it) requires a holistic approach that secures an appropriate balance between control and innovation. Organizations and their leaders need to deal with inherent

BOX 4.4   HOW TO ASSESS THE CURRENT
ORGANIZATION'S RESILIENCE

**Resilient Organisations Research Programme, University of Canterbury,
New Zealand**

The Resilient Organisations Research Programme at the University of Canterbury,
New Zealand (www.resorgs.org.nz), led by Erica Seville and John Vargo (Lee et
al., 2013), has developed some tools for assessing resilience at various levels of
aggregations (employee, organization, community). Among the tools developed
within the research programme, the Resilience Thumbnail Tool is a cut-down
version of their more complete and comprehensive Benchmark Resilience Tool.
The questionnaire considers resilience as 'the ability of an organization to survive
a crisis and thrive in a world of uncertainty', and organization as 'anything from a
one-person small business, to a very large corporation, from a small not-for-profit
to a large Government department'. The questionnaire comprises also the collection of data on some structural features of the organization (full-time employees,
part-time employees, industry) and on its financial solidity. Please take the test
here: www.resorgs.org.nz.

tensions between orientations towards 'defence and progression, consistency and flexibility'. In our terms, they are able to be adaptive in the face
of events and proactive towards such events once they occur. To do so,
they need to embrace "paradoxical thinking" (Lewis and Smith, 2014) that
moves 'beyond "either/or" towards "both/and" outcomes' (Denyer, 2017,
p. 25). As anticipated in Chapter 2, we acknowledge that the existence
of tensions and contradictions between different instances constitutes
resilience. With Benson (1977), we agree that the dialectics between opposing tensions (if not contradictions) is an important conceptual framework
in organizational theory, because organizations as action generators are
constituted by the opposing tensions with which they deal; however, not
all tensions result in paradoxes (e.g., Lewis and Smith, 2014; Cunha and
Putnam, 2017).

BUILDING ORGANIZATIONAL RESILIENCE

There are a variety of processes associated with the construction of organizational resilience, namely adaptive structures, improvisation, managing

internally created constraints, as well as attention to failure. In terms of design, organizational scholars have urged managers to develop designs that facilitate organizational resilience skills (Lee et al., 2013; Whitman et al., 2013). Bahrami and Evans (2011) used Silicon Valley firms to extol the virtues of 'superflexibility': the capacity to adjust to environmental jolts as a normal challenge. Because Silicon Valley organizations know that their environment changes relentlessly, they develop structures that allow them to master change as a survival requirement.

The expression of such a capacity has been explored by Eisenhardt and her colleagues (e.g., Brown and Eisenhardt, 1997; Sull and Eisenhardt, 2012), who have shown that the capacity to design processes semi-structured around simple rules is central to maintaining an organization space in which change can occur naturally, in an emergent fashion, rather than as a centrally designed and planned imposition. In alignment with these findings, it is in the avoidance of top-down, hierarchical structures that inhibit creative responses to emerging problems that resilience resides (Somers, 2009).

An Integrative Model for Organizational Resilience

One interesting tool aiming at helping companies to build resilience was proposed by the BSI group (https://www.bsigroup.com/). BSI presents itself as a 'business standards company that helps organizations make excellence a habit – all over the world'. In partnership with Cranfield School of Management, BSI has published a business report (Denyer, 2017) offering a framework for organizational resilience to help companies 'manage risk and adapt for future business success'.

The proposed model combines the standard 'plan–do–check–act' (PDCA) methodology (Deming, 1982) with something that they call '4Sight': a 'leadership agenda for Organizational Resilience' (Denyer, 2017, p. 20). As the name anticipates, 4Sight considers four 'sights' that leaders should adopt in order to deal with complex problems, those encountered when reality presents itself in the form of 'incomplete or contradictory knowledge' (that is, developing new software applications or a new technology, dealing with major changes, facing a crisis) (Denyer, 2017, p. 20). The four 'sights' are:

1. Foresight: anticipate, predict and prepare for your future.
2. Insight: interpret and respond to your present conditions.
3. Oversight: monitor and review what has happened and assess changes.
4. Hindsight: learn the right lessons from your experience.

PDCA is a simple, perhaps simplistic, method for reproducing consistency over time. The 4Sight approach complements it with planned actions that aim to support continuous improvement of existing systems and processes. While PDCA assumes that all will go as planned, 4Sight leaves room for the role of unanticipated events and the necessity of their sensemaking (see comparison in Table 4.1).

Table 4.1　Comparing PDCA and 4Sight for achieving organizational resilience

PDCA	4Sight
Approach	*Approach*
Plan (definine your policy, objectives and targets)	Foresight (anticipate, predict and prepare your future)
Do (implement your plans within a structured management framework)	Insight (interpret and respond to your present conditions)
Check (measure and monitor your actual results against your planned objectives)	Oversight (monitor and review what has happened and assess changes)
	Hindsight (learn the right lessons from your experience)
Act (correct and improve your plans to meet and exceed your planned results)	Act (respond to and create disruptions and opportunities)
Works well when the challenge . . .	*Works well when the challenge . . .*
Is easy to identify and define	Is difficult to agree; easy to deny
Is resolvable using current expertise and known solutions	Requires new ways of thinking, beliefs, roles, relationships and approaches to work
Has a definite stopping point – when the solution is reached and can be judged as right or wrong	Has no stopping rule – how much is enough? No right or wrong, just better or worse outcomes
Leader's role	*Leader's role*
Agree goals, build commitment, provide answers	Identify the problem, connect people's interests to resolution and ask searching questions
Clarify roles and responsibilities	Empower people to act
Keep emotions out – 'we can solve this'	Let people experience threat – within a productive range of distress
Fit solutions around current ways of working (culture, practices)	Challenge norms – 'we could be very different'
Seek consensus and reduce conflict	Embrace diversity of opinion and scepticism
Focus on 'making what we do better'	Focus on 'doing better things'

Source:　Denyer (2017), p. 23.

RESILIENCE AT THE COMMUNITY LEVEL

Sometimes resilience is depicted as a national or ethnic characteristic, mostly associated with the historical reconstruction of the events that populations had to face during their existence. Examples can be found in *The Economist*'s (2011) synthesis of the country of Pakistan as 'a supreme danger, a fantastically diverse nation and a tough, resilient country'. Lynch (2010) defines Ireland as the 'The world's most resilient country'. More recently, the Resilient Index ranks Switzerland as the most resilient country (Ireland ranks 20th, and Pakistan 125th; see Box 4.5). These are relatively recent examples. Historically, the Volga Tatars (Rorlich, 2017) have been studied as a case of resilience over centuries; Box 4.6.

Such large-scale generalizations are clearly only very proximate caricatures of an enormous range of potential variables and factors, but this does not stop them from being produced: most discussions of national characteristics do not withstand detailed scrutiny. Nonetheless, they are an endless source of fascination and discussion between peoples.

Community resilience may also be seen as a temporary state, a structural feature, or a set or resources that allow a community to face hardship and suffering, or to bounce back and recover after having experienced 'disasters'

BOX 4.5   IS YOUR COUNTRY RESILIENT?

The Resilient Index (RI), released by FM Global (www.fmglobal.com), ranks more than 100 countries based on their enterprise resilience to disruptive events.[1] The index 'is an equally-weighted composite measure of three core resilience factors: economic, risk quality and the supply chain itself. Each factor is comprised of four core drivers. Scores are bound on a scale of 0 to 100 with 0 representing the lowest resilience and 100 being the highest resilience'.[2] Take a look at the RI and search for your country. Search for the most resilient and the least resilient countries. Ask yourself: is it resilience that fosters economic development, or the other way around?

Read the interview of Kevin Ingram, the CEO of FM Global, for Forbes (see Thomson, 2017). Think about the following statement by Ingram: 'For executives who are discovering the index for the first time they now have a resource to help make strategic decisions on: Where in the world to expand; What suppliers to select; How robust their supply chains can be; And what customers may be vulnerable'. What may happen to the less resilient countries if executives of global companies follow this recommendation?

BOX 4.6   A CASE OF NATIONAL RESILIENCE: THE VOLGA
TATARS

Professor Azade-Ayse Rorlich from the University of Southern California (USA)
has reconstructed and analysed the early history of the Tatars (Rorlich, 2017). The
term 'Tatars' was originally applied to a variety of Turco-Mongol semi-nomadic
empires, their people living in and controlling Tartary, a large portion of northern
and central Asia, spanning from the Caspian Sea and the Ural Mountains to the
Pacific Ocean. Nowadays Turkic people, mostly living in Russia and other Post-
Soviet countries, are referred to as Tartars.
   Prof. Rorlich describes the elements contributing to what she describes as the
Tartar national resilience. The process she describes has its roots in controversies
about the Tatars' ethnogenesis, their adoption of Islam, the emergence and the
demise of the Bulgar Khanate (their first political entity), its contacts with
the Russian principalities, the reaction to the Mongol conquest and the creation of
the Kazan Khanate. The Kazan Khanate was lately conquered by Ivan the Terrible
with its territory being annexed by the Muscovite State, entailing coercive conver-
sion to Christianity under the wave of the policies of 'Russification'. Nonetheless,
the Tatars' response to these policies gave rise to an even stronger commitment
to their values, habits, culture, language and religion. The process of moderniza-
tion that began reluctantly in Russia in the late 1800s, including the emancipation
of serfs, enlarged the distance between the Russian and Tatar cultures. The 1917
revolutions and civil war had a deep impact on the Volga Tatars, including a quest
for independence in an area approximately corresponding to the former Kazan
Khanate. During the Soviet period, Tatars coped with nationalism and communism
by defending their national and religious heritage but also enriching and developing it, displaying a nationalist resilience that also lasted into the years following
World War II.

(Manyena, 2006). The case of street vendors in India, that we discuss next,
illustrates the phenomenon.

**From Marginalized Individuals to Resilient Communities (by Chintan
Kella)[3]**

On 1 May 2014, the Street Vendors (Protection of Livelihood and
Regulation of Street Vending) Act, 2014, came into force in India. This Act
affected around 10 million citizens, who engage in the business of street
vending. Street vending is a form of micro entrepreneurship that in most
countries is usually deemed illegal, yet tolerated as a part of the informal
economy. India set a precedent by bringing the informal sector into the

formal economy but on terms and conditions that favour the vendors against the traditional norms of the formal economy. The bill has several provisions to protect the livelihood, social security and human rights of citizens who choose to engage as street vendors, achieved as a result of more than 40 years of struggle and various strategic and structural initiatives carried out by various organizational and individual actors.

While street vending is an ancient form of open market, as trade became more regulated, street vendors were considered, at best, a nuisance to society and open market areas, and at worse, illegal entities evading taxes. Street vendors, especially in developing countries, typically do not engage in this business to evade tax or sell stolen or smuggled goods and products. In fact, they play a very important part in the entire supply chain, primarily of fresh produce such as vegetables, fruits, fish and meat, as well as other small household necessities, offering many other products targeted at low-income households. They also provide convenience for customers by ensuring the availability of products at their doorstep or in residential neighbourhoods.

But city planners think otherwise. In the grandiose ideas and plans of developed cities, there is no space for such urban poor people. While there was no direct law which details street vending as a criminal activity, the police and the municipality would use alternate laws and means to evict street vendors. These forms of harassment range from daily or weekly payments of bribes (significant amounts compared to very low incomes), removal of carts and vending spaces by force or confiscation, wrongly issued fines, even physical violence with beatings from police: harassment that takes the form of systematic institutionalized abuse.

How these socio-economically marginalized, often illiterate and legally weak individuals could change legal institutions characterized by high inertia, while ensuring their own survival, is a telling tale of their resilience. Most studies look at how actors exhibit resilience amid disruption and crises. In these cases, there seems to be an underlying assumption that developing resilience is easy, and resources required to build resilience are easily available. Moreover, management studies tend to look at resilience at the individual or organizational level. In the case of the street vendors of India, the vendors were geographically dispersed because of the nature of their business, and therefore they obviously lacked organizational resilience. In addition, they also lacked individual resilience because of their deep poverty and decades of socio-economic marginalization. The new laws presented them with sudden disruption to their occupation, street vending, from legal authorities. For individual vendors to sustain themselves amid such adversities is difficult, yet these vendors were able to demand and obtain an institutional change through regulatory reform.

The desire for change started when one of the female vendors approached a female member-based trade union, telling the sisters of the struggles and harassment they faced. Since the union organization represented the self-employed and women working in the informal economy, it readily agreed to intervene. Soon, more vendors joined this organization when they started to see the initiatives taken by the officials of the organization on their behalf. With its increasing membership base and a clear project to pursue, the women's unit, a part of a bigger labour union, spun off and created the Self Employed Women's Association (SEWA).

SEWA realized early on that the only way to stand up against harassment of vendors was to organize at grass roots level, within the existing markets, and to develop a community level of resilience against the disruption caused by legal authorities. SEWA also realized that the socio-economic conditions and needs of the street vendors differed to those of other participants in the informal economy. Vendors had to operate in open markets, amid harsh environment conditions and traffic, purchasing their goods daily from central wholesale markets that they then had to transport to local markets, while raising capital, maintaining hygiene and natural biological needs amidst a lack of public toilets, amongst many other challenges. While nearly all street vendors faced these issues, they did so at an individual level. Given the individual resources in terms of time, energy and money that were spent on handling these issues, street vendors lacked any additional resources to handle issues of harassment at the community level.

SEWA had to change the social structures of the market, while creating and developing various social initiatives to ensure that street vendors could become resilient individuals. One discussion led to SEWA deciding to start the Shri Mahila Sewa Sahakari Bank Ltd (the Women's SEWA Cooperative Bank Ltd), so that its members could access financial services that they were currently denied, as illiterates and because of the social and physical distance between the vendors and these institutions, as well as the typical operating hours of such services. Socially, SEWA restructured the markets, by asking the vendors to select and create a Market Committee with an elected leader. In doing so, SEWA was turning individual street vendors into a community of street vendors.

Many local-level issues now became resolvable within the communities, by the organized members. By training and empowering the Market Committee members and its leader, SEWA ensured that they could face and question legal authorities instead of running away from them. In legal cases, members were empowered enough to go and settle the matter at local police stations. Only very critical matters would be escalated to SEWA. For such matters, SEWA would draw on the numbers and power of other communities in different neighbourhoods. Thus, these local-based communities become further resilient by networking and collaborating with members of other communities.

With its bi-monthly meetings of all the market leaders and committee members, the vendors became more aware of the situation of other vendors across the cities. A collective consciousness was coming into being. If a protest had to be carried out, members had additional resources drawn from local market members to attend and support the community that was facing disruption. The purpose of such initiatives was to build resilience by using a two-pronged approach. Individual resilience was primarily built using structural resilience-building mechanisms; while collective resilience created a movement for institutional change, built through strategic resilience-building mechanisms.

By ensuring structural and strategic resilience, SEWA resolved the inability of lone vendors to handle harassment. While the harassment from police diminished over the years, it still continues in different areas and in different forms. When it happened, the vendors were able to view it as a collective threat to their entire community. To overcome these issues, vendors relied on their collective resilience at community level. Eventually, these communities educated their disruptors by collaborating with rather than confronting them. Instead of carrying out surprise eviction drives, especially during festivals and socio-political events, police and municipal authorities informed vendors in advance to plan their activities accordingly. Not only did community-level resilience enable the vendors to bounce back after facing harassment but it also resulted in a drastic reduction of such disruptions.

In 1995, after members of SEWA attended the Bellagio International Declaration of Street Vendors, SEWA started to mobilize these communities at regional and national levels, demanding government and policy-makers change the regulatory framework and develop a policy for street vendors. In 2004, the first policy was drafted, which after various modifications finally became a parliamentary Act in 2014. While the national movement initiated by SEWA was instrumental in passing this law, it was the resilience, built and developed by the members at their individual and, more importantly, community level, that sustained their long fight with institutional forces.

The Best and the Worst as Predictors of Community Resilience

As the case of street vendors in India suggests, communities express resilience when they are exposed to sudden, unexpected traumatic events and yet are able to rebound from and sustain such shocks. In the case of natural disasters (such as earthquakes or tsunamis) or human-generated ones (such as nuclear accidents and wars) that disorganize a specific population and its inhabitants, the ability to recover and restore pre-existing conditions rapidly as well as, in the aftermath of the event, being able to invest in prevention so as to avoid similar misfortune in the future, are signs of resilience. However, in so doing, societal collectivities do not operate with similar resources: the more developed and advanced the state of organization, nationally, civically and organizationally, the more rapid the recovery and the less the damage sustained (and this explains why Switzerland ranks first in the Resilient Index discussed in Box 4.5).

Van der Vegt et al. (2015, p.971) explained that:

> Although adverse events of all kinds are inevitable and have larger impacts, some organizations and societies are better able to rebound from and sustain such shocks than are others. Analyses of recovery processes after the New Zealand earthquakes revealed that businesses with strong pre-existing organizational collaboration networks were better able to access support and organize themselves than those that did not have such networks in place (Stevenson et al., 2014). And although the quadruple disaster – earthquake, tsunami, nuclear alert, and power shortages – that hit Japan in 2011 severely damaged the supply chain of Toyota, resulting in a global production loss for the company of 5% in 2011, Toyota claimed it was able to limit its losses due to the collective and coordinated efforts of suppliers, dealers, and overseas operations (Asano, 2012). In contrast, Haitian businesses and organizations are still struggling to rebuild after the much smaller quake they endured in 2010.

Apart from the crucial role that non-governmental organizations, at their best, may play in helping communities in recovering from disasters and triggering their resilience (Williams and Shepherd, 2016), the New Zealand and Japanese cases testify to the realization that local pre-existing organization and organizations facilitate the construction of more resilient communities. Organizations not only offer resources for resilience, but they also develop the agency of their employees, who are able to transfer organizational practices to their families and communities (Spreitzer, 2007). The history of business presents examples of companies running their business counter-cyclically during times of general crisis as a result of their resilience that become regarded as exemplary by their communities.

Firms such as General Electric, FedEx and Microsoft were created during periods of recession, signalling to communities that – as hard times cannot last forever – cultivating resilience pays off when the economic conditions improve. In so doing, organizations act akin to 'resilience-rich' agents nurturing the development of human skills with a cross-domain impact. Other companies develop specific projects aiming at dealing with specific problems experienced in or by the community. This is the case of

Genentech, a biotechnology corporation that became a subsidiary of Roche in 2009. According to Kristin Campbell Reed, Director of Corporate and Employee Giving, 'The Resilience Effect is part of Genentech's focus on making a big difference in our own backyard in ways that leverage our unique expertise and make an impact on people's health.' Consider the following excerpt from the company website:[4]

> The consequences of adversity can last a lifetime – but they don't have to. Children and communities can heal if the right supports are in place – at home, in the community, at school, and in the doctor's office. Our goal is to support leading thinkers across clinical and community settings to design, test and scale the most effective ways to address childhood trauma. Our support will focus on children under the age of five and their caregivers in low-income communities across the Bay Area. In addition to providing grants, our employees will lend their skills and time to support our partners, and we'll encourage collaboration by convening our grantees, local government, and other health care, philanthropic and community-based organizations.

COMPONENTS OF COMMUNITY RESILIENCE

As discussed above, the concept of 'community resilience' is usually viewed as a positive characteristic or state of a community. It is often represented as increasing local capacity, social support and resources, and decreasing risks, miscommunication and trauma (Patel et al., 2017). However, there is no definitional consensus about community resilience (Patel et al., 2017). For example, the Communities Advancing Resilience Toolkit (CART) considers a resilient community as one that 'has the ability to transform the environment through deliberate, collective action' and 'requires that the community as a whole must cope effectively with and learn from adversity' (Pfefferbaum et al., 2011, p. 1). CART recognizes that five interrelated domains may contribute to community resilience: connection and caring, resources, transformative potential, disaster management, and information and communication (Pfefferbaum et al., 2013; Pfefferbaum et al., 2015; see Table 4.2).

In contrast, the Conjoint Community Resiliency Assessment Measure (CCRAM) defines community resilience as 'the community's ability to withstand crises or disruptions' (Cohen et al., 2013, p. 1732). CCRAM emphasizes variables relating to leadership, collective efficacy, place attachment, preparedness, and social trust. Cox and Perry (2011, p. 396) adopted a different definition: 'a reflection of people's shared and unique capacities to manage and adaptively respond to the extraordinary demands on resources and the losses associated with disasters' (p. 396).

Table 4.2   Some items for measuring community resilience

Domain/ dimension	Items
Connection and caring	People in my community feel like they belong to the community. People in my community are committed to the well-being of the community. People in my community have hope about the future. . . .
Resources	My community supports programmes for children and families. My community has resources it needs to take care of community problems (resources include, for example, money, information, technology, tools, raw materials, and services). . . .
Transformative potential	My community works with organizations and agencies outside the community to get things done. People in my community communicate with leaders who can help improve the community. People in my community work together to improve the community. My community looks at its successes and failures so it can learn from the past. . . .
Disaster management	My community tries to prevent disasters. My community actively prepares for future disasters. . . .
Information and communication	My community keeps people informed (for example, via television, radio, newspaper, Internet, phone, neighbours) about issues that are relevant to them. If a disaster occurs, my community provides information about what to do. . . .

Source: Pfefferbaum et al. (2015). You are invited to refer to the original paper for the complete list of items.

Castleden et al. (2011, p. 370) defined community resilience as 'a capability (or process) of a community adapting and functioning in the face of disturbance'.

Patel et al. (2017) found more than 50 'unique definitions' of community resilience. They identified nine main elements in those definitions:

- Local knowledge (for example, the effects of a disaster may be mitigated if the community understands its existing vulnerabilities).
- Community networks and relationships (for example, members are well connected and form a cohesive whole).
- Communication (for example, the community uses common meanings for all to understand, and there are opportunities for open dialogue).
- Health (for example, the pre-existing health of the community, and the delivery of health services after the disaster are important for community resilience).
- Governance and leadership (for example, infrastructure and services; public involvement and support).
- Resources (for example, tangible supplies such as food, water and first aid kits; technical resources such as shelter, automobiles and essential machinery).
- Economic investment (for example, distribution of financial resources; the economic development of the post-disaster infrastructure).
- Preparedness (for example, actively involving community stakeholders in planning before a disaster; running practice exercises with a focus on risk management).
- Mental outlook (for example, attitudes, feelings and perspectives that occur after a disaster, such as hope, adaptability and acceptance of uncertainty and change).

According to these authors, a focus on such elements 'may be more productive than attempting to define and study community resilience as a distinct concept' (Patel et al., 2017, p. 1).

FROM ORGANIZATIONAL RESILIENCE TO OTHER FORMS OF RESILIENCE

Lengnick-Hall et al.'s (2011) work on organizational resilience may be applied to other larger systems (that is, communities) or smaller ones (that is, families). Accordingly, a system's capacity for developing resilience is dependent on a blend of a system-level cognitive, behavioural and contextual capabilities and routines. Cognitive elements include a sense of purpose, core values, genuine vision and a deliberate use of language. These elements help in building constructive sensemaking (Weick, 1993; see above, *El Milagro De Los Andes*). Behavioural elements include learned resourcefulness, counter-intuitive agility, useful habits and behavioural preparedness. Contextual elements refer to psychological safety, deep social capital, diffuse power and accountability, and broad resource networks. Resilience work takes place through exchanging valuable resources of time, knowledge, skills, energy, expertise and networks with other organizations and communities.

Maslow (1954) argues that the sense of belonging to larger collectivities (that is, society) and smaller collectivities (that is, family) is vital for the individual. Social solidarity across these domains remains vital to the individual's self-realization and identity, whose boundaries tend to be quite permeable (Frone, 2003; Grzywacs and Carlson, 2007). Bakker et al. (2009) pointed out that not only do employees influence one another in the workplace through the frequency of interactions, empathy and similarity, but also that this can extend from work to home, eventually reaching even further into communities. Experiences of resilience inside the family (that is, the loss of a loved one and the absorption of the sense of loss) create opportunities to expand behavioural repertoires and to confront challenges in a way that is mindful.

ANTECEDENTS OF COLLECTIVE RESILIENCE

Similarly to what happens at the individual level (Chapter 3) the presence of some antecedents makes the achievement of resilience in collectivities and the processes that contribute to it easier. Amongst the components of community resilience discussed above, several antecedents may be identified. For example, the pre-existing health of the community, material resources (supplies and technical assets) may help a community to deal more resiliently with a disaster (Patel et al., 2017). Recent research by Rao and Greve (2018) suggested that when disasters are attributed to other community members this weakens cooperation, increases suspicion and reciprocal distrust of the Other, leading to lower community resilience. By contrast, disasters attributed to nature evoke a sense of shared fate within the community and this shared fate fosters cooperation. According to the authors (p. 6), 'disasters are not merely physical events but socially constructed as well'. They also suggested that sociable communities, those characterized by high civic capacity, are more likely to help themselves and be resilient.

At the corporation level, research by Pal et al. (2014), focused on Swedish textile and clothing small and medium-sized enterprises, suggests three categories of enablers that contribute to organizational resilience: (1) assets and resourcefulness (for example, teamwork and trust among employees; collaborative interorganizational relationships); (2) dynamic competiveness (for example, rapid decision-making, rapid and effective internal communications, fast learning, quickly adapting routines and strategies); and (3) learning and culture (for example, resilient leadership, optimism among employees, employee well-being). These enablers make organizations better able to deal resiliently and successfully with economic crises.

In the next sections, we explore some related constructs as antecedents of both adaptive and reactive collective resilience. Redundancy of resources has some common traits with adaptive resilience, as it helps organizations to deploy resources for mobilization, especially in cases where parallel alternative courses of action might be required. Proactive resilience boasts some distinct though related features that can play a positive role in the generation of organizational resilience through constitutive features such as agility and improvisation.

Redundancy as an Antecedent of Adaptive Collective Resilience

Adaptive resilience may benefit from the presence of certain levels of redundancy within organizational contexts. Redundancy expresses the ability of a system to persist even when some of its parts or components are compromised (Powley, 2009). It can be seen as a 'time-tested way to improve the ability' of such systems to persist (Zolli and Healy, 2012, p. 13). Redundancy is nurtured by the creation of backups and other slack resources, via the creation of knowledge repositories and other resource reservoirs.

The availability of such redundant resources can increase the resilience of systems (e.g., McGonigal, 2012): the degree of shock an organization faces is aligned with the resources available to the organization, such as backup databases to be used in case of natural disaster. Backups may be of little use, however, when critical conditions change dramatically from those that informed the creation of redundant resources. In such cases, organizations might create 'repositories' of knowledge and solutions that do not fit emergent challenges such as cyber-attacks that access unprotected backup databases in which redundancy had been created for natural disasters.

Nonetheless, redundancy is not just related to the state of having tangible or intangible assets in excess as a form of defensive, adaptive tactic. Redundancy may inform the process of resilience by helping organizations preserve a culture of learning. International professional firms, in the consultancy sector, for example, encourage the creation of global knowledge repositories that incorporate local solutions that can be studied and distributed as global learning. Similarly, 'relational redundancy' activates relational networks that might enable resilience (Powley, 2009).

Many companies, from semiconductor makers to shipbuilders, had

Figure 4.2   Consequences of a non-resilient system: battling the blazing remnants of the Deepwater Horizon, 20 April 2010

to leverage some non-first-tier suppliers in order to cope with the major supply disruption caused by Japan's devastating earthquake in 2011. The resilience of a system is determined by a set of dynamic capabilities and resources that form a system's adaptive capacity (Norris et al., 2008). In such systems, some redundancy is necessary for the absorption of shocks, eventually building adaptive resilience. It is noteworthy, for example, that BP's Deepwater Horizon (Figure 4.2) lacked the redundancy to absorb the shock of a collapse in a key system, partially because of a fetish for lean management.

Agility and Improvisation as Antecedents of Proactive Collective Resilience

As anticipated in Chapter 2, many constructs can be related to proactive resilience at a collective level. Agility represents the capacity to change purposefully and move nimbly among different domains (Doz and Kosonen,

2008a, 2008b; Martin and Carlile, 2000; Schwaber and Beedle, 2001). In defining agile organizing, Rigby et al. (2016) identified four core agile values and principles: (1) people over processes and tools; (2) responding to change rather than following a plan; (3) working prototypes over excessive documentation; and (4) customer collaboration over rigid contracts. Agile organizations are therefore more ready and inclined to develop fast strategies. Structurally, they are more at ease in 'constantly' adjusting their course of action (Doz and Kosonen, 2008b, p. 95). Prange and Heracleous (2018) notice that while agility has traditionally made organizations more reactive, more fundamental changes in organizational scope, that they label 'Agility.X', are required. Hence, while agility and resilience have in common the same outcome (see later in this chapter), agile organizations are not necessarily resilient, but agility could grant organizations a higher likelihood of becoming resilient (Cunha et al., 2018b).

Improvisation is another possible antecedent of collective resilience. Hadida et al. (2015) distinguish between 'interpersonal improvisation' and 'organizational improvisation'. The former 'transcends' individuals, taking place in small teams, while the latter 'refers both to the ability of the whole organization to improvise and to the institutionalization of structures or practices that enable or lead to improvisation within the organization' (Hadida et al., 2015, p. 448). As an antecedent of resilience, collective improvisation can be seen as either an aggregation of individual improvisations or as a substantially collective and seamless process (Miner et al., 2001).

The same reasoning applies to anticipation, understood as predicting and preventing potential dangers before damage is done (Wildavsky, 1988, p. 77), a cognitive and behavioural 'mode of control'. As such, it may start with individuals (see Chapter 3) and be circulated at interpersonal and collective levels, building resilience (Lengnick-Hall and Beck, 2005, p. 750) when not stigmatized as 'whistle-blowing' (Rothschild, 2008).

When individuals collectively are able to react to jolts, crises and shock by absorbing them and being able to prepare for further events with a similar impact, learning collectively how to face challenging situations, collective resilience proves its existence. The absorption of shocks characterizing adaptive resilience has some aspects in common with other organizational capabilities, such as adaptability and recovery. These facets of resilience, connoting its proactive side, share some commonalities with flexibility, manoeuvrability and robustness.

Related Constructs as Outcomes of Adaptive Collective Resilience

Adaptive resilience can also apply at a collective level. Collectively, adaptability means the capacity to re-establish a state of fit deemed desirable for a changing environment (Chakravarthy, 1982; Waugh et al., 2008); desirability, of course, does not mean success. The adaptations to events that are made are lodged firmly in normal modes of sensemaking and these may well be inappropriate. The adaptation to the environment may be seen as a necessary move to survive, such as a restructuring or a downsizing (e.g., Bowman and Singh, 1993; Giustiniano et al., 2014; Peruffo et al., 2018), limiting the capacity to 'bounce back' or to 'learn' from the experience. Austere responses limit resources and flexibility. So, while organizational resilience is defined as a dynamic process encompassing positive adaptation within the context of significant adversity (Zhang and Liu, 2012), not all forms of adaptability express resilience.

Whether it refers to an ecosystem facing a natural disaster, a population exposed to a disease, a community struggling with an economic crisis, an organization caught in a scandal, or a team hit by a loss, recovery of capabilities is central to resilience. In general terms, recovery entails that a system returns to some baseline conditions (Tax and Brown, 1998). In processual terms, recovery means 'regaining something that has been lost and returning to a former state' (Sonnentag et al., 2012, p. 867). It can mean more, however: resilient systems might emerge from adverse circumstances 'with growth and strengthened capabilities for dealing with future challenges' (Caza and Milton, 2012, p. 898). The restoration to its initial conditions does not necessarily entail that the system has expressed resilience or become resilient. In fact, resilient systems may evolve to a new condition rather than return to a previous one. For instance, an effective service recovery system does not necessarily mean that a system is resilient, when the system was already coded, scripted or prepared (Norris et al., 2008). As a dynamic property of systems, resilience is linked to a system's capacity of response (Gallopi'n, 2006). When present, resilience helps systems to re-form and learn in the process of recovery.

Related Constructs as Outcomes of Proactive Collective Resilience

Flexibility refers to the organization's capacity to change rapidly and without major impediments (McCann, 2004; Bahrami and Evans, 2005, 2011; Ward et al., 2015). Flexible organizations are able to perform 'real-time adjustment of actions in response to actual events' (Eisenhardt et al., 2010, p. 1264). In their study of the United States Emergency Department, Ward et al. (2015) identified five forms of flexibility:

1. Behavioural, expressed via repertoires of behaviours and networks of professionals as sources for facing the unexpected.

2. Conceptual, based on the assumption that not everything can be planned and therefore the adoption of diverse perspectives and ways of thinking are necessary, including the deviation from standards.
3. Physical resources, related to the possibility to use spaces and technology for a variety of purposes.
4. Human resources, linked to the employability of personal skills and competences (that is, generalist versus specialist).
5. Volume, regarding to the ability to maintain operations smoothly in spite of the fluctuation of the demand and the related activities required.

Each form of flexibility might 'individually or in combination with others' respond to organizational needs (that is, customer satisfaction, tackling of emergency situations, and so on) arising in the shape of 'partial flexibility' (Ward et al., 2015, p. 156).

Organizational solutions for flexibility can be found in the adoption of modular structures (e.g., Brusoni et al., 2001), changing position in the value or supply chain in order to generate more value or to reduce risks (Edwards et al., 2004; Nenni and Giustiniano, 2013), or employing virtual freelancers or temporary workers rather than full-time staff (Johns and Gratton, 2013). Collective solutions for flexibility do not necessarily increase collective resilience (see MacCormack et al., 2006; MacCormack et al., 2012). Continuous change in market position as a flexible response can create confusion and dissonance in customers who have become unsure of what a brand signifies in light of these changes, eventually endangering organizational reputation. Similarly, the employment of temporary workers in jobs that have very short duration (some of them under a week, as with some freelancers in the media industries) can create a permanent state of 'indeterminacy of temporariness' that questions the existing mechanisms of coordination and control, forcing the organizations to reinvent and recast continuously (see Morris et al., 2016).

Further, flexibility via a temporary workforce can also endanger the achievement of resilience if freelancers also work for other organizations (for example, avoiding engagement in regressive behaviours; Horne, 1997). Resilience can create flexibility, helping collectivities to adapt to new realities. Nonetheless, the search for flexibility via some organizational forms or solutions may end up harming resilience (for example, use of a part-time, contingent workforce). Just as in natural science, bending (being flexible) does not entail being able to restore the previous shape, state or equilibrium (Crichton et al., 2009).

Similarly to flexibility and agility, manoeuvrability also emphasizes the capability to react to jolts in a timely manner. Manoeuvrability 'concerns the quickness of a controlled system's planned change from one trajectory to another' (Nissen and Burton, 2011, p. 423). Manoeuvrability differs from adaptability, which merely aims at re-establishing an a priori condition, while manoeuvrability implies dynamic capabilities. In studying organization from a 'fluxing' approach (alternative to the 'equilibrating' one), Nissen (2014) sees flexibility as the alternative pole to efficiency (efficiency–flexibility tension). Similarly, when an organization reacts to stressors, 'the stability–manoeuvrability tension is fundamental to organizational dynamics, as is the classic tension between efficiency and flexibility' (Nissen, 2014, p. 37). Organizations are manoeuvrable when they are able to redesign in a routine, integrative way. In such situations, 'maintaining organizational performance through fluxing designs represents a central responsibility of management' (Nissen, 2014, p. 38).

Resilient organizations are manoeuvrable (Nissen and Burton, 2011) because they are able to return dynamically to stable states after disruptions (Bhamra et al., 2011). They do by searching for a new point of equilibrium that differs from that which previously existed. Manoeuvrability requires dynamic fit (Burton and Obel, 2004, 2013; Nissen, 2014) between the organization and the source of stress; where systems are exposed to multiple stressors and survive they are becoming more resilient (Du et al., 2010). Whether adjustments and reconfigurations take place as expressions of agility, flexibility or manoeuvrability, they might be effective in the short run, but that does not guarantee organizational learning and the implementation of 'lessons learned' (e.g., Buchanan and Denyer, 2013) concerning how to bounce back (see also Boin, 2004; Carroll, 1998). Such learning and its implementation is a central element in promoting proactive resilience.

Resilience minimizes the harm and damage that individuals and collectivities might endure. Resilience entails robustness: 'taking hits with minimal damage to functional capability' (Bahrami and Evans, 2005, p. 423). Robustness can be increased by hardening the characteristics of a system's strategic design or by redesigning the system's structural architecture in view of experiences (Miller, 1993). In a classic example, as the environment becomes more uncertain, the organization adopts a simpler and more organic design (e.g., Burns and Stalker, 1961). Nonetheless, collectivities may become progressively more robust without gaining any resilience. They may be hard to bend, but under pressure break, rather than bouncing back (Miller, 1993).

COLLECTIVE NON-LEARNING THREATENS RESILIENCE

In Chapter 3 we learned that individuals might very easily 'exaggerate stressors', creating vicious circles in consequence (Bonnanno, quoted in Konnikova, 2016). A similar dynamic might take place in groups via groupthink. Groupthink is a psychological collective phenomenon occurring in groups of individuals in whom the desire for harmony or conformity leads to irrational or dysfunctional decision-making (Janis, 1972, 1982). Team cohesion may be a source of team resilience. But, paradoxically, it may also facilitate disastrous decisions and catastrophic consequences (see Box 6.2 in Chapter 6). A typical case of groupthink occurs when group members try to avoid or minimize conflict during a decision-making process via the suppression of dissenting viewpoints or the restitution of agendas to 'safe' issues, resulting in severe limiting of the range of alternative viewpoints. When groupthink takes place, the deep understanding of 'what happened' and the evaluation of possible alternatives, vital to organizational learning, may be suffocated by (a pseudo) rationality that is too bounded, too constrained. An exaggerated commitment to social cohesiveness and organizational robustness that reflects this conformism may endanger resilience.

Another possible danger for resilience comes from an excess of agility and flexibility. In their study of 100 high-tech companies listed in *Fortune*, Sanner and Bunderson (2018) suggest dismissing a myth of contemporary management: that hierarchy within organizations is essentially useless. The study argues for the characteristic role of hierarchy (or rather, of the 'boss') in reducing decision-making options and choosing the skills necessary to execute them. The study points out that hierarchy, even if it is exercised in a temporary form, effectively delivers decision-making that can lose momentum in the illusory search for absolute consensus. The excessive pursuit of agility and flexibility might trap organizations in vicious circles of political stasis, eventually endangering time-based innovation and competition and making the teams and the organizations involved more vulnerable, and therefore less resilient. That flat, non-hierarchical or holacratic organization (e.g., Bernstein et al., 2016; Robertson, 2015) may well have these effects leads some management theorists to defend the necessity for hierarchy in contemporary organizations (Pfeffer, 2013; Box 4.7).

The next chapter introduces a conceptual model highlighting how different levels in an organization can participate in the construction of resilience via virtuous circles and how the unfolding of vicious circles impedes resilience of the overall system. We also specify the role of interactions at each level as a prerequisite for resilience to flow across levels. The

BOX 4.7   HIERARCHY: WITH OR WITHOUT IT?

Hierarchy: friend or foe? On the one hand, organizations need hierarchy because it instils order and coordination in a simple, clear, effective way. On the other hand, hierarchy typically comes associated with bureaucracy, command, fear and rigidity. Holacracy is a practice of organizing based on a holarchy of decentralized management and organizational governance originally developed by HolacracyOne, a company founded in 2007 that proudly presents itself as follows: 'We're a non-conventional company in many ways: we're based in the USA but all our business partners work from home. We don't have any employees, we're all legal partners in the company, and we've adopted Holacracy in our bylaws' (https://www. holacracy.org/holacracyone). In opposition to vertical hierarchy, the practice of holacracy is based on distributed (rather than centralized) decision-making and self-organizing teams (rather than stable organizational units). So, is hierarchy good or bad? Read Pfeffer's paper, 'You're still the same' (Pfeffer, 2013) and Robertson's pledge for holacracy (Bernstein et al., 2016). Do also consider the interview with Zappos CEO, Tony Hsieh (De Smet and Gagnon, 2017). When asked about 'What does holacracy mean for Zappos?', Hsieh replied:

> We've always encouraged employees to move around to find the intersection of what they are passionate about, what they are good at, and what adds value to the company, even in the 'old days.' For me personally, calling it 'holacracy' was more a way of codifying or making explicit what was already implicit in our culture. We shouldn't have to be dependent on a benevolent manager or CEO to allow employees to move around within the organization, because that's a single point of failure. Our org chart is available in real-time online and changes probably 50 times a day, and every one of our 1500 employees can transparently view what every employee's purposes and accountabilities are. We have self-organized governance methods and meetings that happen on a regular basis, and it's all browsable and updateable online, along with, occasionally, policy updates – all of which enables any employee to contribute to the evolving structure of the organization. So it's not so much about 'holacracy' as it is about 'self-organization'.

Reflect about the pros and cons of hierarchy and holocracy. What is your position? Does hierarchy or holacracy best aid or hinder organizational resilience, and under what conditions?

concept of employee engagement, originally introduced by Kahn (1990) as the willingness of employees to invest themselves cognitively, emotionally and physically in their work role, which has been investigated at various levels of analysis, from the individual and team level (e.g., Rich et al., 2010;

Carmeli et al., 2015) to the whole firm (e.g., Harter et al., 2002; Macey et al., 2011), will be introduced. We follow this example of multi-level analysis.

NOTES

1. See https://www.fmglobal.com/research-and-resources/tools-and-resources/resilienceindex/explore-the-data/?&cr=BGD&sn=6&vd=1.
2. https://www.fmglobal.com/research-and-resources/tools-and-resources/resilienceindex/explore-the-data/?&cr=BGD&sn=6&vd=1.
3. The author of this sub-section is Chintan Kella, LUISS Guido Carli University and Tilburg School of Economics and Management.
4. https://www.gene.com/good/local-initiatives/childhood-adversity/the-resilience-effect.

5. The diffusion of resilience via cross-level interactions

> Strong leadership that promotes cohesive and interdependent teams is a critical component of a resilient organization. Organizational resilience evolves over time as management and teams adhere to the mission and to the core values of the organization.
> (Southwick et al., 2017, p. 315)

THE DIFFUSION OF RESILIENCE: HOW RESILIENT INDIVUALS MAKE COLLECTIVES MORE RESILIENT, AND VICE VERSA

As organizational environments have become more and more unstable, uncertain and equivocal, resilience has entered the core of management studies as the organizational, team and individual capacity to absorb external shocks and to learn from them while simultaneously preparing for and responding to external shifts. A vulnerable organization can still survive; a resilient organization is expected to face adversity and yet prosper.

As a spur to cross-level resilience research, in this chapter we propose a multi-level model of resilience in organizations. The model is based on the nature and dynamics of resilience flowing across levels, and builds on interactive components: regular patterns that can be identified both at the lower level (for example, individuals) and in higher level units (for example, teams) up to the organization considered as a whole. Our model highlights the importance of interactions as the foundation for resilience emergence at different levels, and suggests ways for competitive organizations to increase their overall resilience.

RESILIENCE AT THE INDIVIDUAL LEVEL

As anticipated in Chapter 2, resilience can be considered a state-like construct (open to development) or as a process. As a state-like individual characteristic, resilience is a core feature of the overall construct of positive psychological capital (Luthans et al., 2007). Resilient individuals are able 'to overcome, steer through, bounce back and reach out to pursue new knowledge and experiences, deeper relationships with others and [find] meaning in life' (Luthans et al., 2007, p. 123). As a process, resilience is considered to be 'a developmental trajectory characterized by demonstrated competence in the face of, and professional growth after, experiences of adversity in the workplace. Each enables an individual to handle future challenges' (Caza and Milton, 2012, p. 896).

Various dispositions can make some individuals more resilient than others, including personal traits such as optimism, confidence (Bonanno et al., 2006) or faith (Pargament, 1997), and relational aspects such as involvement in rich social networks (Pressman et al., 2005). The individual level of analysis is critical because an understanding of what differentiates resilient individuals from others provides a useful starting point for defining resilience at higher levels.

Studies on individual resilience have demonstrated that resilience is related to problem-solving capabilities, favourable perceptions, positive reinforcement and strong faith (Zolli and Healy, 2012). Resilience also relates to workplace performance (Caverley, 2005; Coutu, 2002; Luthans et al., 2005; Luthans et al., 2010; Waite and Richardson, 2004), as well as to a number of other coping processes, such as employability (Chen and Lim, 2012). Resilience is a capability that can be deliberately cultivated (Caza and Milton, 2012; Luthans et al., 2006a). Therefore, it can be the object of overall system intervention.

The Interactive Component

Rich interactions are central to the processes of personal development at work, including those offered by coaching and mentoring (e.g., MacNeil, 2004). In these processes, the fact that one feels supported and respected increases the capacity to act (Rogers and Ashford, 2017). As shown by Carmeli et al. (2015), in order to be effective, interactions at the individual and team levels have to be grounded on respectful engagement. Respectful engagement depends on how the individual is seen and valued within the organization (e.g., Wrzesniewski and Dutton, 2001). Respectful engagement, as the development processes of new solutions, may create the conditions for predisposing employees both to share their personal crises with others and to seek help (adaptive resilience), as well as to experiment with new solutions (proactive resilience) within a framework of psychological safety (for example, no-blame culture).

Within this framework, coaching practices may play a crucial role in developing a climate for positive interactions and creating and maintaining the conditions for psychological safety. Coaches energize relationships

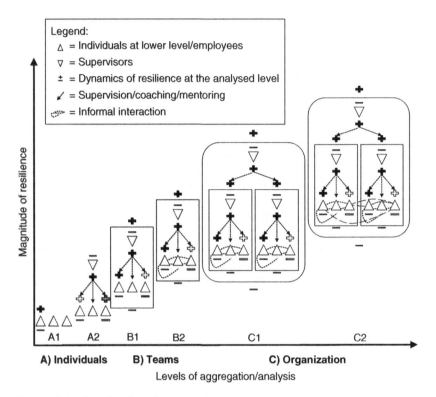

Figure 5.1   Levels of resilience and interaction components

and counter feelings of isolation and loneliness. This is critical at several levels of analysis, including newcomers but also experienced leaders, such as chief executive officers (CEOs). Positive, constructive relationships equip individuals under strain with psychological resources that increase resilience (Masten, 2001; Hallowell, 1999), which in turn can facilitate the construction of more resilient contexts (Figure 5.1, Level A2).

RESILIENCE AT THE TEAM LEVEL

Chapter 2 has discussed different definitions of resilience that have developed over time and across disciplines (Caza and Milton, 2012). Two consistent aspects emerge from almost all definitions (Figure 5.1, Level A1): (1) resilience requires the presence of some negative stressors (−) and an individual being exposed to significant threats (Luthar et al., 2000); (2) resilient individuals perform a positive adaptation (+) in the face of those stressful or threatening events. Chapter 4 anticipated that resilient teams develop the capacity to see failure and imperfection as sources of learning and progress (Edmondson, 2012). They develop an appreciation for imperfection as possessing an aesthetic quality (Weick, 1979, 1995) that increases their collective mindfulness and consequent alertness to opportunities for improvement (Figure 5.1, Level B1). Resilient teams are potentially more able to adapt and bounce back from failures, setbacks, threats and other adverse circumstances (−), are more cohesive, and more willing to support other members to maintain their positivity and to adopt more prosocial behaviours, thus improving their performance (+) (Clapp-Smith et al., 2009; West et al., 2009; Walumbwa et al., 2011).

Edmondson (1999, 2008, 2012) proposed that a combination of psychological safety and accountability are critical ingredients for the emergence of resilience at the group level. Resilient teams are not those that protect people from mistakes, but those that recognize mistakes but protect people (for example, a no-blame culture). Confronting mistakes constructively is required to cultivate resilience. The learned capacity to expose mistakes but not those who made them results in growing confidence to tackle problems and develop a learning attitude that embeds resilience in team functioning. Resilient teams develop this capacity to cultivate rich relationships among team members (Pentland, 2012), by avoiding the attribution of mistakes to individuals (Deming, 1982) as well as by attenuating the disadvantages of hierarchy in unstable environments (Anderson and Brown, 2010). Exposed to extreme conditions, resilient teams can also generate positive energies out of previously 'unthinkable' behaviours via the development of sensemaking (Box 5.1).

The Interactive Component

Resilient teams exemplify rich interactions. Research suggests that they have more and more diversified internal connections, not necessarily mediated by the leader (Dutton and Heaphy, 2003; Pentland, 2012). Richer interactive patterns (Figure 5.1, level B2) are created that can be seen as relational information processes, meant as basic units of human interactions essential to organizational communication (Ford and Ford, 1995). Intense communicative interactions have a positive effect upon the development of respectful engagement and, in turn, on persistence and resilience (Carmeli et al., 2015). In addition, due to their interactions, resilient teams are probably more connected to other teams both inside and outside the organization (Ancona et al., 2002). These connections allow them to gain more access to resources of various kinds which, in turn, potentially increases their effectiveness. Higher accessibility to cognitive resources is linked to the presence of 'shared perceptions' of engagement (Klein et al., 2001; Barrick et al., 2015).

BOX 5.1   SURVIVING IN EXTREME CONDITIONS: A
'MIRACLE' IN A MINE

Watch the movie '*33*', which narrates the real story of the 33 miners trapped in the San
José Mine in Chile. The 33 were rescued after being trapped underground for 69 days
(Figure 5.2). Experts had estimated that the probability of locating and rescuing the
missing workers alive was less than 1 per cent (Rashi et al., 2013). Analyse the similarities and differences with the *El Milagro* (in Chapter 4). Read the works of Rashi et
al. (2013) and Useem et al. (2011) on the same topic. Read the timeline of the event
on the CNN webpage (https://edition.cnn.com/2013/07/13/world/americas/chilean-
mine-rescue/index.html). Then reflect: (1) What are the main lessons for resilience?
(2) Why did René Aguilar, one member of the rescue team, feel that 'It was the happiest
day in my life. More than happy, total jubilation!' (Useem et al., 2011, p. 54)? (3) What
factors nourished the resilience of the 33 and the members of the rescue team?

Source: Photo: Gobierno de Chile, https://commons.wikimedia.org/wiki/File:Mina_
San_Jos%C3%A9_-_Luis_Urz%C3%BAa_-_Gobierno_de_Chile.jpg. File is licensed
under the Creative Commons Attribution 2.0 Generic license.

*Figure 5.2   Celebrating the 'miracle': Luis Urzúa, the leader of the
trapped miners and the last to be lifted to freedom,
celebrates with Sebastián Piñera, the then President of
Chile, 13 October 2010*

Engagement nurtures the social capital that is necessary to spread resilience within the organization. Additionally, if the social capital embeds psychological safety, engagement should also counter passivity.

Interaction is critical to sustain organizational resilience. Garud et al.'s (2006) study of the transformation of Infosys illustrates the importance of organizationally framed interactions for the cultivation of resilience at the level of organizations (Figure 5.1, level C2). These authors highlight, first, the role of clear goals, namely a purpose that orients organizational action. Second, at Infosys, fundamental change was represented internally as 'an opportunity to transform the company' (p. 279). Third, Infosys emphasized decentralized decision-making and a culture of 'learnability'.

Critical for 'learnability' to occur was the cultivation of an 'asking culture' and the nurturance of an interactive infrastructure. The culture was distilled through norms such as, 'if you can help someone, you should' (p. 280), the notion that employees should stay 'in touch', as well as the importance of the creation of 'binding aspects' (p. 280) in the absence of which learnability would be just an empty word. The whole process is fuelled by the habit of inquiring (for example, asking 'why' or 'why not' within 'framing experiments') as an organizational, established practice.

CULTIVATING RESILIENCE ACROSS LEVELS: TOWARDS AN INTERACTIVE MODEL OF DIFFUSION

As previously described, proactive resilience refers to the cultivated preparedness to cope with surprise. It leads to organizational resilience as an intentional, enduring organizational characteristic. Adaptive resilience refers to the ability to bounce back and to absorb strain with minimal disruption. Doing so requires resilient organizing and the willingness of individuals to frame organizational problems as their own problems. Assuming that organizational problems are an individual issue requires the constant reaccomplishment of psychological safety, otherwise potentially individual negative outcomes may emerge.

Psychological Safety

Resilience is supported by relationships that help people to activate resources as required. Resilience is favoured by interactions that strengthen social relationships and helps in coping with stressful circumstances (Lyubomirsky et al., 2005). Studies on social resilience have highlighted the effects of processes such as gratitude (Grant and Gino, 2010; Gino and

Staats, 2012), human touch (Fuller et al., 2011), helping (Schein, 2009), expressing a tolerance for failure (Edmondson, 2012) and developing habits of positive connecting with others (Stephens et al., 2012; Stephens et al., 2013). All these elements may be fundamental to the creation of psychological safety, as part of wider occupational health and safety (e.g., Zanko and Dawson, 2012).

Psychological safety is a group process that, while preserving individual accountability, frames the team as a social buffer against adversity and failure. Resilience is favoured by psychological safety, 'individuals' perceptions regarding the consequences of interpersonal risks in their work environment' (Edmondson, 2012, p. 146), because individuals feel that the team is a safe place to take risks. Because resilience is inherently risky, psychological safety is critical for individuals to consciously expose themselves to the possibility of failure. Thus, individual contributions to team psychological safety will facilitate resilience by motivating team members to risk responding to adversity (Box 5.2). Leaders are particularly relevant in

---

BOX 5.2   IS YOUR TEAM PSYCHOLOGICALLY SAFE?

Take the study from Liang et al. (2012). Think about your team and compute your score. The mean score in the Liang et al. (2012) study was around between 3.5 and 3.6. Is your score lower or higher?

Read Duhigg's (2016) article published in the *New York Times*, about 'What Google learned from its quest to build the perfect team'. The text explains that Matt Sakaguchi, a team leader, once shared with his team: 'I think one of the things most people don't know about me,' he told the group, 'is that I have Stage 4 cancer'. Is your team a place where both the leader and the team members may share their own vulnerabilities? What does this kind of frankness do for the individual and the team resilience? If you are a leader, do you behave as a builder of team psychological safety, or rather do you kill the messenger of the bad news? Measure the psychological safety of your team by asking all team members to answer (anonymously) the five questions mentioned above. If the score is not what you would like, do not point the finger at others – point it at yourself. Explore the reasons behind such a score. Develop yourself in order to be a builder of team psychological safety.

fostering team psychological safety. Google's Project Aristotle showed that psychological safety, 'more than anything else' (Duhigg, 2016, p. MM20), was critical to build a 'perfect team'.

Organizations should cultivate psychological safety. Without psychological safety, people may not contribute to identify and expose problems: 'psychological safety is critical for diagnosis . . . Without it, people may not be speaking up about the problems and errors they know exist' (Edmondson, 2012, p. 244). They can do so by nurturing the idea that error is the source of learning (MacPhail and Edmondson, 2012), and by creating caring cultures (Spreitzer and Porath, 2012), where secure learning is possible (Hodgkinson and Healey, 2011). They can train leaders to function as coaches oriented towards improvement, rather than as control-oriented supervisors. And they can institute formal mechanisms to facilitate learning.

Again, asking 'why' rather than 'who' helps to create learning as a collective endeavour, empowering action in preference to protection through rule tropism. Cultivating accountability and safety processes may be critical for supporting a culture of resilience. The process, however, may be difficult for several reasons, including existing implicit leadership theories (Detert and Edmondson, 2011) by employees who may retain the representations of leaders as directive and threatening rather than inclusive and supportive. The formal adoption by organizations of 'speak up' types of policies can be important as a signal, but the actual expression of psychological safety depends on the everyday leader's actions (Cunha et al., forthcoming-b). It also depends on the level of power distance that characterizes the context (Hu et al., 2017; Liang et al., 2012). In team and organizational cultures characterized by high power distance, a low level of psychological safety to (not) show disagreement toward authority figures may be the norm; and the consequences may be catastrophic, including for air crashes (Hagen, 2013). Creating a culture of psychological safety requires 'more than words' (Box 5.3).

The Diffusion of Proactive Resilience

Proactive and adaptive forms of resilience may occur across levels (in both directions, that is, top-down and bottom-up) and the greater the fluidity between levels, the greater the organization's resilience potential. We illustrate the two processes below by analysing connections between successive levels (see Figure 5.3). Higher-level capabilities are not only additive composites of capabilities expressed at some lower level. Micro-actions matter to define the emergence of system behaviours, but interaction effects are equally important (Morgeson and Hofman, 1999).

BOX 5.3   MORE THAN WORDS

A study by Cunha et al. (forthcoming-b) in the healthcare industry indicates that speaking about 'speak up' and formally proclaiming the value of speaking up is very different from allowing people to speak up and to nurture a culture of psychological safety. In other words: speaking about resilience does not result in greater resilience. As such, in practice managers need to walk the talk: they need to create the contexts favourable for resilience and this requires more than words.

Think about the reasons why defending the value of speaking up does not necessarily translate into superior levels of speaking up.

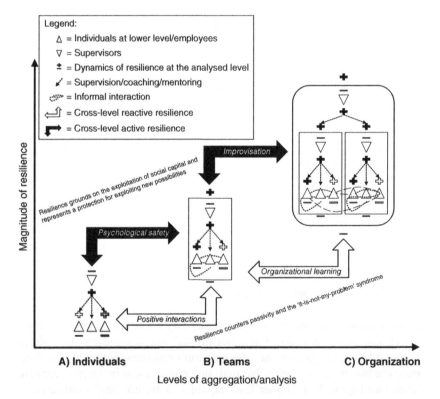

Figure 5.3   Multi-level cultivation of resilience

In the proposed model, proactive resilience is induced by the organization itself and, in this sense, seen as a relatively enduring organizational attribute. Proactive resilience is less an exercise in hierarchy than a culture of proactivity supported by organizational culture and management practice: companies with superior management have been shown to fare better in times of adversity (Carvalho and Areal, 2016). This macro approach materializes a culture of rich, positive interaction nurtured by supportive leaders that 'show positive regard, build cooperative relationships, and help people cope with stressful situations' (Yukl, 2012, p. 71). Without supportive leadership practices, cultural messages will not translate into action and will not lead to resilience. Such leadership development, however, is politically sensitive, culturally complex and institutionally embedded (Mabey, 2013).

Individual and team: positive interactions
Individuals may activate resilience by creating and sustaining positive relationships as a normal and recurrent pattern of action. When positive interactions prevail, individuals will be more willing to initiate response from the base (Frohman, 1997), to express proactivity and to lead change efforts via a local, proactive approach (Grant and Ashford, 2008). Organizational support for proactivity is a catalyst for resilience. When those in substantial leadership positions who are 'resilience-rich' embrace positivity, this resilience nurtures the cross-domain development of human capabilities (e.g., Hougaard et al., 2018). Positive interactions can also emerge in extreme conditions of negative expectations about the success of individuals and teams by the external context.

Organizations can train individuals to engage in positive rather than negative interactions, and use trained individuals, particularly those in central network positions (for example, leaders) to energize and sustain positive relationships (Dutton, 2003), for example by displaying grit and humility (Rego et al., 2018). These individuals, be they 'naturally' dispositional energizers or trained to be so, may have an important role in nurturing the types of positive relationships that increase resilience. These interactions may stabilize in teams as patterns, points out Pentland (2012). Individuals, particularly those in leadership positions, may thus represent their roles as providers of interactional micro-processes that will support the creation of resilience from the ground up. As Story et al. (2013) observed, leader resilience positively influences follower resilience where there is a high-quality relationship and frequent interaction. From this we suggest that positive interactions will facilitate individual and team resilience by energizing teams and team members to be more proactive in their tackling of problems.

Team and organization: learning processes

Teams can be used to support organizational resilience as the preferential locus for organizational learning (Edmondson, 2012). Teams operate within the constraints established by the existing rules, but in some cases organizations develop teams with the mission of countering inertial pressures and existing assumptions to facilitate learning and preparedness for change. These teams embed resilience in the system, disrupting routines (Cunha and Chia, 2007).

The literature offers several examples of these types of teams operating at the boundaries of the existing organization, with the aim of reimagining some organizational processes in anticipation of external shocks. Informal project teams coordinated with the formal structure may be used to go beyond the status quo and assist the organization in thinking about the future, increasing preparedness and flexibility with regard to change processes from the inside (Kotter, 2012). Teams have also been designed to explore the organization's periphery, the space where threats and opportunities incubate, often without capturing the organization's attention (Day and Schoemaker, 2004). Their role is to alert the organization to possibilities yet to be explored, and to help it avoid trapping itself in exploitative dynamics (March, 1991) that will render it progressively simpler (Miller, 1993), against an increasingly complex and turbulent organizational environment (D'Aveni, 1995). Groups may also increase resilience by tracking small failures, creating situational awareness and developing sensitivity to operations (Weick and Sutcliffe, 2001 [2007]). Organizations can thus become more proficient in anticipating and tackling surprises by shifting decision to teams closer to the problem rather than by resorting to the hierarchy to do so. Hence, learning to learn (Andersen, 2016) at the level of psychologically safe teams and organizations facilitates resilience by helping people come to terms with failing and to bounce back. Conversely, overconfidence and hubris may prevent team learning and lead to repeated disasters (see Box 5.4).

The Diffusion of Adaptive Resilience

Adaptive resilience is triggered in response to events (Deroy and Clegg, 2011). Responding to issues that arise is better conducted at the group level when groups combine psychological safety with an intention to act (that is, proactivity; Grant et al., 2011). Adaptive resilience can be interpreted as: (1) induced by the organizational environment as potentially temporary and fleeting; (2) a process that articulates higher levels with increasingly lower levels, turning problems of the organization into problems of their

BOX 5.4   THE SILENT RESILIENCE OF THE UNDERDOGS –
PART II: THE *'MARACANAÇO'*

The Uruguay versus Brazil match, played on 16 July 1950 in Rio de Janeiro for the FIFA World Cup, is probably the most famous in the history of football, not for the quality of the match itself but rather for its social implications. The match took place at the iconic Maracanã Stadium in Rio de Janeiro, then the capital of Brazil. Although in the 1950 edition of the World Cup the winner was determined in a 'round robin' played by four teams, that match was the equivalent of a final. In fact, after having heavily dominated the two other finalists (Spain 6-1 and Sweden 7-1), Brazil was one point ahead of Uruguay, needing just a draw to claim the title while Uruguay needed a win. At the same time, Brazil had won the Copa America just one year before with the remarkable record of 46 goals in eight matches, and during the World Cup had destroyed all the opponents with its aggressive attack-minded style; Uruguay, on the other hand, drew 2-2 with Spain and marked a late-minutes narrow victory over Sweden (3-2).

As a matter of fact, Brazil was so sure to win that, in an impetus of collective hubris, the press and the population started to celebrate the team as the new world champions days before the final match. The entire population was envisioning a clear victory, supporters were practising and chanting a victory song composed for the occasion, and even an impromptu carnival was organized the very morning of the match, while the Brazilian newspaper *O Mundo* released an early edition with the picture of the team labelled 'These are the world champions' (later remembered by White, 2014, as one of the 100 most significant sentences in the history of football); in a pre-match speech addressed to the players, the Mayor of Rio de Janeiro dared to state that having 'no rivals in the entire hemisphere', 'in less than a few hours' they would be 'hailed as champions by millions of compatriots!' (White, 2014).

On the other side, the preparation of this match in this 'hostile' environment by the Uruguayan team was quite different, in particular in the mind of Uruguay's Captain, Obdulio Varela. The morning of the match, Varela gathered all the possible copies of the newspaper *O Mundo* anticipating the victory of Brazil, brought them to the dressing room, laid them on the bathroom floor and encouraged his teammates to piss all over them. Additionally, in the pre-match meeting, after the Uruguay coach Juan López asked the team to adopt a defensive strategy, as the only possible way to resist the blasting Brazilian attack, Varela waited for the coach to leave and delivered a moving inspirational speech claiming that this time the coach was wrong. Being the rank outsiders, the underdogs, playing defensively against Brazil would doom them to be beaten, as were Spain and Sweden. He instead said impassionedly: *'Muchachos, los de afuera son de palo. Que comience la función'* ('Boys, outsiders don't play. Let's start the show'; Pougatch 2011).

At 3 pm the game began at the Maracanã Stadium with a record attendance

Figure 5.4   *'Campeones mundiales de 1950' ('World Champions of
1950'): Uruguayan monument in Montevideo*

estimated to be about 200 000. Predictably, Brazil took the lead. Nonetheless,
Uruguay was able to draw. At 11 minutes before the end, Alcides Ghiggia from
Uruguay scored the winning goal, fixing the final result 2-1 for Uruguay, making
them the World Champions (Figure 5.4). That moment left a whole country open-
mouthed, and is remembered as one of the biggest upsets in sporting history,
giving rise to the term *Maracanaço* (Maracanazo, 'The Maracanã Blow') and later
in the years to the 'Phantom of '50'.

In preparing for the eventual Maracanazo, Varela turned the underdogs into
national heroes, encouraging his teammates not to be intimidated by what the
press said, by the roaring crowd and all the media speculations; having done so,
he is considered one of the principal figures forging modern Uruguayan national
identity (Giulianotti, 1999).

Homework: The '*Mineiraço*' of 2014

And now another piece of homework. On 8 July in the 2014 World Cup, Brazil played against Germany in the Mineirão Stadium in Belo Horizonte. The responsibility on Brazil's shoulders was very high. At the end, the score was an impressive 7-1 . . . to the Germans. The disaster became known as the '*Mineiraço*'. What similarities can you identify between the cases? What does one episode tell about the other? And what do they both say about resilience?

---

individual members or teams who interpreted and framed them in the first place, as issues that could be acted upon.

DIFFUSION AND CULTIVATION OF RESILIENCE IN PRACTICE

We have discussed the multi- and cross-level dynamics of resilience in organizations. The analysis opens a number of practical possibilities for management research and practice. Figure 5.3 summarizes the cross-level dynamics of cultivation here presented in terms of nature of resilience and levels of interactions. Psychological safety is addressed above, and building on that, we next explore possibilities revealed by a number of interactive practices that demand respectful forms of engagement: positive interactions, organizational learning and improvisation.

Positive Interactions

Organizations may develop norms of positive interacting in several ways. They can create cultures of inquiry (Schoemaker et al., 2013) by inviting people to ask 'why' and by stimulating curiosity and learning (Sinek, 2011). Asking 'why' breeds curiosity and counters the sort of political communication that undermines rich organizational relationships (Heynoski and Quinn, 2012). Promoting a culture rich in other-awareness, perspective-taking, mutual respect and help (Stephens et al., 2012), cultivating positive emotions (Stephens et al., 2012) and positivity is also an important cultural practice.

Positive capital can be influenced via assessment, training and development (Luthans et al., 2007) as well as via less conventional approaches, such as meditation (Peterson et al., 2008). Managers can also cultivate listening skills and empathy (Powley, 2013; Stephens et al., 2012). Listening suggests consideration and creates opportunities for focusing on the other (Losada and Heaphy, 2004). Listening also stimulates mutual appreciation and a culture of civility (Porath, 2012). The introduction of the 'Wow' awards at Zappos, for instance, established that any employee who observes a colleague doing something special could award them a 'Wow'. These awards illustrate how to develop appreciation and appreciative interactions as an organizational practice (Porath and Pearson, 2013), helping to build the necessary confidence to face adversity.

Organizational Learning

To create the learning necessary for resilience to be expressed, organizations can use teams to counter inertia. Self-managing teams can be instituted to increase exploratory competences. Teams can be specifically assigned to explore the organization's periphery (that is, the spaces around organizational attention that are habitually ignored, populated by customers, competitors, new entrants, recent technological developments) and to bring in new learning. Project teams can be used to pursue learning possibilities that are difficult to tackle in a hierarchical mode and context. Organizing people in teams rather than assigning them individual tasks is often taken as a source of competitive advantage through people (Pfeffer, 1994). One explanatory possibility for this type of advantage is the added resilience that empowered teams bring to organizations when used to explore new possibilities. Empowerment offers a sense of control and mutual support that stimulates the desire for learning and problem solving (Spreitzer and Porath, 2012).

Improvisation

The capacity to adjust to environmental change on an ongoing basis as problems emerge, in the absence of planning and of the appropriate resources, has been called improvisation (Miner et al., 2001). Organizational processes oriented towards the prediction of environmental change are critical in assisting organizations in their responses to environmental jolts (Meyer, 1982). Prediction, however, is not enough. Organizations have to express a capacity for improvisation in response to relevant challenges even when these are coded as weak signals (Vogus and Sutcliffe, 2012). Improvisation in teams equips organizations with the skill of responding to the unexpected without the benefit of planning (e.g., Hadida et al., 2015). By creating structures and cultures supportive of improvisation

(Barrett, 2012; Eisenhardt et al., 2010), organizations develop the capacity of responding to threats with resilience and openness, instead of relying on standard procedures. Improvisation at the level of teams and organizations will facilitate resilience by equipping them with the skill of responding to unexpected changes without the benefit of planning, instead of waiting for instructions from the hierarchical command system.

Improvisation has been presented as a 'core skill' for the resilient organization (Coutu, 2002, p. 55). To facilitate improvisation, organizations must, first, develop an appreciation for impromptu action (Barrett, 2012). Improvisation is often perceived as dangerous and risky, which means that honing and developing this skill is a precondition for teams to act spontaneously in the face of challenges. Second, organizations will have to empower teams to make decisions on their behalf. Improvisation does not occur naturally in traditional hierarchies – at least in the open. Hierarchies have many advantages but also significant limitations (Anderson and Brown, 2010), including slowness in responding to change, which may impair resilience. Another facilitator of improvisation is the diffusion of strategy throughout the organization so that people can strategize via improvisation. This goes against the traditional strategy–execution gap; to prosper in turbulent environments, organizations need to decentralize strategy and to empower employees as 'strategizers' in addressing emergent problems in real time.

FURTHER REFLECTIONS

The model proposed here has some limitations that are partly related to the assumptions underpinning its formulation in line with the dominant literature that sees resilience as positive. Other studies show the 'dark side' of resilience (Williams et al., 2017; see also Chapter 1). But rigidity may be more favourable when facing some contingencies (Staw et al., 1981). In fact, as with an excess of control, an excess of resilience may cause organizations to drift (Ciborra, 2002). Resilience embeds interactions based on employee engagement as interactive features, but different organizational ecologies may require different types of resilience (for example, the right amount of resilience in one environment may be excessive or insufficient in others; e.g. Burns and Stalker, 1961). Finally, based on research conducted at the micro level (e.g., Luthans et al., 2006a), we assumed that resilience could be designed and managed. But ecosystems research suggests that resilience is a natural, emergent property of healthy ecosystems (Mars et al., 2012). In this sense, it may be un-managed rather than designed, a possibility that should also be considered. Further reflection will be reported in Chapter 6.

6. Resilience as dialectical synthesis

> The concept of resilience is becoming a pervasive idiom of global governance.
> (Walker and Cooper, 2011, p. 144)

> 'Resilience' of human systems [is] the capacity of a system to absorb human/
> natural shocks or disturbances and reorganise while undergoing change that
> either retains, or develops further, essential functions, structures, identities, and
> feedbacks that characterise the system. (Wilson, 2018, p. 90)

RESILIENCE AND ITS TENSIONS

The embeddedness of resilience across different levels relies on the multidimensional nature of human interactions and possible aggregations (Chapter 5). Resilience can be recognized, absorbed, learned by individuals, teams, organizations and collectivities. Chapter 5 has clarified that individuals should be able to 'recognize the pattern' of resilience at the higher levels of aggregation (teams, organizations). On the other hand, organizations should be able to appreciate individuals and teams' resilient behaviours. The case of the Lower Manhattan trading room in the aftermath of the 9/11 (2001) terrorist attack shows the management team regrouping in an emergency facility in New Jersey. While the expected time to resume operations was estimated to be from three to 12 weeks, the business was actually running again after only six days, as soon as the financial markets reopened (Beunza and Stark, 2003, p. 144):

> In New Jersey they [the managers] camped on a table partly occupied by two photocopiers and three fax machines ... They camped, but they stayed together ... When the managers of the agency and special situation desks found themselves sitting again in front of each other, they reverted to their old routine of checking perceptions against each other, probing into each other's belief and designing together new arbitrage trades.

Considering what was described in Chapter 5, the case shows how individual engagement could lead to a distributed cognition, which in turn is able dialectically to synthetize some apparent extremes, such as recovery from extreme damage, with business innovation.

The dialectical interaction between adaptive and proactive forces results in permanent dialectics, which is constitutive of organizational resilience that extends the role of the 'positive feedback loop to an organization's capabilities', as expressed by Sutcliffe and Vogus (e.g., Sutcliffe and Vogus, 2008, p. 499). Organizational resilience ultimately expresses a socially constructed process, embedding minimal conditions of constraints and deviation or construction, allowing individuals and organizations to be adaptive and flexible as action unfolds (e.g. Cunha et al., 2002). Resilience, as a multi-level construct, connects the organization and its environment, spanning at least three levels of aggregation (e.g., Drazin et al., 1999; Hackman, 2003; Sutcliffe and Vogus, 2003): intrasubjective (individual), intersubjective (team), and collective (organization). At different levels of aggregation, agents that are resilience-rich are better prepared to generate sustainable creative ideas for problem-solution (e.g., Luthar and Cicchetti, 2000; Luthar et al., 2000; see Box 6.1). They are also able to conserve adaptive capacity (Gratton and Ghoshal, 2003; Zolli and Healy, 2012). Resilience-poor agents, on the other hand, make choices that unintentionally but consistently point them in the direction of failure (Diamond, 2005).

As Baxter (2004, pp. 182–183) put it, 'the core concept in dialectical perspectives is, after all, the contradiction – a unity of opposites'. Therefore, instead of looking for resolution, a dialectical framework represents organizational resilience as the productive outcome of a tension between two forms of resilience well established in the literature: adaptive and proactive.

The interdependence between levels of aggregation appears to be a constitutive property of organizational resilience. As Egeland et al. (1993) note, facing challenging conditions translates into 'a hierarchical integration of behavioural systems whereby earlier structures are incorporated into later structures in increasingly complex forms' (p. 518). However, the process is not cumulative: resilience at a higher level is not the sum of resilience resources at a lower level (for example, as explained, a team constituted from resilient individuals is not necessarily a resilient team). Considering the potential negative impact that disasters may have in organizational operations, studying resilience at multiple levels, as a way of overcoming challenges, is of paramount importance. Understanding the mechanisms of organizational resilience (Sutcliffe and Vogus, 2003; Vogus and Sutcliffe, 2007) can permit decision-makers to understand how to cultivate or inhibit it and allow them to use this knowledge as a source of competitive advantage (e.g., Pfeffer, 1994; Spreitzer and Porath, 2012).

As for the dialectics of resilience, Figure 6.1 shows how engagement is able to blend adaptive (Template 1) and proactive (Template 2) resilience in a unique and comprehensive template, synthetizing both adaptive and proactive expressions of resilience (Template 3). The idea of resilience as

BOX 6.1   TONY HSIEH, THE ZAPPOS CEO, TALKING ABOUT THE RESILIENCE OF CITIES AND ORGANIZATIONS

Read the following excerpt from an interview with Zappos Chief Executive Officer (CEO) Tony Hsieh for *McKinsey Quarterly* (De Smet and Gagnon, 2017), and then think about the implications for managing organizations:

> Imagine a greenhouse with lots of plants, and each plant represents an employee. Maybe at a typical company, the CEO is the tallest, strongest plant that the other plants aspire to one day become. That's not how I think of my role. Instead, I think of my role as the architect of the greenhouse, and to help figure out the right conditions within the greenhouse to enable all of the other plants to flourish and thrive. Cities are another example of self-organization. Cities are the man-made organizations that have best stood the test of time. Cities last much longer than companies. Cities are resilient. Cities are adaptable. And cities aren't hierarchical the way most companies are. I read somewhere that all of Manhattan has literally three days of food supply. But there's no central food planner for Manhattan. Instead, you've got consumers and businesses 'selfishly' consuming food in a self-organized manner, which creates opportunities for suppliers and so on. And that self-organized system works if there is a natural disaster; a bridge can go out and Manhattan still doesn't run out of food.
>
> Not only do cities stand the test of time, there's plenty of evidence they actually scale in terms of productivity and innovation. One interesting statistic is that whenever the size of a city doubles, innovation or productivity per resident increases 15 percent. But in companies you get the opposite effect. As companies get bigger, they usually get more bureaucratic and less innovative per employee. The mayor of a city doesn't tell its residents what to do or where to live; there is a certain infrastructure that a city must provide, such as the grid: water, power, and sewage. And there are certain basic laws that a city enforces. But for the most part, what happens when a city grows and innovates is a result of the self-organization that happens with a city's residents, businesses, and other organizations.

a process highlights the dynamics through which individuals and aggregative forms create or retain resources (cognitive, emotional, structural, or relational) necessary to successfully cope with and learn from the unexpected (Sutcliffe and Vogus, 2003). Furthermore, as a construct, resilience is unique but shares some characteristics with other well-known organizational processes. Such similarities can be classified according to the adaptive or proactive nature of resilience.

We present the process of resilience as dialectical in nature, with adaptation and pro-action informing one another in a permanent tension that can be dynamic and generative. As noted in Chapter 2, taken singularly, adaptive resilience and proactive resilience represent two opposite ways of facing challenges. Reaction without (future) anticipation, that is adaptive without proactive resilience, is 'learning but forgetting'. Proactive resilience in the absence of adaptive resilience corresponds to contemplative reflection without correspondent action. The synthesis between the two templates articulates action and reflection, which eventually grants the cultivation of ongoing reflective practice. In fact, the sublated achievement of Template 3 overcomes the logic alternative of pursuing either adaptation (action) or reaction (reflection). In this sense adaptive/proactive resilience becomes a sort of reflective reactivity: a reaction based on previous reflection and followed by more reflection that will inform future action (see the arrows in Figure 6.1).

A dialectical concept of resilience will therefore help us to understand how organizations deal resiliently with unpredictable and challenging events. In this vein, viewed at a micro level, resilience is one of the 'four positive psychological resources' that compose an individual's psychological capital; it has a 'positive impact on attitudes, behaviours and performance' (Luthans and Youssef, 2004, 2007; Avey et al., 2011). At the same time, at a macro level, it constitutes 'a unique blend of cognitive, behavioural, and contextual properties that increase a firm's ability to

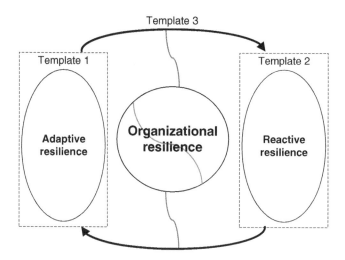

Figure 6.1   Organizational resilience as a dialectical synthesis

understand its current situation and to develop customized responses that reflect that understanding' (Lengnick-Hall and Beck, 2005, p. 750).

ORGANIZATIONAL RESILIENCE AS SYNTHESIS

In this section we develop our third conceptual template by articulating the two previous templates through the notion of permanent dialectics (Clegg et al., 2002). Resilience in this case is not about the capacity to respond or about the cultivation of resilience abilities, but about the dynamic interplay between these two forces. It is the very capacity dynamically to articulate reaction and proactivity that sustains resilient organizing. Permanent dialectics (Clegg et al., 2002) regards organizational phenomena as involving opposite forces. In dialectical terms, these constitute thesis and antithesis. In the logic of permanent dialectics, these two elements will not converge towards a synthesis but will rather sustain one another dynamically without one subsuming the other. The two conceptual templates are not only critical in themselves but also, fundamentally, articulate a process of permanent dialectics:

- Adaptive resilience is rapid, instinctive, ad hoc. It unfolds when an episode pushes the organization beyond the boundary of habitually established action repertoires. When the system is perturbed the capacity to bounce back after pressure is important because it allows the organization to respond in an adaptive way, a form of reaction that is possible, in a dialectical lens, because of the work undertaken in the alternative template: proactive resilience.
- Proactive resilience is the process of regularly questioning the system and the assumptions that sustain it, cultivating reflective practice, appreciating slow thinking (Kahneman, 2011), cultivating voice, dealing with errors as opportunities to make the system more robust (e.g., Hollnagel, 2012). Proactive resilience offers the organization experiences of failure that constitute an opportunity for learning (Birkinshaw and Haas, 2016). Proactive resilience relates to double-loop learning (e.g., Meyer, 1982), leading the system to question itself, to reflect upon its practice, through reflective practice and learning from experience (Yanow and Tsoukas, 2009).
- A dialectical view regards the two modes as important in and of themselves, but especially because they support and challenge each other. The process of resilience can be approached via adaptation and proactivity, but organizational resilience exists when the two templates are articulated in dialectics of reciprocal constitution.

Resilience works by incorporating the ability to bounce back as the result of organizational testing episodes being treated as opportunities for inquiring and learning. The resilient organizational system constantly oscillates between using shocks as opportunities to respond, and responses as opportunities to learn about shocks. Action without reflection is mere reaction, which can be positive in the immediate term but inconsequential for future reference; reflection in the absence of action will be contemplation. It is the dynamic tension between pragmatic action in the face of urgency and the cultivation of learning without immediate need that defines organizational resilience.

The permanent dialectics of reaction and anticipation allows organizations to cultivate resilience as a systemic attribute. A dialectical view of resilience thus contributes to the literature by integrating the views of resilience as rapid responding (that is, in a crisis; e.g., Bigley and Roberts, 2001), which expresses reliance in the here and now, with the view of resilience as slow preparation and incubation of learning that can be deployed while facing a crisis. Dialectically, resilience can be described as the simultaneous capacity to act fast and to think slow. Reactions to stressors, crises and jolts must often be fast, in order to reduce the magnitude of the damage and the exposure of the organization to risks (e.g., Perrow, 1984; Weick, 1993). The reflection on what happened, what are the lessons learned, and how a higher readiness can inform future reactions, requires instead slow thinking (Kahneman, 2011), to be conducted via the analytical and conscious efforts in the elaboration and reflection on the actual facts experienced and on other potential risks avoided (e.g., Yanow and Tsoukas, 2009).

The dynamic interplay of fast action and slow thinking leads to the accumulation of different sorts of resources and helps to tackle the tensions between the adaptive and proactive views of resilience. A dialectical lens reveals that one perspective is not superior to the other and that one ultimately depends upon the presence of the other. For example, to express the capacity to improvise, a possible ingredient of the resilience process (Coutu, 2002), organizational members will need to cultivate the necessary skills over long periods of time (Vera and Crossan, 2004) such that improvisation can be utilized when necessary.

The dialectical framework also helps to explain that resilience, as a complex process, resides both in the agents and in the structures. At the agent level, resilience arises as an individual propensity to respond. At the structural level, it manifests as the activation of tacit knowledge and organizational memory (Moorman and Miner, 1998; Tsoukas and Vladimirou, 2001; Vogus and Sutcliffe, 2012). Therefore, organizations need to equip their members with an infrastructure enabling them to act when organizational routines fail. In other words, when habitual routines fail, the lack of organization is pre-empted by individual resources embedded in the organization, namely self-confidence to act in face of risk and ambiguity, and the social support that protects people with the psychological safety necessary to act in the face of crisis or ambiguity (Edmondson, 1999).

In the absence of a dialectical view, scholars can study reaction without opening the black box of preparation. On the other hand, while studying preparation they witness the occurrence of reflection and preparation without practical expression. Considering resilience as preparation, they would be able to assist the rehearsal but not the actual performance. The dialectical view thus indicates that the two processes compose a duality (Farjoun, 2010) in which a thesis and the antithesis mutually constitute each other. Therefore, what appears as an individual 'magic' (Masten, 2001) is in fact an expression of individual abilities embedded in a system and namely in its social capital. In this sense, resilience is an individual expression of a systemic quality. Dialectics thus synthesizes the presence of opposites (for example, episodic responding versus dynamic learning) in the two originating templates (1 and 2) (e.g. Clegg et al., 2002; Cunha et al., 2015).

Resilience, to summarize, involves the capacity to adjust positively, to recognize limitations and imperfections, to reconfigure processes, to avoid cognitive traps and biased team processes (see Box 6.2), and to go beyond established routines in a dynamic expression of adjustment to adversity. Such manifestation of positive adjustment outcomes cannot be prespecified or designed in advance (Luthar and Cicchetti, 2000; Välikangas and Romme, 2013). Therefore, resilience involves preparation to recognize and even to appreciate imperfection as a source of learning on an ongoing basis, the process of creating psychological safety over time (Powley, 2009), plus the capacity to respond in real time when the system is put under pressure. It is about understanding events as manifestations of processes, and processes as sources of events.

IMPLICATIONS FOR PRACTICE AND RESEARCH

Previous psychological research on resilience recommended that scholars develop conceptual work on the process (Luthar et al., 2000). In response, we established the foundations for a dialectical view of resilience in organizations, identifying the building blocks of the process as well as uncovering possibilities for further theorizing. In doing so we accepted and maintained the assumption that resilience is a phenomenon that can take place at different levels of aggregation: from individuals to the whole organization, networks and communities.

BOX 6.2 *THE THREE MUSKETEERS*

Consider the motto of the famous novel by Alexandre Dumas père, published in 1844: 'one for all and all for one' (Figure 6.2). In fact, the expression is older: *Unus pro omnibus, omnes pro uno*. What does it mean? Is it possible that the famous quartet succeeded in confronting adversity because of this state of collaboration? What does it say about resilience?

Are more cohesive teams more resilient? If you think so, take into account literature about groupthink (Choi and Kim, 1999; Esser, 1998; Garvin and Roberto, 2001; Janis, 1982). Remember that groupthink explains, at least in part, the disaster of the *Challenger* space shuttle (Esser and Lindoerfer, 1989; Maier, 2002), and other disasters. Read the interview with Roger Boisjoly in the *Journal of*

Source: Retrieved from https://commons.wikimedia.org/wiki/File:The_three_ musketeers_fairbanks.jpg. This media file is in the public domain in the United States.

Figure 6.2 Poster for film version of The Three Musketeers, *1921*

Management Inquiry (Armenakis, 2002). Boisjoly recommended and defended the original no-launch decision of *Challenger*. Unfortunately, his concerns were underestimated.

When cohesion leads team members to conceal their dissonant voices, the risks are huge. In healthy teams, dissonant voices are welcome and constructive conflict is fostered (Turner and Pratkanis, 1997). Therefore, team cohesion is a double-edged sword: it can make the team stronger or weaker, depending on how dissonant voices and the logic of contradiction (Livingstone et al., 2002) are, or are not, allowed.

We then articulated these two major conceptual templates or building blocks, each contributing to a 'satisfactory [yet partial] explanation' (Langley, 1999, p. 698) in a dialectical frame that presents dialectical resilience as a process rich in tension and contradiction, similarly to organizational processes in general (Putnam et al., 2016). We suggested that instead of trying to solve the tension, organizations could frame the tension between proactive preparation and adaptive responding as the very source of resilience. When organizations are exposed to unpredictable events, resilience can be thought of as a panacea for organizational problems that cannot be resolved by increasing efficiency and resorting to habituated ways of responding (Weick, 1993). Organizations need to hone the capacity to change both in response to shocks as well as in anticipation of them, the dual ability at the core of resilience.

In this light, resilience is a paradoxical combination of using reaction and anticipation to build organizations that work on opposite plans simultaneously (Figure 6.3):

- They focus on the present and the future.
- They anticipate and respond.
- They zoom in (to problems in the here and now) and zoom out (seeing the big picture).
- They consider the trees (the small things, the operations) and the forest (the big things, the strategy).

Resilience is thus hard to accomplish because it involves the skill to act on the opposite horns of paradox, trying to reach higher states of synthesis while knowing that every new accomplished synthesis will become the input for a next paradoxical state (Smith and Lewis, 2011). The construction of resilience is thus a permanent construction, a process propending towards infinity (Cunha and Clegg, 2018), a never-ending story.

A dialectical concept of resilience will therefore help us to understand

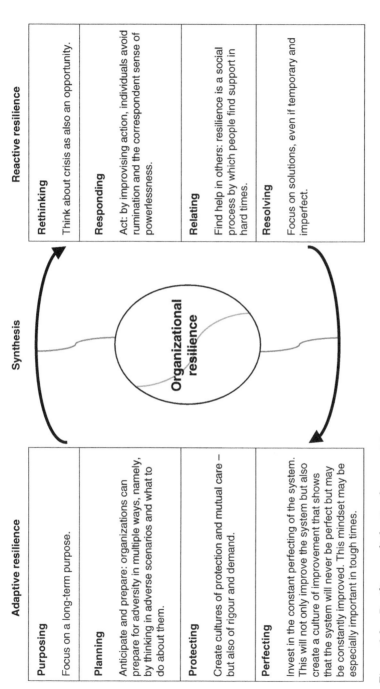

Adaptive resilience

Purposing

Focus on a long-term purpose.

Planning

Anticipate and prepare: organizations can prepare for adversity in multiple ways, namely, by thinking in adverse scenarios and what to do about them.

Protecting

Create cultures of protection and mutual care – but also of rigour and demand.

Perfecting

Invest in the constant perfecting of the system. This will not only improve the system but also create a culture of improvement that shows that the system will never be perfect but may be constantly improved. This mindset may be especially important in tough times.

Synthesis

Organizational resilience

Reactive resilience

Rethinking

Think about crisis as also an opportunity.

Responding

Act: by improvising action, individuals avoid rumination and the correspondent sense of powerlessness.

Relating

Find help in others: resilience is a social process by which people find support in hard times.

Resolving

Focus on solutions, even if temporary and imperfect.

Figure 6.3   Resilience: dialectics for practitioners

how organizations deal resiliently with unpredictable and challenging events. In this vein, viewed at a micro level, resilience is one of the 'four positive psychological resources' that compose an individual's psychological capital; it has a 'positive impact on attitudes, behaviors and performance' (Avey et al., 2011; Luthans and Youssef, 2004, 2007; Luthans and Youssef-Morgan, 2017). At the same time, at a macro level, it constitutes 'a unique blend of cognitive, behavioural, and contextual properties that increase a firm's ability to understand its current situation and to develop customized responses that reflect that understanding' (Lengnick-Hall and Beck, 2005, p. 750). The collective resilience capacities of a company predict how effective the company is in responding to disruptions (Parker and Ameen, 2018).

7. Future trajectories for research on resilience

> Disruptions are inevitable, yet there are striking differences in how firms cope with disruptions. Why do some firms fail in the face of disruptions, while others survive, thrive, and emerge more resilient?
>
> (Parker and Ameen, 2018)

This book is based on an academic literature review (see the Appendix), a collection of vignettes sourced from scholarly work and publications, as well as reflections by the authors. The models proposed potentially pave the way for future investigations in at least three directions: holography, dialectics and organizational design.

RESPECTFUL ENGAGEMENT AS A HOLOGRAPHIC COMPONENT OF RESILIENCE

The model presented in Chapter 6 acknowledges the dynamics of resilience, as a phenomenon potentially flowing across levels of analysis. Empirical studies can test whether the regular patterns identified across levels may boast complete holographic properties. For example, the cross-level dynamics see employees' respectful engagement as having holographic properties, representing a constant stimulus of interaction. Sutcliffe and Vogus (2003, p. 101) considered the existence of parallel resilience processes across levels. With Lengnick-Hall et al. (2011, p. 247), they agree that 'resilient organizations are not managed hierarchically. Instead, they rely on self-organization, dispersed influence, individual and group accountability, and similar factors that create a "holographic" structure (Morgan, 1986 [1997]), where each part is a fractional replica of the whole organization'. Since some common elements can be found at multiple levels, we argue that organizational resilience also carries some holographic regularity in the overall presence of 'interactions'. Furthermore, we posit that such a common element can be found in employee engagement.

Resilience starts with externally challenging or adverse conditions: actual (in the case of reactive resilience) or potential (in the case of proactive resilience). When these conditions are interpreted as challenging and relevant, the system expresses resilience by activating three parallel, mutually supporting competencies. First, expandable competencies are mobilized to face the challenge. We call these competencies expandable because their services are expected to express value while being applied to new fields of organizational action. Second, the expansion of competencies (individual, team, organizational) is supported by social resources, namely by social capital. Because resources will be put to a test, social support is critical both to explore new possibilities via their combination with additional resources provided by other agents (part of their expansion comes from this social nature), and for protection if the response fails (e.g., Lawton et al., 2013). Third, a problem-solving orientation must be in place. Otherwise people will prefer to adopt a defensive rather than a resilient approach. When these three conditions are met, the unit will express a resilient orientation.

Despite their potential in driving organizational behaviour, expandable competencies, social resources and problem-solving orientation alone cannot enact proactive resilience. In fact, the triggering of the learning effects requires a willingness to invest cognitive and intellectual energies by employees. Such a triggering role can be played by employees' respectful engagement, given the pivotal role of respect in the assertion of human existence and self-worth (Rawls, 1971). Respectful engagement refers to behaviours that convey respect among members of an organization or team (Carmeli et al., 2015), which include listening and attending to others' needs, highlighting one's qualities, and empathizing, among others (Rosenberg, 2003).

For Barrick et al. (2015), 'engagement can potentially manifest as a property of the organization; that is employees throughout the organization may share perceptions that members of the organization collectively invest their full selves into their work roles' (p. 112). Building on that point, engagement and resilience overlap as affective-motivational states, spreading a positive attitude within the organization, which becomes contagious and transferable within organizational boundaries (Pugh, 2001). Engagement amplifies the willingness of employees (and their aggregated social forms) to invest their self fully into their work roles. Nonetheless, in the case of the trading room reinstalled in New Jersey (Beunza and Stark, 2003), the traders were able to replicate the floor plan but not the technology. So despite individual engagement to overcome difficulties, they were exposed to organizational constraints. 'Thus, the traders had to do real trades with data they did not consider real' (Beunza and Stark, 2003, p. 147). In that case, the progressive aggregation of engagement, along with resilience, is also testified by the evidence that the traders – using improvisational bricolage (Cunha et al., 2009) – were also proactive as teams and 'in the face of damaged technologies and missing tools, they recombined old and new tools to be able to trade again' (Beunza and Stark, 2003, p. 147). As one of the executives summarized it: 'Without that human element of commitment to the task, commitment to each other, preparedness wouldn't have done anything. The best plan would have never opened up' (Beunza and Stark, 2003, p. 149).

Employee engagement, in summary, confers resilience with holographic properties by energizing teams and team members to be proactive in their response to adversities. The following section will describe how employee engagement could contribute to the development of holographic properties for both reactive and adaptive resilience.

Considering the dialectical synthesis defended in Chapter 6, with engagement one might be able to synthesize the presence of opposites (for example, static versus dynamic equilibrium) in the two originating templates (1 and 2) (e.g., Clegg et al., 2002; Cunha et al., 2015). Considering the models proposed in Chapters 5 and 6 in synergy, the holographic property of engagement is to be found in embeddedness in the interactions between levels.

A DIALECTICAL RESEARCH AGENDA ON RESILIENCE

A dialectical view of resilience opens a number of important possibilities for future research. We explore possible avenues in four areas: the preconditions, the antecedents, processes and consequences.

Preconditions

In terms of the preconditions, taking resilience as a dialectical phenomenon allows one to articulate conceptually why it is so difficult to construct resilience in organizations. Resilience articulates opposite processes, namely slow thinking and fast acting, modesty in dealing with error and boldness in the face of crises. As research on organizational contradictions suggests, dealing with competing demands poses a number of difficulties that companies are not necessarily prepared to face (Smith and Lewis, 2011) and that force leaders to think in 'both/and' terms (Smith et al., 2016). Organizational tensions are embedded in every organization (Smith and Tracey, 2016). The ways that organizations surface tensions, handle their constitutive poles and use the poles to support one another are highly consequential for the resilience of an organization.

Antecedents

With regards to antecedents, it is tempting to see resilience as initiated by external factors. In fact, resilience can result from exposure to some external stressor, but it is also possible to argue that the true antecedent of resilience is a cultural infrastructure, an embedded habit, which allows for responding. Therefore, instead of conceptualizing resilience causally, our theorizing indicates that there is possibly space for exploring the mutual constitution of resilience as cause and consequence of a permanent tension between the proactive and reactive components.

Processes

In terms of process, researchers can adopt recent theorizing on process organization studies and explore the sensitivity of resilience to factors such as time and feedback loops (Langley et al., 2013). From a process perspective, resilience is not something that organizations have; it is something that they express or fail to express over time. This capacity, itself, changes as time goes by. As Smith and Tracey (2016, p. 458) point out, 'dialectics emphasize contradictory and interrelated elements but assume that these relationships morph over time'. Exploring the role of time and feedback loops can help in understanding why organizations may dynamically reinforce or harm their resilience. By studying the unfolding of the process of resilience, researchers will be able to investigate how maintaining a vibrant relationship between resilience's constitutive poles helps to explain its dynamics, as previous research on paradoxes predicts (Smith and Tracey, 2016). Research shows that positive processes such as resilience are inherently paradoxical (Cameron, 2008), expressing even dialectical qualities when the poles originate syntheses between opposites.

The dynamics of paradox in the construction of resilience remain an area rich in research possibilities. For example, research has indicated that high-quality connections are critical for the expression of resilience (Beunza and Stark, 2003) but that, after a threshold, social proximity will degrade the quality of team and organizational functioning and therefore its capacity to express resilience, replaced by an excess of cohesion (Esser, 1998).

Consequences

In terms of consequences, research has to be conducted to test how thesis and antithesis can be affected by organizational attempts to solve the dialectics. The dialectical framework proposed here indicates that resilience results from the very existence of the tension. Therefore, attempts to resolve the tension may end up threatening the process and reducing resilience. For example, training people to gain skills in rapid responding, through improvisation, may instil the sense of self-confidence that they will be prepared to deal with unexpected tensions when they happen. This sense of confidence can disrupt the generativity of the dialectical tension by reducing the inclination to learn and reflect, therefore reducing the potential for resilience. In line with research on dialectics and contradiction, attempts at the resolution of tension can be escalatory rather than ameliorative (Smith and Tracey, 2016).

An important practice implication of our proposal resides in the difficulties associated with the management of duality. In a duality, two processes are interdependent but contradictory. What reinforces one debilitates the other. Thinking can lead to precaution and be perceived as a substitute for action (Pfeffer and Sutton, 2013); action can be perceived as dispensing with the need for thinking (Bruch and Ghoshal, 2004). Cultivating the dialectic can be a demanding practical exercise as it puts contradictions shoulder to shoulder, creates dissonance and is emotionally painful (Vince and Broussine, 1996). More research is needed to specifically study the dialectics of resilience as an innovative theoretical object.

ORGANIZATIONAL DESIGN FOR RESILIENCE

Previous research on resilience recommended that scholars develop conceptual work on the process (Luthar et al., 2000). In response, we established the foundations for a dialectical view of resilience in organizations, identifying the building blocks of the process as well as uncovering possibilities for further theorizing. In so doing we accepted and maintained the assumption that resilience is a phenomenon that can take place at different levels of aggregation: from individuals to the whole organization, networks and communities.

We then articulated these two major conceptual templates or building blocks, each contributing to a 'satisfactory [yet partial] explanation' (Langley, 1999, p.698) in a dialectical frame that presents dialectical resilience as a process rife with tension and contradiction, just like organizational processes in general (Putnam et al., 2016). We suggested that instead of trying to solve the tension, organizations could instead frame the tension between proactive preparation and adaptive responding as the very source of resilience.

When organizations are exposed to unpredictable events, resilience can be thought of as a panacea for organizational problems that cannot be resolved by increasing efficiency and resorting to habituated ways of responding (Weick, 1993). Organizations need to hone the capacity to change both in response to shocks as well as in anticipation of them, the dual ability at the core of resilience. In trying to answer the question of how to build organizational resilience, Linnenluecke (2017, p. 19) admits:

> the literature offers at times contradictory recommendations for how organizations should build resilience. Tensions between the need for organizational stability on the one hand (habits, routines, consistency, control, and low deviation) and organizational change on the other hand (search, mindfulness, redundancy, openness, preoccupation with failure, imagination, experimentation and variety) have not yet been resolved and require future work. (See also Farjoun, 2010)

In an attempt to provide an answer to the same question, Giustiniano and Cantoni (2018) propose an organizational 'design' for resilience (see also Box 7.1). The design is inspired by the metaphors of 'sponge' and 'titanium': the sponge, as an absorbent property; titanium, as an alloy, with a strength-to-density ratio that is the highest of any metallic element.

Hence, in design terms, what is crucial is the ability to absorb change while preserving and maintaining core organizational functions. How this is possible is by finding and implementing organizational micro and macro structures that, in line with the organization's current exigencies, are able to transform adversity into new opportunity, uncertainty into novel solutions. Tensions thus become seen as sources of energy and the dialectical synthesis can be seen as the means of benefiting from the creative energy

---

BOX 7.1   A RESILIENT MARKERS FRAMEWORK

In order to express resilience, organizations are often asked to seek for responses to jolts and stressors outside the scope of their designed formal procedures. The reaction to stressors can be assessed by the usage of markers that identify the 'potential strategies that may be created and invoked in response to the specifics of the situation at a particular point in time' (Furniss et al., 2011, p.3). The paper 'Reliability engineering and system safety' (Furniss et al., 2011), presents a 'resilience markers framework' operating at several levels, and illustrates the application of the framework through discussing the case study of the performance of nuclear power plant operators taking part to an experiment at the Halden Man-Machine Laboratory (HAMMLAB) in the United States. Read the paper and try to use the markers framework in your team or organization.

that the tension generates (Cunha et al., 2002). Resilience, in summary, and as we have discussed throughout the book, is not a process free of tension but the understanding of tension as a part of growth. The representation of resilience as a dialectical process involves not the avoidance of the negative but the extraction of positive lessons from the negativity of life, to mine wisdom from the inevitable difficulty.

Appendix: methodology

Our analysis of resilience starts with a systematic review of the literature (e.g., Tranfield et al., 2003; Brock, 2006; Denyer et al., 2008; Denyer and Tranfield, 2009; Fisher, 2010; Lawton et al., 2013; Turner et al., 2013; Hadida et al., 2015) by using several databases. We systematically searched for papers and books published in English that investigated concepts related to organizational resilience. We started from investigation of the founding constructs of resilience formulated in the natural and psychological sciences. We initially clarified the constituting foundations of resilience as a construct, and then focused on its usage in the fields of strategy, organization theory, organizational behaviour, organization design and innovation. Such disciplines were selected in consideration of the growing importance of strategic, organizational and behavioural resilience.

Vogus and Sutcliffe (2007) posit that 'the recurrent interplay between resilience and its constitutive capabilities . . . suggests that organizations can continuously bolster and refine their capability in a manner that allows them to see, remain flexible, and avoid the inertial tendencies that traditionally accrue with success' (p. 3420). Our study delivers a tri-partition of the concept of resilience as adaptive, reactive or 'organizational' (active and proactive), considering the latter as the comprehensive form of resilience, as suggested by several founding studies (e.g., Luthar et al., 2000; Weick and Sutcliffe, 2001 [2007]; Hamel and Välikangas, 2003; Sutcliffe and Vogus, 2003). The systematic review of the literature was based on a nomological network that scanned the presence of related constructs, meant as constitutive capabilities (Vogus and Sutcliffe, 2007). Interestingly such related constructs present an element of commonality with resilience, either in terms of antecedents or outcomes (see Table 2.3 in Chapter 2), while individually differing in other aspects. Some related constructs were also associated with 'organizational resilience', meant concomitantly as both adaptive and proactive, but differing either in terms of level of analysis (that is, limited just to individuals) or process. We present the process of resilience as dialectical in nature, with adaptation and proaction informing one another in a permanent tension that can be dynamic and generative.

Cronbach and Meehl's (1955) founding contributions on construct validity inform the literature review generating the nomological network.

A construct is 'some postulated attribute of people [and their aggregations] assumed to be reflected in test performance . . . [it] has certain associated meanings carried in statements' (Cronbach and Meehl, 1955, p.178). Using nomological networks can validate the association of meanings with constructs. Cronbach and Meehl (1955) remark that the nomological network is an 'interlocking system of laws which constitute a theory' (p. 187). The nomological network makes clear what the meaning of something is ('what'), via stating the laws in which it occurs (occurrences equalling to 'where'). In the case of a literature review, the related system of laws must therefore reciprocally relate observable properties, theoretical constructs to observable phenomena ('observables'), or different theoretical constructs to one another. To this extent, a construct acquires validity *à la* Cronbach and Meehl (1955) as it occurs in a nomological net, 'at least *some* of whose laws involve observables' (p. 187).

The data collection was carried out in four subsequent steps. First, resilience-related subjects were searched in academic databases (ISI Web of Science, EBSCO, ProQuest and Emerald). The search covered the time period from 1973, when Garmezy and Holling published their first research findings on resilience (Garmezy, 1973; Holling, 1973), to December 2015. In ISI Web of Science and ProQuest the search used the key words 'resilien*', using the asterisk (*) as a wildcard symbol to intercept the variations of the term. The research was limited to the fields of title, abstract and keywords. In order to limit the scope of the book, the search was refined by using Boolean operators associated with 'business', 'management', 'organization*' and 'behaviour*'.

Most of the papers found were published recently, between 2011 and 2015, a reflection of the growing interest in the potential of resilient systems (e.g., Linnenluecke, 2017; Van Der Vegt et al., 2015). All papers identified were considered and analysed, except those referring only to sectorial and territorial aspects of the phenomenon. An additional search conducted through Emerald, using the same time span and keywords, produced similar results: few papers were related to managerial aspects of resilience. Furthermore, out of the search executed through EBSCO a number of other papers were considered marginal because of their particular focus on specific aspects related to developmental or child psychology.

The total amount of records (papers) collected was 479. The authors, acting as reviewers, determined the suitability of the sources by manually filtering the overall dataset. In order to exhibit both the interdisciplinary nature of the study and the focus on organizational resilience, the following criteria filtered the dataset: the study examined dealt with organizational resilience (levels: individuals and/or groups and/or organizations) or contained elements of analysis of discussion with significant managerial implications. When at least two authors agreed on exclusion, the paper was erased from the dataset. The number dropped to 331 as some papers were considered marginal because they were specific to aspects of developmental or child psychology, economics (that is, crisis of macroeconomic systems) or disaster management.

Such preliminary appraisal led to greater appreciation of the origins of the term 'resilience' in management and business. Although most papers neglect this aspect, the term arose initially from the fields of engineering and physics, where it is considered as the capacity to bounce back quickly after stress, to endure greater stresses and be less malformed by a given amount of stress (Campbell, 2008). These definitions are commonly applied to the object world and constitute the origin of 'adaptive resilience'. 'Proactive resilience' relates instead to social systems. Holling (1996) notes that engineering resilience is defined by 'operating near to an equilibrium far from instability', while ecological systems can learn at different levels of aggregation. So 'management and institutional regimes can . . . preserve or expand resilience of systems as well to provide developmental opportunity' (Holling, 1996, p. 41). Socially, most global risks are systemic in nature and a system – unlike an object – may show resilience not by returning exactly to its previous state but instead by finding different ways to carry out its essential functions.

Social and natural forms of resilience are related (Holling, 1986, 1996; Adger, 2000). It was this consideration that led us from the papers explicitly addressing resilience in broad managerial terms to other constructs linked to resilience (see Table 2.3 in Chapter 2). Using a nomological network has validated the relatedness of such concepts to resilience. As remarked by Pinto (2014), nomological networks can also be used 'more loosely to refer to a group of constructs that are related to one another and conflated with the phrase "family of constructs" (Mowshowitz, 1997)' (p. 293). Similarly to other studies (e.g., Sun and Anderson, 2010; Pinto, 2014), we constructed the nomological networks of adaptive and proactive resilience by looking at their theoretical background and to the ontological characteristics of other related constructs.

The nomological network was framed around the two dimensions of: (1) 'adaptation' as a post-shock reaction (relatedness to adaptive resilience); and (2) 'adoption' of new practice or organizational form as a preparation for the next jolt (relatedness to proactive resilience). The identification of such related constructs provided another set of keywords: 'agility', 'anticipation/prevention', 'flexibility', 'improvisation', 'robustness', 'manoeuvrability' (associated to proactive resilience), and 'adaptability', 'coping', 'hardiness', 'recovery', 'redundancy', 'posttraumatic growth', 'healing' (associated to adaptive resilience).

Finally, some constructs were ascribable to 'organizational resilience', meant as both adaptive and proactive: 'thriving' and 'grit'. As anticipated, such related constructs, meant as constitutive capabilities of all the forms of resilience, were classified as either antecedents and/or outcomes. What qualifies and distinguishes resilience is the process that we will later describe in dialectical terms.

The second step was conducted by carrying out systematic and electronic searches for all papers published on resilience and its 'related constructs'.[1] The journals were selected because of their high impact factor and their centrality in academic debate. In the third step, the search was completed by considering articles and books cited by papers from these top journals, published in outlets with wider audiences.[2] In the fourth step, books and book chapters were included. The search was conducted by searching 'resilience', 'resiliency' and 'resilient' in Google Scholar (last search 31 December 2015). Results were filtered to exclude papers, articles and other sources. We used cursory content analysis to filter books and book chapters. In contrast to other studies focused on constructs of resilience (Luthar and Cicchetti, 2000; Luthar et al., 2000) or on the generation and consolidation process (Egeland et al., 1993), we have sought to advance a synthetic framework that jointly considers adaptive and proactive resilience.

NOTES

1. The search was conducted in (although not totally limited to) the *Academy of Management Annals, Academy of Management Review, Academy of Management Journal, Strategic Management Journal, Administrative Science Quarterly, Organization Science, Journal of Management Studies, Journal of Organizational Behavior, Organization Studies, International Journal of Management Reviews, Management Decision, Journal of Management, Research in Organizational Behavior, Human Resources Management* and *Human Resource Management Review.*
2. The journals consulted included *California Management Review, Harvard Business Review, MIT Sloan Management Review* and *Academy of Management Executive.* Further, the same process of direct references and analogy brought into consideration other relevant journals, including (but not limited to): *Psychological Bulletin, Long Range Planning, Organizational Dynamics, Journal of Managerial Psychology, Psychological Science, Human Resource Management Journal, Journal of Organization Design, International Journal of Human Resource Management* and *Journal of Change Management.* Additionally, such journals were monitored up to the moment of submission.

References

Adger, W.N. (2000). Social and ecological resilience: Are they related? *Progress in Human Geography*, **24**, 347–364.

Agência Lusa (2015). Maria da Conceição quer tirar da pobreza 100 crianças no Bangladesh. *Observador*, 25 March, https://observador.pt/2015/03/25/maria-da-conceicao-quer-tirar-da-pobreza-100-criancas-no-bangladesh/.

Ahrne, G. and Brunsson, N. (2011). Organization outside organizations: The significance of partial organization. *Organization*, **18**, 83–104.

Aitken, J. (1996). *Nixon: A Life*. Washington, DC: Regnery Publishing.

Alliger, G.M., Cerasoli, C.P., Tannenbaum, S.I. and Vessey, W.B. (2015). Team resilience. *Organizational Dynamics*, **44**, 176–184.

Ancona, D., Bresman, H. and Kaeufer, K. (2002). The comparative advantage of X-teams. *MIT Sloan Management Review*, **43**, 33–39.

Andersen, E. (2016). Learning to learn. *Harvard Business Review*, **94** (3), 98–101.

Anderson, C. and Brown, C.E. (2010). The functions and dysfunctions of hierarchy. *Research in Organizational Behavior*, **30**, 55–89.

Annarelli, A. and Nonino, F. (2016). Strategic and operational management of organizational resilience: Current state of research and future directions. *Omega*, **62**, 1–18.

Armenakis, A.A. (2002). Boisjoly on ethics: An interview with Roger M. Boisjoly. *Journal of Management Inquiry*, **11** (3), 274–281.

Armenakis, A.A., Harris, S.G. and Mossholder, K.W. (1993). Creating readiness for organizational change. *Human Relations*, **46**, 681–703.

Armour, N. (2018), Nick Foles, Philadelphia Eagles are no longer underdogs after Super Bowl LII win. *USA Today Sports*, 4 February, https://www.usatoday.com/story/sports/nfl/2018/02/04/nick-foles-philadelphia-eagles-underdogs-win-super-bowl/305947002/.

Asano, K. (2012). Rethinking a business continuity plan (BCP): What should companies learn from the Great East Japan earthquake? NRI Papers no. 173. Tokyo: Nomura Research Institute, https://www.nri.com/global/opinion/papers/2012/pdf/np2012173.pdf.

Asch, S. and Mulligan, T. (2016). *ROAR: How to Build a Resilient Organization the World-Famous San Diego Zoo Way*. New York: Highpoint Executive Publishing.

Ashmos, D.P. and Huber, G.P. (1987). The systems paradigm in organization theory: Correcting the record and suggesting the future. *Academy of Management Review*, **12**, 607–621.

Atkins, R. (2016). Ex-Zurich chief's suicide highlights executive stress. *Financial Times Europe*, 1 June, 12.

Ausmus, H.J. (1978). Nietzsche and eschatology. *Journal of Religion*, **58**, 347–364.

AutoList (2016). The People vs. VW. https://www.autolist.com/volkswagen-jetta-bostonma#section=model-reviews (accessed 20 May 2016).

Avey, J.B., Reichard, R.J., Luthans, F. and Mhatre, K.H. (2011). Meta-analysis of the impact of positive psychological capital on employee attitudes, behaviors, and performance. *Human Resource Development Quarterly*, **22**, 127–152.

Bach, R. (ed.) (2015). *Strategies for Supporting Community Resilience: Multinational Experiences*. CRISMART Vol. 41. Stockholm: Swedish Defence University, http://www.diva-portal.se/smash/get/diva2:795117/FULLTEXT01.pdf.

Bahrami, H. and Evans, S. (2005). *Super-Flexibility for Knowledge Enterprises*. Berlin: Springer.

Bahrami, H. and Evans, S. (2011). Super-flexibility for real-time adaptation: Perspectives from Silicon Valley. *California Management Review*, **53**, 21–39.

Baker, P. (2015). Abraham Lincoln, the one President all of them want to be more like. *New York Times*, 15 April, A11.

Bakker, A.B., Westman, M. and Hetty van Emmerik, I.J. (2009). Advancements in crossover theory. *Journal of Managerial Psychology*, **24** (3), 206–219.

Balachandra, L., Crossan, M., Devin, L., Leary, K. and Patton, B. (2005). Improvisation and teaching negotiation: Developing three essential skills. *Negotiation Journal*, October, 435–441.

Bandura, A. (2008). An agentic perspective on positive psychology. In Lopez, S.J. (ed.), *Positive Psychology: Exploring the Best in People*, Vol. 1 (pp. 167–196). Westport, CT: Greenwood Publishing.

Barrett, F.J. (2012). *Yes to the Mess*. Boston, MA: Harvard Business School Press.

Barrick, M.R, Thurgood, G.R., Smith, T.A. and Courtright, S.H. (2015). Collective organizational engagement: Linking motivational antecedents, strategic implementation, and firm performance. *Academy of Management Journal*, **50**, 111–135.

Barsade, S.G. and O'Neil, O.A. (2014). What's love got to do with it?: The influence of a culture of companionate love in the long-term care setting. *Administrative Science Quarterly*, **59** (4), 551–598.

Baxter, L.A. (2004). A tale of two voices: Relational dialectics theory. *Journal of Family Communication*, **4**, 181–192.

BCI – Business Continuity Institute (2015). *Supply Chain Resilience, 2015: An International Survey to Consider the Origin, Causes and Consequences of Supply Chain Disruption*. Caversham: Business Continuity Institute.

Beasley, M., Thompson, T. and Davidson, J. (2003). Resilience in response to life stress: The effects of coping style and cognitive hardiness. *Personality and Individual Differences*, **34**, 77–95.

Beck, H. (2012). The evolution of a point guard. *New York Times*, 25 February, http://www.nytimes.com/2012/02/25/sports/basketball/the-evolution-of-jeremy-lin-as-a-point-guard.html?_r=1andpagewanted=all.

Beck, U. (1999). *World Risk Society*. Malden, MA: Polity.

Beermann, M. (2011). Linking corporate climate adaptation strategies with resilience. *Journal of Cleaner Production*, **19**, 836–842.

Bell, M.A. (2002). *The Five Principles of Organizational Resilience*. Gartner Research, http://www.gartner.com/id=351410 (accessed 18 March 2015).

Bennett, J.B., Aden, C.A., Broome, K., Mitchell, K. and Rigdon, W.D. (2010). Team resilience for young restaurant workers: Research-to-practice adaptation and assessment. *Journal of Occupational Health Psychology*, **15** (3), 223.

Benson, J.K. (1977). Organizations: A dialectical view. *Administrative Science Quarterly*, **22**, 1–21.

Bernstein, E., Bunch, J., Canner, N. and Lee, M. (2016). Beyond the holacracy hype. *Harvard Business Review*, **94** (7), 13.

Beunza, D. and Stark, D. (2003). The organization of responsiveness: Innovation and recovery in the trading rooms of Lower Manhattan. *Socio-Economic Review*, **1**, 35–164.

Bhamra, R., Dani, S. and Burnard, K. (2011). Resilience: The concept, a literature review and future directions. *International Journal of Production Research*, **49**, 5375–5393.

Bigley, G.A. and Roberts, K.H. (2001). The incident command system: High-reliability organizing for complex and volatile task environments. *Academy of Management Journal*, **44**, 1281–1299.

Birkinshaw, J. and Haas, M. (2016). Increase your return on failure. *Harvard Business Review*, **94**, 88–93.

Blatt, R. (2009). Tough love: How communal schemas and contracting practices build relational capital in entrepreneurial teams. *Academy of Management Review*, **34** (3), 533–551.

Block, J. and Kremen, A.M. (1996). IQ and ego-resiliency: Conceptual and empirical connections and separateness. *Journal of Personality and Social Psychology*, **70**, 349–361.

Boin, A. (2004). Lessons from crisis research. *International Studies Review*, **6**, 165–174.

Bonanno, G.A. (2004). Loss, trauma, and human resilience: Have we underestimated the human capacity to thrive after extremely aversive events? *American Psychologist*, **59**, 20–28.

Bonanno, G.A., Galea, S., Bucciarelli, A. and Vlahov, D. (2006). Psychological resilience after disaster: New York City in the aftermath of the September 11th terrorist attack. *Psychological Science*, **17**, 181–186.

Booth, R. (2018). 'We fear what's next': Oxfam reels from prostitution scandal. *Guardian*, 11 February, https://www.theguardian.com/world/2018/feb/11/we-fear-whats-next-oxfam-reels-from-prostitution-scandal.

Bowman, E.H. and Singh, H. (1993). Corporate restructuring: Reconfiguring the firm. *Strategic Management Journal*, **14** (S1), 5–14.

Bridges, W. (1995). *Jobshift: How to Prosper in a Workplace without Jobs*. New York: DaCapo.

Brock, D.M. (2006). The changing professional organization: A review of competing archetypes. *International Journal of Management Reviews*, **8**, 157–174.

Brodsky, A.E., Welsh, E., Carrillo, A., Talwar, G., Scheibler, J. and Butler, T. (2011). Between synergy and conflict: Balancing the processes of organizational and individual resilience in an Afghan women's community. *American Journal of Community Psychology*, **47** (3/4), 217–235.

Brooks, D. (2016). Putting grit in its place. *New York Times*, 10 May, A23.

Brown, A.D. (2015). Identities and identity work in organizations. *International Journal of Management Reviews*, **17**, 20–40.

Brown, S.L. and Eisenhardt, K.M. (1997). The art of continuous change: Linking complexity theory and time-paced evolution in relentlessly shifting organizations. *Administrative Science Quarterly*, **42**, 1–34.

Bruch, H. and Ghoshal, S. (2004). *A Bias for Action*. Boston, MA: Harvard Business School Press.

Brusoni, S., Prencipe, A. and Pavitt, K. (2001). Knowledge specialization, organizational coupling, and the boundaries of the firm: Why do firms know more than they make? *Administrative Science Quarterly*, **46** (4), 597–621.

Buchanan, D.A. and Denyer, D. (2013). Researching tomorrow's crisis: Methodological innovations and wider implications. *International Journal of Management Reviews*, **15**, 205–224.

Buchanan, L. (2017). How to gain strength from your darkest moments. *Inc.*, 24 April, https://www.inc.com/leigh-buchanan/adam-grant-on-how-to-gain-strength-from-your-darkest-moments.html.

Buckle, P., Mars, G. and Smale, S. (2000). New approaches to assessing vulnerability and resilience. *Australian Journal of Emergency Management*, **15**, 8–15.

Burns, T. and Stalker, G.M. (1961). *The Management of Innovation*. Oxford: Oxford University Press.

Burton, R.M. and Obel, B. (2004). *Strategic Organizational Diagnosis and Design: The Dynamics of Fit*, 3rd edn. Newell, MA: Kluwer Academic Publishers.

Burton, R.M. and Obel, B. (2013). Design rules for dynamic organization design: The contribution of computational modeling. In Grandori, A. (ed.), *Handbook of Economic Organization: Integrating Economic and Organization Theory* (pp. 223–244). Cheltenham, UK and Northampton, MA, USA: Edward Elgar Publishing.

Butts, C.T., Acton, R.M. and Marcum, C.S. (2012). Interorganizational collaboration in the Hurricane Katrina response. *Journal of Social Structure*, **13**, 1–36.

Cameron, K.S. (2008). Paradox in positive organizational change. *Journal of Applied Behavioral Science*, **44**, 7–24.

Campbell, A. (2010). Oxytocin and human social behavior. *Personality and Social Psychology Review*, **14**, 281–295.

Campbell, F.C. (2008). *Elements of Metallurgy and Engineering Alloys*. Materials Park, OH ASM International.

Cappelli, D. (2011). Mujica, el presidente más pobre. *El Mundo*, 25 May, http://www.elmundo.es/america/2012/05/25/noticias/1337961914.html.

Carmeli, A., Dutton, J.E. and Hardin, A.E. (2015). Respect as an engine for new ideas: Linking respectful engagement, relational information processing and creativity among employees and team, *Human Relations*, **68** (6), 1021–1047.

Carmeli, A., Friedman, Y. and Tishler, A. (2013). Cultivating a resilient top management team: The importance of relational connections and strategic decision comprehensiveness. *Safety Science*, **51**, 148–159.

Carmeli, A. and Gittell, J. (2009). High-quality relationships, psychological safety, and learning from failures in work organizations. *Journal of Organizational Behavior*, **30**, 709–729.

Carr, L.J. (1932). Disaster and the sequence-pattern concept of social change. *American Journal of Sociology*, **38**, 207–218.

Carroll, J. (1998). Organizational learning activities in high-hazard industries: The logics underlying self-analysis. *Journal of Management Studies*, **35**, 699–717.

Cartwright, S. and Pappas, C. (2008). Emotional intelligence, its measurement and implications for the workplace. *International Journal of Management Reviews*, **10**, 149–171.

Carvalho, A. and Areal, N. (2016). Great Places to Work®: Resilience in times of crisis. *Human Resource Management*, **55** (3), 479–498.

Cascio, W.F. and Luthans, F. (2014). Reflections on the metamorphosis at Robben Island: The role of institutional work and positive psychological capital. *Journal of Management Inquiry*, **23** (1), 51–67.

Castleden, M., McKee, M., Murray, V. and Leonardi, G. (2011). Resilience thinking in health protection. *Journal of Public Health*, **33** (3), 369–377.

Caverley, N. (2005). Civil Service resilience and coping. *International Journal of Public Sector Management*, **18**, 401–413.

Caza, B.B. and Milton, L.P. (2012). Resilience at work: Building capability in the face of adversity. In Cameron, K.S. and Spreitzer, G. (eds), *The Oxford Handbook of Positive Organizational Scholarship* (pp. 895–908). Oxford: Oxford University Press.

Chakravarthy, B.S. (1982). Adaptation: A promising metaphor for strategic management. *Academy of Management Review*, **7**, 35–44.

Chamorro-Premuzic, T. and Lusk, D. (2017). The dark side of resilience. *Harvard Business Review*, August, https://hbr.org/2017/08/the-dark-side-of-resilience.

Chapman, B. and Sisodia, R. (2015). *Everybody Matters: The Extraordinary Power of Caring for Your People Like Family*, New York: Portfolio/ Penguin.

Chen, D.J.Q. and Lim, V.K.G. (2012). Strength in adversity: The influence of psychological capital on job search. *Journal of Organizational Behavior*, **33**, 811–839.

Choi, J.N. and Kim, M.U. (1999). The organizational application of groupthink and its limitations in organizations. *Journal of Applied Psychology*, **84** (2), 297–306.

Ciborra, C. (2002). *The Labyrinths of Information: Challenging the Wisdom of Systems*. Oxford: Oxford University Press.

Cicotto, G., De Simone, S., Giustiniano, L. and Pinna, R. (2014). Psychosocial training: A case of self-efficacy improvement in an Italian school. *Journal of Change Management*, **14**, 475–499.

Clair, J.A. and Dufresne, R.L. (2007). Changing poison into medicine: How companies can experience positive transformation from a crisis. *Organizational Dynamics*, **36** (1), 63–77.

Clapp-Smith, R., Vogelgesang, G.R. and Avey, J.B. (2009). Authentic leadership and positive psychological capital: The mediating role of trust at the group level of analysis. *Journal of Leadership and Organizational Studies*, **15**, 227–240.

Clegg, S. (2010). The state, power, and agency: Missing in action in institutional theory? *Journal of Management Inquiry*, **19**, 4–13.

Clegg, S. and Cunha, M.P. (2017). Organizational dialectics. In Lewis,

M.W., Smith, W.K., Jarzabkowski, P. and Langley, A. (eds), *The Oxford Handbook of Organizational Paradox: Approaches to Plurality, Tensions, and Contradictions* (pp. 105–124). New York: Oxford University Press.

Clegg, S.R., Cunha, J.V. and Cunha, M.P. (2002). Management paradoxes: A relational view. *Human Relations*, **55**, 483–503.

Cohen, O., Leykin, D., Lahad, M., Goldberg, A. and Aharonson-Daniel, L. (2013). The conjoint community resiliency assessment measure as a baseline for profiling and predicting community resilience for emergencies. *Technological Forecasting and Social Change*, **80** (9), 1732–1741.

Cohn, M.A., Fredrickson, B. Brown, S.L., Mikels, J.A. and Conway, A.M. (2009). Happiness unpacked: Positive emotions increase life satisfaction by building resilience. *Emotion*, **9** (3), 361–368.

Cole, S. (2014). 11 famous companies with enviable pet-friendly policies. *Fast Company*, 22 October, https://www.fastcompany.com/3037384/pet-week/11-famous-companies-with-enviable-pet-friendly-policies.

Collins, J.C. and Porras, J.I. (1994). *Built to Last: Successful Habits of Visionary Companies*. New York: HarperCollins.

Comfort, L.K., Sungu, Y., Johnson, D. and Dunn, M. (2001). Complex systems in crisis: Anticipation and resilience in dynamic environments. *Journal of Contingencies and Crisis Management*, **9**, 144–158.

Compas, B.E., Connor-Smith, J.K., Saltzman, H., Thomsen, A.H. and Wadsworth, M.E. (2001). Coping with stress during childhood and adolescence: Problems, progress, and potential in theory and research. *Psychological Bulletin*, **127**, 87–127.

Cornum, R., Mathews, M.D. and Seligman, M.E.P. (2011). Comprehensive soldier fitness: Building resilience in a challenging institutional context. *American Psychologist*, **66** (1), 4–9.

Coutu, D.L. (2002). How resilience works. *Harvard Business Review*, **80**, 46–55.

Cox, R., and Perry, K. (2011). Like a fish out of water: Reconsidering disaster recovery and the role of place and social capital in community disaster resilience. *American Journal of Community Psychology*, **48** (3/4), 395–411.

Crichton, M.T., Ramsay, C.G. and Kelly, T. (2009). Enhancing organizational resilience through emergency planning: Learnings from cross-sectoral lessons. *Journal of Contingencies and Crisis Management*, **17**, 24–37.

Cronbach, L.J. and Meehl, P.E. (1955). Construct validity in psychological tests. *Psychological Bulletin*, **52**, 281–302.

Cunha, J.V., Clegg, S.R. and Cunha, M.P. (2002). Management, paradox, and permanent dialectics. In Clegg, S. (ed.), *Management and Organization Paradoxes* (pp. 11–40). Amsterdam: Benjamins.

Cunha, M.P., Abrantes, A., Clegg, S., Giustiniano, L. and Rego, A. (2018a). Freelance improvisation and resilience: Lessons from the EN236-1 tragedy. Paper LAM-012, LAEMOS 2018 Conference, Buenos Aires, Argentina, 22–24 March.

Cunha, M.P. and Chia, R. (2007). Using teams to avoid peripheral blindness. *Long Range Planning*, **40**, 559–573.

Cunha, M.P. and Clegg, S. (2018). Persistence in paradox. In Farjoun, M., Smith, W.K., Langley, A. and Tsoukas, H. (eds), *Perspectives on Process Organization Studies: Dualities, Dialectics and Paradoxes in Organizational Life*, Vol. 8 (pp. 14–34). Oxford: Oxford University Press.

Cunha, M.P., Clegg, S.R. and Kamoche, K. (2006). Surprises in management and organization: Concept, sources, and a typology. *British Journal of Management*, **17**, 317–329.

Cunha, M.P. and Cunha, J.V. (2006). Towards a complexity theory of strategy. *Management Decision*, **44**, 839–850.

Cunha, M.P., Cunha, J.V. and Clegg, S.R. (2009). Improvisational bricolage: A practice-based approach to strategy and foresight. In Costanzo, L.A. and MacKay, R.B. (eds), *Handbook of Research on Strategy and Foresight* (pp. 182–199). Cheltenham, UK and Northampton, MA, USA: Edward Elgar Publishing.

Cunha, M.P., Cunha, J.V. and Kamoche, K. (1999). Organizational improvisation: What, when, how and why. *International Journal of Management Reviews*, **1**, 299–341.

Cunha, M.P., Giustiniano, L., Neves, P. and Rego, A. (2018b). Improvising agility: Organizations as structured-extemporaneous hybrids. In Boccardelli, P., Annosi, M.C., Brunetta, F. and Magnusson, M. (eds), *Learning and Innovation in Hybrid Organizations* (pp. 231–254). Cham: Palgrave Macmillan.

Cunha, M.P., Giustiniano, L., Rego, A. and Clegg, S. (forthcoming-a). 'Heaven or Las Vegas': Competing institutional logics and individual experience. *European Management Review*. DOI: 10.1111/emre.12156.

Cunha, M.P., Miner, A.S. and Antonacopoulou, E. (2017). Improvisation processes in organizations. In Langley, A. and Tsoukas, H. (eds), *The SAGE Handbook of Process Organization Studies* (pp. 559–573). London: SAGE.

Cunha, M.P.E. and Putnam, L.L. (2017). Paradox theory and the paradox of success. *Strategic Organization*, 1476127017739536.

Cunha, M.P., Rego, A., Clegg, S. and Lindsay, G. (2015). The dialectics of serendipity. *European Management Journal*, **33**, 9–18.

Cunha, M.P., Rego, A. and Munro, I. (2018c). Dogs in organizations. *Human Relations*. DOI: 10.1177/0018726718780210.

Cunha, M.P., Simpson, A.V., Clegg, S. and Rego, A. (forthcoming-b).

Speak! Paradoxical effects of a managerial culture of 'speaking up'. *British Journal of Management*. doi.org/10.1111/1467-8551.12306.

Cunha, M.P. and Tsoukas, H. (2015). Reforming the state: Understanding the vicious circles of reform. *European Management Journal*, **33** (4), 225–229.

Damásio, B.F., Borsa, J.C. and Silva, J.P. (2011). 14-item resilience scale (RS-14): Psychometric properties of the Brazilian version. *Journal of Nursing Measurement*, **19** (3), 131–145.

D'Aveni, R.A. (1995). Coping with hypercompetition: Utilizing the new 7-S's framework. *Academy of Management Executive*, **9**, 45–57.

Day, G.S. and Schoemaker, P. (2004). Peripheral vision: Sensing and acting on weak signals. *Long Range Planning*, **37**, 117–121.

Decroos, S., Lines, R.L., Morgan, P.B., Fletcher, D., Sarkar, M., Fransen, K., Boen, F. and Vande Broek, G. (2017). Development and validation of the characteristics of resilience in sports teams inventory. *Sport, Exercise, and Performance Psychology*, **6** (2), 158–178.

Deming, W.E. (1982). *Out of the Crisis*. Cambridge, MA: MIT Press.

Denyer, D. (2017). Organizational resilience: A summary of academic evidence, business insights and new thinking. BSI and Cranfield School of Management, https://www.cranfield.ac.uk/~/media/images-for-new-website/som-media-room/images/organisational-report-david-denyer.ashx (accessed 7 February 2018).

Denyer, D. and Tranfield, D. (2009). Producing a systematic review. In Buchanan, D.A. and Bryman, A. (eds), *The SAGE Handbook of Organizational Research Methods* (pp. 671–689). Thousand Oaks, CA: SAGE.

Denyer, D., Tranfield, D. and Van Aken, J.E. (2008). Developing design propositions through research synthesis. *Organization Studies*, **29**, 393–414.

Deroy, X. and Clegg, S.R. (2011). When events interact with business ethics, *Organization*, **18**, 637–653.

De Smet, A. and Gagnon, C. (2017). Safe enough to try: An interview with Zappos CEO Tony Hsieh. *McKinsey Quarterly*, October, https://www.mckinsey.com/business-functions/organization/our-insights/safe-enough-to-try-an-interview-with-zappos-ceo-tony-hsieh?cid=other-eml-alt-mkq-mck-oth-1710.

Detert, J. and Edmonson, A.C. (2011). Implicit voice theories: Taken-for-granted rules of self-censorship at work. *Academy of Management Journal*, **54**, 461–488.

Diamond, J. (2005). *Collapse: How Societies Choose to Fail or to Survive*. London: Penguin.

Dooley, K.J. (1997). A complex adaptive systems model of organization change. *Nonlinear Dynamics, Psychology, and Life Sciences*, **1**, 69–97.

Doz, Y. and Kosonen, M. (2008a). *Fast Strategy: How Strategic Agility will Help You Stay Ahead of the Game*. Philadelphia, PA: Wharton School Publishing.

Doz, Y. and Kosonen, M. (2008b). The dynamics of strategic agility: Nokia's rollercoaster experience. *California Management Review*, **50**, 95–118.

Drazin, R., Glynn, M.A. and Kazanjian, R.K. (1999). Multilevel theorizing about creativity in organizations: A sensemaking perspective. *Academy of Management Review*, **24**, 286–307.

Du, S., Bhattacharya, C.B. and Sen, S. (2010). Maximizing business returns to corporate social responsibility (CSR): The role of CSR communication. *International Journal of Management Reviews*, **12**, 8–19.

Duckworth, A. (2016). *Grit: The Power of Passion and Perseverance*. New York: Simon & Schuster.

Duckworth, A.L., Peterson, C., Matthews, M.D. and Kelly, D.R. (2007). Grit: Perseverance and passion for long-term goals. *Journal of Personality and Social Psychology*, **92**, 1087–1101.

Duckworth, A.L. and Quinn, P.D. (2009). Development and validation of the short grit scale. *Journal of Personality Assessment*, **91** (2), 166–174.

Duhigg, C. (2016). What Google learned from its quest to build the perfect team. *New York Times, Sunday Magazine*, 28 February, MM20.

Dutton, J.E. (2003). *Energize Your Workplace*. San Francisco, CA: Jossey Bass.

Dutton, J.E. and Heaphy, E. (2003). Coming to life: The power of high quality connections at work. In Cameron, K., Dutton, J. and Quinn, R. (eds), *Positive Organizational Scholarship* (pp. 263–278). San Francisco, CA: Berrett-Koehler.

Dylan, B. (1965). Love minus zero/no limit. *Bringing it all Back Home* (LP). New York: Columbia.

The Economist (2011). Books of the month: Pakistan. We've read them all. 12 May, http://www.economist.com/blogs/multimedia/2011/05/books_month_pakistan.

The Economist (2014). Uruguay: A conversation with President José Mujica. 21 August, http://www.economist.com/blogs/americasview/2014/08/uruguay.

The Economist (2018). Telephone tower v rubber boots. 10 March, 59–60.

Edgeman R. (2014). Modeling and analytics of sustainable, resilient and robust enterprises. *Business Systems Review*, **3**, 75–99.

Edgeman, R. and Williams, J.A. (2014). Enterprise self-assessment analytics for sustainability, resilience and robustness. *TQM Journal*, **26**, 368–381.

Edmondson, A. (1999). Psychological safety and learning behavior in work teams. *Administrative Science Quarterly*, **44**, 350–383.

Edmondson, A.C. (2008). The competitive imperative of learning. *Harvard Business Review*, **86**, 60–67.

Edmondson, A.C. (2012). *Teaming*. Boston, MA: Harvard Business School Press.

Edmondson, A.C. and Lei, Z. (2014). Psychological safety: The history, renaissance, and future of an interpersonal construct. *Annual Review of Organizational Psychology and Organizational Behavior*, **1**, 23–43.

Edwards, T., Battisti, G. and Neely, A. (2004). Value creation and the UK economy: A review of strategic options. *International Journal of Management Reviews*, **5**, 191–213.

Egeland, B., Carlson, E. and Sroufe, L.A. (1993). Resilience as process. *Development and Psychopathology*, **5**, 517–528.

Eichenwald, K. (2006). Verdict on an era. *New York Times*, 26 May, C1.

Eisenhardt, K.M., Furr, N.R. and Bingham, C. (2010). Microfoundations of performance: Balancing efficiency and flexibility in dynamic environments. *Organization Science*, **21**, 1263–1273.

Endo, T., Delbridge, R. and Morris, J. (2015). Does Japan still matter? Past tendencies and future opportunities in the study of Japanese firms. *International Journal of Management Reviews*, **17**, 101–123.

Esser, J.K. (1998). Alive and well after 25 years: A review of groupthink research. *Organizational Behavior and Human Decision Processes*, **73** (2/3), 116–141.

Esser, J.K. and Lindoerfer, J.S. (1989). Groupthink and the space shuttle Challenger accident: Toward a quantitative case analysis. *Journal of Behavioral Decision Making*, **2** (3), 167–177.

Ewing, J. (2017). *Faster, Higher, Farther: The Inside Story of the Volkswagen Scandal*. New York: Random House.

Farjoun, M. (2010). Beyond dualism: Stability and change as a duality. *Academy of Management Review*, **35**, 202–225.

Feldman, M.S. and Orlikowski, W.J. (2011). Theorizing practice and practicing theory. *Organization Science*, **22**, 1240–1253.

Fiksel, J., Polyviou, M., Croxton, K.L. and Pettit, T.J. (2015). From risk to resilience: learning to deal with disruption. *MIT Sloan Management Review*, **56**, 79–86.

Finkel, M. (2011). *On Flexibility: Recovery from Technological and Doctrinal Surprise on the Battlefield*. Stanford, CA: Stanford Security Studies.

Fisher, C.D. (2010). Happiness at work. *International Journal of Management Reviews*, **12**, 384–412.

Flint-Taylor, J. and Cooper, C.L. (2017). Team resilience: Shaping up for the challenges ahead. In Crane, M.F. (ed.), *Managing for Resilience: A Practical Guide for Employee Wellbeing and Organizational Performance* (pp. 129–149). London, UK and New York, USA: Taylor & Francis.

Folke, C. (2006). Resilience: The emergence of a perspective for social-ecological systems analyses. *Global Environmental Change*, **16**, 253–267.

Ford, J.D. and Ford, L.W. (1995). The role of conversations in producing intentional change in organizations. *Academy of Management Review*, **20**, 541–570.

Frazier, M.L., Fainshmidt, S., Klinger, R.L., Pezeshkan, A. and Vracheva, V. (2017). Psychological safety: A meta-analytic review and extension. *Personnel Psychology*, **70**, 113–165.

Fredrickson, B.L., Tugade, M.M., Waugh, C.E. and Larkin, G.R. (2003). What good are positive emotions in crisis? A prospective study of resilience and emotions following the terrorist attacks on the United States on September 11th, 2001. *Journal of Personality and Social Psychology*, **84**, 365–376.

Freeman, S.F., Hirschhorn, L. and Maltz, M. (2004). The power of moral purpose: Sandler O'Neill and Partners in the aftermath of September 11th, 2001. *Organization Development Journal*, **22** (4), 69–81.

French, L. (2016). The six biggest brand disasters of the last decade. *World Finance*, 19 October, https://www.worldfinance.com/special-reports/the-six-biggest-brand-disasters-of-the-last-decade (accessed 10 February 2018).

Frohman, A.L. (1997). Igniting organizational change from below: The power of personal initiative. *Organizational Dynamics*, **25**, 3953.

Frone, M.R. (2003). Work–family balance. In Quick, J.C. and Tetrick, L.E. (eds), *Handbook of Occupational Health Psychology* (pp. 143–162). Washington, DC: American Psychological Association.

Fuller, B., Simmering, M.J., Marler, L.E., Cox, S.S., Bennett, R.J. and Cheramie, R.A. (2011). Exploring touch as a positive workplace behavior. *Human Relations*, **64**, 231–256.

Furniss, D., Back, J., Blanford, A., Hildebrand, M. and Broberg, H. (2011). A resilience markers framework for small teams. *Reliability Engineering and System Safety*, **96**, 2–10.

Furu, P. (2013). The art of collaborative leadership in jazz bands. In Caust, J. (ed.), *Arts Leadership: International Case Studies* (pp. 210–223). Prahan, Australia: Tilde University Press.

Gallopi'n, G.C. (2006). Linkages between vulnerability, resilience, and adaptive capacity. *Global Environmental Change*, **16**, 293–303.

Gardner, W. and Rogoff, B. (1990). Children's deliberateness of planning according to task circumstances. *Developmental Psychology*, **26**, 480–487.

Garmezy, N. (1973). Competence and adaptation in adult schizophrenic patients and children at risk. In Dean, S.R. (ed.), *Schizophrenia: The First Ten Dean Award Lectures* (pp. 163–204). New York: MSS Information Corp.

Garmezy, N. (1991). Resilience and vulnerability to adverse developmental outcomes associated with poverty. *American Behavioral Scientist*, **34**, 416–430.

Garud, R., Kumaraswamy, A. and Sambamurthy, V. (2006). Emergent by design: Performance and transformation at Infosys. *Organization Science*, **17**, 277–286.

Garvin, D.A. and Roberto, M.A. (2001). What you don't know about making decisions. *Harvard Business Review*, **79** (8), 108–116.

Geher, G. (2015). Failure as the single best marker of human success. *Psychology Today*, 5 September, https://www.psychologytoday.com/blog/darwins-subterranean-world/201409/failure-the-single-best-marker-human-success.

Gibbert, M. and Välikangas, L. (2004). Boundaries and innovation: Special issue introduction by the guest editors. *Long Range Planning*, **37** (6), 495–504.

Gibson, C.B. and Zellmer-Bruhn, M.E. (2001). Metaphors and meaning: An intercultural analysis of the concept of teamwork. *Administrative Science Quarterly*, **46** (2), 274–303.

Gilbert, M., Eyring, M. and Foster, R.N. (2012). Two routes to resilience. *Harvard Business Review*, **90**, 67–73.

Gillespie, B.M., Chaboyer, W. and Wallis, M. (2007). Development of a theoretically derived model of resilience through concept analysis. *Contemporary Nurse*, **25** (1/2), 124–135.

Gino, F. and Staats, B.R. (2012). The microwork solution. *Harvard Business Review*, **90**, 92–96.

Gittell, J.H., Cameron, K., Lim, S. and Rivas, V. (2006). Relationships, layoffs, and organizational resilience: Airline industry responses to September 11. *Journal of Applied Behavioral Science*, **42**, 300–329.

Gittell, J.H. and Douglass, A. (2012). Relational bureaucracy: Structuring reciprocal relationships into roles. *Academy of Management Review*, **37**, 709–733.

Giulianotti, R. (1999). Built by the two Varelas: The rise and fall of football culture and national identity in Uruguay. *Culture, Sport Society*, **2** (3), 134–154.

Giustiniano, L. and Cantoni, F. (2018). Between sponge and titanium: Designing micro and macro features for the resilient organization. In

Boccardelli, P., Annosi, M.C., Brunetta, F. and Magnusson, M. (eds), *Learning and Innovation in Hybrid Organizations* (pp. 167–190). Cham: Palgrave Macmillan.

Giustiniano, L., Cunha, M.P. and Clegg, S. (2016a). Organizational zemblanity. *European Management Journal*, **34** (1), 7–21.

Giustiniano, L., Cunha, M.P. and Clegg, S. (2016b). The dark side of organizational improvisation: Lessons from the sinking of Costa Concordia. *Business Horizons*, **59** (2), 223–232.

Giustiniano, L., Marchegiani, L., Peruffo, E. and Pirolo, L. (2014). Understanding outsourcing of information systems. In Tsiakis, T., T. Kargidis and P. Katsaros (eds), *Approaches and Processes for Managing the Economics of Information Systems* (pp. 199–220). Hershey, PA: IGI.

Goldberg, S.D. and Harzog, B.B. (1996). Oil spill: Management crisis or crisis management? *Journal of Contingencies and Crisis Management*, **4**, 1–9.

Goodman, D. and Mann, S. (2008). Managing public human resources following catastrophic events: Mississippi's local governments' experiences post-Hurricane Katrina. *Review of Public Personnel Administration*, **28**, 3–19.

Goodwin, D.K. (2005). *Team of Rivals: The Political Genius of Abraham Lincoln*. New York: Simon & Schuster.

Grandori, A. and Furnari, S. (2008). A chemistry of organization: Combinatory analysis and design. *Organization Studies*, **29** (3), 459–485.

Grant, A. (2017). To be resilient, don't be too virtuous. *LinkedIn*, 13 May, https://www.linkedin.com/pulse/resilient-dont-too-virtuous-adam-grant.

Grant, A.M. and Ashford, S.J. (2008). The dynamics of proactivity at work. *Research in Organizational Behavior*, **28**, 3–34.

Grant, A.M. and Gino, F. (2010). A little thanks goes a long way: Explaining why gratitude expressions motivate prosocial behavior. *Journal of Personality and Social Psychology*, **98**, 946–955.

Grant, A.M., Nurmohamed, S., Ashford, S.J. and Dekas, K. (2011). The performance implications of ambivalent initiative: The interplay of autonomous and controlled motivations. *Organizational Behavior and Human Decision Processes*, **116**, 241–251.

Gratton, L. and Ghoshal, S. (2003). Managing personal human capital: New ethos for the 'volunteer' employee. *European Management Journal*, **21**, 1–10.

Grimm, D. (2015). How dogs stole our hearts. *Online News, Science*, 16 April, http://www.sciencemag.org/news/2015/04/how-dogs-stole-our-hearts.

Grzywacs, J.G. and Carlson, D.S. (2007). Conceptualizing work family balance: Implications for practice and research. *Advances in Developing Human Resources*, **9**, 455–471.

Hackman, J. (2003). Learning more by crossing levels: Evidence from airplanes, hospitals, and orchestras. *Journal of Organizational Behavior,* **24,** 905–922.

Hadida, A.L. (2009). Motion picture performance: A review and research agenda. *International Journal of Management Reviews,* **11,** 297–335.

Hadida, A.L., Tarvainen, W. and Rose, J. (2015). Organizational improvisation: A consolidating review and framework. *International Journal of Management Reviews,* **17** (4), 437–459.

Hagen, J.U. (2013). *Confronting Mistakes: Lessons from the Aviation Industry when Dealing with Error.* New York: Palgrave Macmillan.

Hallowell, E.M. (1999). The human moment at work. *Harvard Business Review,* January–February, 58–66.

Hamel, G. and Välikangas, L. (2003). The quest for resilience. *Harvard Business Review,* **81** (9), 52–63.

Harlinger, M. and Blazina, C. (2016). Exploring the role of playfulness with canine companions in coping with stress. In Blazina, C. and Kogan, L.R. (eds), *Men and Their Dogs* (pp. 151–174). Cham: Springer.

Harms, P.D., Vanhove, A. and Luthans, F. (2017). Positive projections and health: An initial validation of the implicit psychological capital health measure. *Applied Psychology,* **66** (1), 78–102.

Harter, J.K., Schmidt, F.L. and Hayes, T.L. (2002). Business-unit-level relationship between employee satisfaction, employee engagement, and business outcomes: A meta-analysis. *Journal of Applied Psychology,* **87,** 268–279.

Harvey, S. (2014). Creative synthesis: Exploring the process of extraordinary group creativity. *Academy of Management Review,* **39,** 324–343.

Heinrichs, M., von Dawans, B. and Domes, G. (2009). Oxytocin, vasopressin, and human social behavior. *Frontiers in Neuroendocrinology,* **30,** 548–557.

Helton, W.S., Feltovich, P.J. and Velkey, A.J. (2009). Skill and expertise in working dogs: A cognitive science perspective. In Helton, W.S. (ed.), *Canine Ergonomics: The Science of Working Dogs* (pp. 17–42). Boca Rato, FL: CRC Press.

Heynoski, K., and Quinn, E.R. (2012). Seeing and realizing organizational potential: Activating conversations that challenge assumptions. *Organizational Dynamics,* **41,** 118–125.

Hirschhorn, L., Maltz, M. and Freeman, S.F. (2004). The power of moral purpose: Sandler O'Neill and Partners in the aftermath of September 11, 2001. *Organizational Development Journal,* **22,** 69–81.

Hodgkinson, G.P. and Healey, M.P. (2011). Psychological foundations of dynamic capabilities: Reflexion and reflection in strategic management. *Strategic Management Journal,* **32,** 1500–1516.

Holling, C.S. (1973). Resilience and stability of ecological systems. *Annual Review of Ecology and Systematics*, **4**, 1–23.

Holling, C.S. (1986). The resilience of terrestrial ecosystems: Local surprise and global change. In Clark, W.C. and Munn, R.E. (eds), *Sustainable Development of the Biosphere* (pp. 292–317). Cambridge: Cambridge University Press.

Holling, C.S. (1996). Engineering resilience versus ecological resilience. In Schultze, P. (ed.), *Engineering within Ecological Constraints* (pp. 31–44). Washington, DC: National Academy Press.

Hollnagel, E. (2012). When things go wrong: Failures as the flip side of successes. In Hoffman, D.A. and Frese, M. (eds), *Errors in Organizations* (pp. 225–244). New York: Routledge.

Holt, R. and den Hond, F. (2013). Sapere aude. *Organization Studies*, **34** (11), 1587–1600.

Horne, J.F.I. (1997). The coming age of organizational resilience. *Business Forum*, **22**, 24–28.

Hougaard, R., Carter, J. and Brewerton, V. (2018). Why do so many managers forget they're human beings? *Harvard Business Review*, January, https://hbr.org/2018/01/why-do-so-many-managers-forget-theyre-human-beings (accessed 13 July 2018).

Howard-Grenville, J., Buckle, S.J., Hoskins, B.J. and George, G. (2014). Climate change and management. *Academy of Management Journal*, **57**, 615–623.

Hsu, T. (2017). 4,800 file suits claiming cancer from baby powder. *New York Times*, 19 September, B1.

Hu, J., Erdogan, B., Jiang, K., Bauer, T.N. and Liu, S. (2017). Leader humility and team creativity: The role of team information sharing, psychological safety, and power distance. *Journal of Applied Psychology*, **103** (3), 313–323.

Jackall, R. (1988). *Moral Mazes: The World of Corporate Managers*. New York: Oxford University Press.

Janis, I.L. (1972). *Victims of Groupthink: A Psychological Study of Foreign-Policy Decisions and Fiascoes*. Oxford: Houghton Mifflin.

Janis, I. (1982). *Groupthink*. Boston, MA: Houghton Mifflin Company.

Jhabvala, N. (2018). Reasons to worry? Against underdog Eagles, Patriots have plenty in Super Bowl LII. *Denver Post*, 3 February, https://www.denverpost.com/2018/02/03/philadelphia-eagles-embrace-underdog-role-super-bowl-lii-new-england-patriots/.

Johns, T. and Gratton, L. (2013). The third wave of virtual work. *Harvard Business Review*, **91**, 66–73.

Jones, R.H. (2014). *Nagarjuna: Buddhism's Most Important Philosopher*, 2nd edn. New York: Jackson Square Books.

Jung, J.C. and Park, S.B.A. (2017). Volkswagen's diesel emissions scandal. *Thunderbird International Business Review*, **59** (1), 127–137.

Kahn, W.A. (1990). Psychological conditions of personal engagement and disengagement at work. *Academy of Management Journal*, **33**, 692–724.

Kahn, W.A. (1998). Relational systems at work. In Staw, B.M. and Cummings, L.L. (eds), *Research in Organizational Behavior*, Vol. 20 (pp. 39–76). Greenwich, CT: JAI Press.

Kahn, W.A., Barton, M.A. and Fellows, S. (2013). Organizational crises and the disturbance of relational systems. *Academy of Management Review*, **38**, 377–396.

Kahneman, D. (2011). *Thinking, Fast and Slow*. New York: Macmillan.

Kaplan, R.S. and Mikes, A. (2012). Managing risks: A new framework. *Harvard Business Review*, **90**, 48–60.

Keeler, J.R., Rothm, E.A., Neuser, B.L., Spitsbergen, J.M., Waters, D.J.M. and Vianney, J.-M. (2015). The neurochemistry and social flow of singing: Bonding and oxytocin. *Frontiers in Human Neuroscience*, **9**, 518.

Kendra, J.M. and Wachtendorf, T. (2003). Elements of resilience after the World Trade Center disaster: Reconstituting New York City's emergency operations center. *Disasters*, **27**, 37–53.

Khan, Z., Rao-Nicholson, R., Akhtar, P., Tarba, S.Y., Ahammad, M.F. and Vorley, T. (2017). The role of HR practices in developing employee resilience: A case study from the Pakistani telecommunications sector. *International Journal of Human Resource Management*, 1–28. DOI: 10.1080/09585192.2017.1316759.

King, D.D., Newman, A. and Luthans, F. (2016). Not if, but when we need resilience in the workplace. *Journal of Organizational Behavior*, **37** (5), 782–786.

Kingson, J.A. (2016). A President's best friends often have four legs. *New York Times*, 30 September, http://www.nytimes.com/2016/10/01/us/politics/presidential-pets-clinton-trump.html.

Kingwell, B.A., Lomdhal, A. and Anderson, W.P. (2001). Presence of a pet dog and human cardiovascular responses to mild mental stress. *Clinical Autonomic Research*, **11**, 313–317.

Klehe, U., Van Vianen, A.E.M. and Zikic, J. (2012). Coping with economic stress: Introduction to the special issue. *Journal of Organizational Behavior*, **33**, 745–751.

Klein, K.J., Conn, A.B., Smith, D.B. and Sorra, J.S. (2001). Is everyone in agreement? An exploration of within-group agreement in employee perceptions of the work environment. *Journal of Applied Psychology*, **86**, 3–16.

Klein, K.J. and Kozlowski, S.W.J. (2000). A multilevel approach to theory and research in organizations: Contextual, temporal, and emergent processes. In Klein, K.J. and Kozlowski, S.W.J. (eds), *Multilevel Theory, Research, and Methods in Organizations: Foundations, Extensions, and New Directions* (pp. 3–90). San Francisco, CA: Jossey-Bass.

Kleindorfer, P.R. and Saad, G.H. (2005). Managing disruption risks in supply chains. *Production and Operations Management*, **14** (1), 53–68.

Kobasa, S.C. (1979). Stressful life events, personality and health: An inquiry into hardiness. *Journal of Personality and Social Psychology*, **37**, 1–11.

Kobasa, S.C. and Puccetti, M.C. (1983). Personality and social resources in stress resistance. *Journal of Personality and Social Psychology*, **45**, 839–850.

Koehn, N.F. (2013). Lincoln's School of Management. *New York Times*, 2 January, BU1.

Kohlrieser, G., Goldsworthy, S. and Coombe, D. (2012). *Care to Dare: Unleashing Astonishing Potential through Secure Base Leadership*. San Francisco, CA: Jossey-Bass.

Kokalitcheva, K. (2016). Here are the 12 most pet-friendly companies. *Fortune*, 8 March, http://fortune.com/2016/03/08/here-are-the-12-most-pet-friendly-companies/.

Konnikova, M. (2016). How people learn to become resilient. *New Yorker*, 11 February, http://www.newyorker.com/science/maria-konnikova/the-secret-formula-for-resilience?mbid=rss.

Kossek, E.E. and Perrigino, M.B. (2016). Resilience: A review using a grounded integrated occupational approach. *Academy of Management Annals*, **10** (1), 729–797.

Kotter, J. (2012). Accelerate! *Harvard Business Review*, **90**, 44–58.

Kroll, M.J., Toombs, L.A. and Wright, P. (2000). Napoleon's tragic march home from Moscow: Lessons in hubris. *Academy of Management Executive*, **14** (1), 117–128.

Langley, A. (1999). Strategies for theorizing from process data. *Academy of Management Review*, **24**, 691–710.

Langley, A.N.N., Smallman, C., Tsoukas, H. and Van de Ven, A.H. (2013). Process studies of change in organization and management: Unveiling temporality, activity, and flow. *Academy of Management Journal*, **56**, 1–13.

Lawton, T., McGuire, S. and Rajwani, T. (2013). Corporate political activity: A literature review and research agenda. *International Journal of Management Reviews*, **15**, 86–105.

Lazarus, R.S. and Folkman, S. (1984). *Stress, Appraisal, and Coping*. New York: Springer.

Lee, A.V., Vargo, J. and Seville, E. (2013). Developing a tool to measure and compare organizations' resilience. *Natural Hazards Review*, **14** (1), 29–41.

Lee, J.E.C., Sudom, K.A. and McCreary, D.R. (2011). Higher-order model of resilience in the Canadian Forces. *Canadian Journal of Behavioural Science*, **43**, 222–234.

Leitch, W. (2012). Rocket Man. *GQ*, November, https://www.gq.com/story/jeremy-lin-gq-november-2012-cover-story?printable=true.

Lengnick-Hall, C.A. (2008). Organizational resilience. In Clegg, S. and Bailey, J. (eds), *International Encyclopedia of Organization Studies* (pp. 1160–1161). London: SAGE.

Lengnick-Hall, C.A. and Beck, T.E. (2005). Adaptive fit versus robust transformation: How organizations respond to environmental change. *Journal of Management*, **31**, 738–757.

Lengnick-Hall, C.A., Beck, T.E. and Lengnick-Hall, M.L. (2011). Developing a capacity for organizational resilience through strategic human resource management. *Human Resource Management Review*, **21**, 243–255.

Leong, Y.M.J. and Crossman, J. (2016). Tough love or bullying? New nurse transitional experiences. *Journal of Clinical Nursing*, **25** (9/10), 1356–1366.

Lewis, M.W. and Smith, W.K. (2014). Paradox as a metatheoretical perspective: Sharpening the focus and widening the scope. *Journal of Applied Behavioral Science*, **50** (2), 127–149.

Liang, J., Farh, C.I. and Farh, J.L. (2012). Psychological antecedents of promotive and prohibitive voice: A two-wave examination. *Academy of Management Journal*, **55** (1), 71–92.

Linnenluecke, M.K. (2017). Resilience in business and management research: A review of influential publications and a research agenda. *International Journal of Management Reviews*, **19** (1), 4–30.

Linnenluecke, M.K. and Griffiths, A. (2015). *The Climate Resilient Organization: Adaptation and Resilience to Climate Change and Weather Extremes*. Cheltenham, UK and Northampton, MA, USA: Edward Elgar Publishing.

Livingstone, L.P., Palich, L.E. and Carini, G.R. (2002). Promoting creativity through the logic of contradiction. *Journal of Organizational Behavior*, **23**, 321–326.

Losada, M. and Heaphy, E. (2004). The role of positivity and connectivity in the performance of business teams: A nonlinear dynamics model. *American Behavioral Scientist*, **47** (6), 740–765.

Lowe, S. (2018). André Gomes may feature against Chelsea despite Barcelona 'hell'. *Guardian*, 13 March, https://www.theguardian.com/football/2018/mar/13/andre-gomes-chelsea-barcelona-hell-champions-league.

Luscombe, B. (2017). Life after death. *Time*, 13 April, http://time.com/sheryl-sandberg-option-b/?xid=newsletter-brief.

Luthans, F., Avey, J.B., Avolio, B.J., Norman, S.M. and Combs, G.M. (2006a). Psychological capital development: Toward a micro-intervention. *Journal of Organizational Behavior*, **27** (3), 387–393.

Luthans, F., Avey, J.B., Avolio, B.J. and Peterson, S.J. (2010). The development and resulting performance impact of positive psychological capital. *Human Resource Development Quarterly*, **21** (1), 41–67.

Luthans, F., Avey, J.B. and Patera, J.L. (2008). Experimental analysis of a web-based intervention to develop positive psychological capital. *Academy of Management Learning and Education*, **7** (2), 209–221.

Luthans, F., Avolio, B.J., Avey, J.B. and Norman, S.M. (2007). Positive psychological capital: Measurement and relationship with performance and satisfaction. *Personnel Psychology*, **60** (3), 541–572.

Luthans, F., Avolio, B.J., Walumbwa, F.O. and Li, W. (2005). The psychological capital of Chinese workers: Exploring the relationship with performance. *Management and Organization Review*, **1**, 249–271.

Luthans, F., Vogelgesang, G.R. and Lester, P. (2006b). Developing the psychological capital of resiliency. *Human Resource Development Review*, **5** (1), 25–44.

Luthans, F. and Youssef, C. (2004). Human, social, and now positive psychological capital management: Investing in people for competitive advantage. *Organizational Dynamics*, **33** (2), 143–160.

Luthans, F. and Youssef, C.M. (2007). Emerging positive organizational behavior. *Journal of Management*, **33**, 321–349.

Luthans, F., Youssef, C.M. and Avolio, B.J. (2007). *Psychological Capital*. Oxford: Oxford University Press.

Luthans, F. and Youssef-Morgan, C.M. (2017). Psychological capital: An evidence-based positive approach. *Annual Review of Organizational Psychology and Organizational Behavior*, **4**, 339–366.

Luthans, F., Youssef-Morgan, C.M. and Avolio, B.J. (2015). *Psychological Capital and Beyond*. Oxford: Oxford University Press.

Luthar, S.S. (2006). Resilience in development: A synthesis of research across five decades. In Cicchetti, D. and Cohen, D.J. (eds), *Developmental Psychopathology: Risk, Disorder and Adaptation*, 2nd edn (pp. 739–795). Hoboken, NJ: John Wiley & Sons.

Luthar, S.S. and Cicchetti, D. (2000). The construct of resilience: Implications for interventions and social policies. *Development and Psychopathology*, **12**, 857–885.

Luthar, S.S., Cicchetti, D. and Becker, B. (2000). The construct of resilience: A critical evaluation and guidelines for future work. *Child Development*, **71**, 543–562.

Luthar, S.S. and Zigler, E. (1991). Vulnerability and competence: A review of research on resilience in childhood. *American Journal of Orthopsychiatry*, **61**, 6–22.

Lynch, D. (2010). *When the Luck of the Irish Ran Out: The World's Most Resilient Country and its Struggle to Rise Again*. New York: Palgrave Macmillan.

Lyubomirsky, S., Sheldon, K.M. and Schkade, D. (2005). Pursuing happiness: The architecture of sustainable change. *Review of General Psychology*, **9**, 111–131.

Mabey, C. (2013). Leadership development in organizations: Multiple discourses and diverse practice. *International Journal of Management Reviews*, **15**, 359–380.

MacCormack, A., Baldwin, C. and Rusnak, J. (2012). Exploring the duality between product and organizational architectures: A test of the 'mirroring' hypothesis. *Research Policy*, **41** (8), 1309–1324.

MacCormack, A., Rusnak, J. and Baldwin, C.Y. (2006). Exploring the structure of complex software designs: An empirical study of open source and proprietary code. *Management Science*, **52** (7), 1015–1030.

Macey, W.H., Schneider, B., Barbera, K.M. and Young, S.A. (2011). *Employee Engagement: Tools for Analysis, Practice, and Competitive Advantage*, Vol. 31. Malden, MA: John Wiley & Sons.

MacNeil, C.M. (2004). Exploring the supervisor role as a facilitator of knowledge sharing in teams. *Journal of European Industrial Training*, **28**, 93–102.

MacPhail, L.H. and Edmondson, A.C. (2012). Learning domains: The importance of work context in organizational learning from error. In Hoffman, D.A. and Frese, M. (eds), *Errors in Organizations* (pp. 177–188). New York: Routledge.

Maddi, S.R. (2013). *Hardiness: Turning Stressful Circumstances into Resilient Growth*. Dordrecht: Springer.

Maddi, S.R. and Khoshaba, D.M. (2005). *Resilience at Work*. New York: American Psychological Association.

Magni, M., Proserpio, L., Hoegl, M. and Provera, B. (2009). The role of team behavioral integration and cohesion in shaping individual improvisation. *Research Policy*, **38**, 1044–1053.

Maier, M. (2002). Ten years after a major malfunction . . . Reflections on 'The Challenger Syndrome'. *Journal of Management Inquiry*, **11** (3), 282–292.

Maitlis, S. (2012). Posttraumatic growth: A missed opportunity for positive organizational scholarship. In Cameron, K.S. and Spreitzer, G.M. (eds), *The Oxford Handbook of Positive Organizational Scholarship* (pp. 909–923). Oxford: Oxford University Press.

Maitlis, S. (2018). Out of darkness: Stories of trauma and growth at work.

keynote speech, LAEMOS 2018 Conference, Buenos Aires, Argentina, 22–24 March.

Mallak, L.A. (1997). How to build a resilient organization. *Proceedings of the Industrial Engineering Solutions, 1997 Conference* (pp. 170–177). Miami, FL, May.

Manyena, S.B. (2006). The concept of resilience revisited. *Disasters*, **30** (4), 434–450.

March, J.G. (1991). Exploration and exploitation in organizational life. *Organization Science*, **2**, 71–87.

Margolis, J.D. and Stoltz, P.G. (2010). How to bounce back from adversity. *Harvard Business Review*, January–February, 86–92.

Mars, M.M., Bronstein, J.L. and Lusch, R.F. (2012). The value of a metaphor: Organizations as ecosystems. *Organizational Dynamics*, **41**, 271–280.

Marston, A. and Marston, S. (2018). To handle increased stress, build your resilience. *Harvard Business Review*, 19 February, https://hbr.org/2018/02/to-handle-increased-stress-build-your-resilience.

Martin, J.A. and Carlile, P.R. (2000). Designing agile organizations: Organizational learning at the boundaries. In Quinn, R.E., O'Neill, R.M. and St Clair, L. (eds), *Pressing Problems in Modern Organizations* (pp. 129–152). New York: Amacom.

Maslow, A.H. (1954). *Motivation and Personality*. New York: Harper.

Masten, A.S. (2001). Ordinary magic: Resilience process in development. *American Psychologist*, **56**, 227–239.

Masten, A.S. and Monn, A.R. (2015). Child and family resilience: A call for integrated science, practice, and professional training. *Family Relations*, **64**, 5–21.

McCann, J. (2004). Organizational effectiveness: Changing concepts for changing environments. *Human Resource Planning*, **27**, 42–50.

McConnell, A.R., Brown, C.M., Shoda, T.M., Stayton, L.E. and Martin, C.E. (2011). Friends with benefits: On the positive consequence of pet ownership. *Journal of Personality and Social Psychology*, **101**, 1239–1252.

McFarlane, A.C. and Norris, F.H. (2006). Definitions and concepts in disaster research. In Norris, F., Galea, S., Friedman, M. and Watson, P. (eds), *Methods for Disaster Mental Health Research* (pp. 3–19). New York: Guilford Press.

McGonigal, J. (2012). Building resilience by wasting time. *Harvard Business Review*, **90**, 38.

McManus, S., Seville, E., Vargo, J. and Brunsdon, D. (2008). Facilitated process for improving organizational resilience. *Natural Hazards Review*, **9**, 81–90.

Meneghel, I., Borgogni, L., Miraglia, M., Salanova, M. and Martínez, I.M. (2016). From social context and resilience to performance through job satisfaction: A multilevel study over time. *Human Relations*, **69** (11), 2047–2067.

Meyer, A.D. (1982). Adapting to environmental jolts. *Administrative Science Quarterly*, **27**, 515–537.

Meyer, C. (2017). Tough love: When mentoring marks a turning point. *Journal of Accountancy*, **224** (4), 42–44.

Meyer, R.E. and Höllerer, M.A. (2014). Does institutional theory need redirecting? *Journal of Management Studies*, **51** (7), 1221–1233.

Miller, D. (1993). The architecture of simplicity. *Academy of Management Review*, **18**, 116–138.

Miner, A.S., Bassoff, P. and Moorman, C. (2001). Organizational improvisation and learning: A field study. *Administrative Science Quarterly*, **46**, 304–337.

Mitchell, A. (2013). Risk and resilience: From good idea to good practice. OECD Development Co-operation Working Papers, No. 13, Paris: OECD Publishing, http://dx.doi.org/10.1787/5k3ttg4cxcbp-en.

Mitroff, I.I. (2005). *Why Some Companies Emerge Stronger and Better from a Crisis*. New York: Amacom.

Moenkemeyer, G., Hoegl, M. and Weiss, M. (2012). Innovator resilience potential: A process perspective of individual resilience as influenced by innovation project termination. *Human Relations*, **65** (5), 627–655.

Moorman, C. and Miner, A.S. (1998). Organizational improvisation and organizational memory. *Academy of Management Review*, **23**, 698–723.

Morgan, G. (1986 [1997]). *Images of Organization*, Newbury Park, CA: SAGE. (1997), 2nd edn, Thousand Oaks, CA: SAGE.

Morgan, G. and Ramirez, R. (1984). Action learning: A holographic metaphor for guiding social change. *Human Relations*, **37**, 1–27.

Morgan, P.B., Fletcher, D. and Sarkar, M. (2013). Defining and characterizing team resilience in elite sport. *Psychology of Sport and Exercise*, **14** (4), 549–559.

Morgeson, F.P. and Hofman, D.A. (1999). The structure and function of collective constructs: Implications for multilevel research and theory development. *Academy of Management Review*, **24**, 249–265.

Morris, J., Farrell, C. and Reed, M. (2016). The indeterminacy of 'temporariness': Control and power in neo-bureaucratic organizations and work in UK television. *Human Relations*, **69** (12), 2274–2297.

Mowshowitz, A. (1997). Virtual organization. *Communications of the ACM*, **40**, 30–37.

Mueller, M.K. and Callina, K.S. (2014). Human–animal interaction as a context for thriving and coping in military-connected youth: The role of pets during deployment. *Applied Developmental Science*, **18** (4), 214–223.

Nagasawa, N., Mitsui, S., En, S., Ohtani, N., Ohta, M., Sakuma, Y., Onaka, T., Mogi, K. and Kikusu, T. (2015). Oxytocin–gaze positive loop and the coevolution of human–dog bonds. *Science*, **348** (6232), 333–336.

Nakanishi, H., Black, J. and Matsuo, K. (2014). Disaster resilience in transportation: Japan earthquake and tsunami, 2011. *International Journal of Disaster Resilience in the Built Environment*, **5**, 341–361.

Nenni, M.E. and Giustiniano, L. (2013). Increasing integration across the supply chain through an approach to match performance and risk. *American Journal of Applied Sciences*, **10**, 1009–1017.

Newman, A., Ucbasaran, D., Zhu, F. and Hirst, G. (2014). Psychological capital: A review and synthesis. *Journal of Organizational Behavior*, **35**, S120–S138.

Nietzsche, F. (1889 [1968]). *Götzen-Dämmerung: oder, Wie man mit dem Hammer philosophiert*. Leipzig: Alfred Kröner Verlag. Translated by R.J. Hollingdale (1968), *Twilight of the Idols*. Harmondsworth: Penguin.

Nishi, D., Uehara, R., Yoshikawa, E., Sato, G., Ito, M. and Matsuoka, Y. (2013). Culturally sensitive and universal measure of resilience for Japanese populations: Tachikawa resilience scale in comparison with resilience scale 14-item version. *Psychiatry and Clinical Neurosciences*, **67**, 174–181.

Nissen, M. (2014). Organization design for dynamic fit: A review and projection. *Journal of Organization Design*, **3** (2), 30–42.

Nissen, M.E. and Burton, R.M. (2011). Designing organizations for dynamic fit: System stability, maneuverability, and opportunity loss. *IEEE Transactions on Systems, Man and Cybernetics, Part A: Systems and Humans*, **41**, 418–433.

Norman, S., Luthans, B. and Luthans, K. (2005). The proposed contagion effect of hopeful leaders on the resiliency of employees and organizations. *Journal of Leadership and Organizational Studies*, **12** (2), 55–64.

Norris, F.H., Stevens, S.P., Pfefferbaum, B., Wyche, K.F. and Pfefferbaum, R.L. (2008). Community resilience as a metaphor, theory, set of capacities, and strategy for disaster readiness. *American Journal of Community Psychology*, **41**, 127–150.

OutSystems (2013). *The Small Book of the Few Big Rules*. http://www. outsystems.com/the-small-book/.

Ozbay, F., Fitterling, H., Charney, D. and Southwick, S. (2008). Social support and resilience to stress across the life span: A neurobiologic framework. *Current Psychiatry Reports*, **10**, 304–310.

Ozbay, F., Johnson, D.C., Dimoulas, E., Morgan, C.A., Charney, D. and

Southwick, S. (2007). Social support and resilience to stress: From neurobiology to clinical practice. *Psychiatry*, **4** (5), 35–40.

Özbilgin, M.F., Beauregard, T.A., Tatli, A. and Bell, M.P. (2011). Work–life, diversity and intersectionality: A critical review and research agenda. *International Journal of Management Reviews*, **13**, 177–198.

Pal, R., Torstensson, H. and Mattila, H. (2014). Antecedents of organizational resilience in economic crises: an empirical study of Swedish textile and clothing SMEs. *International Journal of Production Economics*, **147**, 410–428.

Pargament, K.I. (1997). *The Psychology of Religion and Coping: Theory, Research, Practice*. New York: Guilford.

Parker, H. and Ameen, K. (2018). The role of resilience capabilities in shaping how firms respond to disruptions. *Journal of Business Research*, **88**, 535–541.

Parrado, N. (2007). *Miracle in the Andes: 72 Days on the Mountain and My Long Trek Home*. London: Broadway Books.

Patel, S.S., Rogers, M.B., Amlôt, R. and Rubin, G.J. (2017). What do we mean by 'community resilience'? A systematic literature review of how it is defined in the literature. *PLoS Currents Disasters*, **1** February, Edition 1. doi:10.1371/currents.dis.db775aff25efc5ac4f0660ad9c9f7db2.

Pearson, C.M. and Clair, J.A. (1998). Reframing crisis management. *Academy of Management Review*, **23**, 59–76.

Pelling, M. and Uitto, J.I. (2001). Small island developing states: Natural disaster vulnerability and global change. *Environmental Hazards*, **3**, 49–62.

Pentland, A.S. (2012). The new science of building great teams. *Harvard Business Review*, **90**, 60–70.

Perkins-Gough, D. (2013). The significance of grit: A conversation with Angela Lee Duckworth. *Educational Leadership*, **71**, 14–20.

Perrow, C. (1984). *Normal Accidents: Living with High-Risk Technologies*. New York: Basic Books.

Peruffo, E., Marchegiani, L. and Vicentini, F. (2018). Experience as a source of knowledge in divestiture decisions: emerging issues and knowledge management implications. *Journal of Knowledge Management*, **22** (2), 344–361.

Peterson, S.J., Balthazard, P.A., Waldman, D.A. and Thatcher, R.W. (2008). Neuroscientific implications of psychological capital: Are the brains of optimistic, hopeful, confident, and resilient leaders different? *Organizational Dynamics*, **37** (4), 342–353.

Pfeffer, J. (1994). *Competitive Advantage through People*. Boston, MA: Harvard Business School Press.

Pfeffer, J. (2013). You're still the same: Why theories of power hold over time and across contexts. *Academy of Management Perspectives*, **27** (4), 269–280.

Pfeffer, J. and Sutton, R.I. (2013). *The Knowing–Doing Gap: How Smart Companies Turn Knowledge into Action*. Cambridge, MA: Harvard Business Press.

Pfefferbaum, R.L., Pfefferbaum, B., Nitiéma, P., Houston, J.B. and Van Horn, R.L. (2015). Assessing community resilience: An application of the expanded CART survey instrument with affiliated volunteer responders. *American Behavioral Scientist*, **59** (2), 181–199.

Pfefferbaum, R.L., Pfefferbaum, B. and Van Horn, R.L. (2011). *Communities Advancing Resilience Toolkit (CART): The CART Integrated System*. Oklahoma City, OK: Terrorism and Disaster Center at the University of Oklahoma Health Sciences Center.

Pfefferbaum, R.L., Pfefferbaum, B., Van Horn, R.L., Klomp, R.W., Norris, F.H. and Reissman, D.B. (2013). The Communities Advancing Resilience Toolkit (CART): An intervention to build community resilience to disasters. *Journal of Public Health Management and Practice*, **19** (3), 250–258.

Pinto, J. (2014). Expanding the content domain of workplace aggression: A three-level aggressor-target taxonomy. *International Journal of Management Reviews*, **16** (3), 290–313.

Plowman, D.A., Baker, L.T., Beck, T., Kulkarni, M., Solansky, S. and Travis, D. (2007). Radical change accidentally: The emergence and amplification of small change. *Academy of Management Journal*, **50**, 515–543.

Ponomarov, S.Y. and Holcomb, M.C. (2009). Understanding the concept of supply chain resilience. *International Journal of Logistics Management*, **20**, 124–143.

Porath, C.L. (2012). Civility. In Cameron, K.S. and Spreitzer, G.M. (eds), *The Oxford Handbook of Positive Organizational Scholarship* (pp. 439–448). Oxford: Oxford University Press.

Porath, C.L. and Pearson, C. (2013). The price of incivility. *Harvard Business Review*, **91**, 115–121.

Pougatch, M. (2011). *Three Lions Versus the World: England's World Cup Stories from the Men Who Were There*. Edinburgh: Mainstream Publishing.

Powley, E.H. (2009). Reclaiming resilience and safety: Resilience activation in the critical period of crisis. *Human Relations*, **62**, 1289–1326.

Powley, E.H. (2013). The process and mechanisms of organizational healing. *Journal of Applied Behavioral Science*, **49**, 42–68.

Prange, C. and Heracleous, L. (2018). *Agility.X: How Organizations Thrive in Unpredictable Times*. Cambridge: Cambridge University Press.

Pressman, S.D., Cohen, S., Miller, G.E., Barkin, A., Rabin, B. and Treanor, J.J. (2005). Loneliness, social network size, and immune response to influenza vaccination in college freshmen. *Health Psychology*, **24**, 297–306.

Pugh, S.D. (2001). Service with a smile: Emotional contagion in the service encounter. *Academy of Management Journal*, **44**, 1018–1027.

Putnam, L.L., Fairhurst, G.T. and Banghart, S.G. (2016). Contradictions, dialectics, and paradoxes in organizations: A constitutive approach. *Academy of Management Annals*, **10** (1), 65–171.

Rak, C. and Patterson, L. (1996). Promoting resilience in at-risk children. *Journal of Counseling and Development*, **74**, 368–373.

Rao, H. and Greve, H. (2018). Disasters and community resilience: Spanish flu and the formation of retail cooperatives in Norway. *Academy of Management Journal*, **61** (1), 5–25.

Rashi, F., Edmondson, A.C. and Leonard, H.B. (2013). Leadership lessons from the Chilean mine rescue. *Harvard Business Review*, July–August, 113–119.

Rawls, J. (1971). *A Theory of Justice*. Cambridge, MA: Harvard University Press.

Read, P.P. (1974). *Alive: The Story of the Andes Survivors*. Washington, DC: Lippincott.

Reay, T. and Hinings, C.R. (2009). Managing the rivalry of competing institutional logics. *Organization Studies*, **30** (6), 629–652.

Rego, A., Owens, B., Leal, S., Melo, A., Cunha, M.P., Gonçalves, L. and Ribeiro, L. (2017a). How leader humility helps teams to be humbler, psychologically stronger, and more effective: A moderated mediation model. *Leadership Quarterly*, **28**, 639–658.

Rego, A., Owens, B., Yam, K.C., Bluhm, D., Cunha, M.P., Silard, T., Gonçalves, L., Martins, M., Simpson, A.V. and Liu, W. (2017b). Leader humility and team performance: Exploring the mediating mechanisms of team PsyCap and task allocation effectiveness. *Journal of Management*. DOI: 10.1177/0149206316688941.

Rego, A., Vitória, A., Owens, B., Cunha, M.P., Ventura, A., Leal, S., Valverde, C. and Lourenço-Gil, R. (2018). The interplay of leader's grit and humility in fostering employees' improvisational behavior through PsyCap. Unpublished.

Rego, A., Yam, K.C., Owens, B., Story, J., Cunha, M.P., Bluhm, D. and Lopes, M.P. (2017c). Conveyed leader PsyCap predicting leader effectiveness through positive energizing. *Journal of Management*. DOI: 10.1177/0149206317733510.

Reinmoeller, P. and Baardwijk, N. van. (2005). The link between diversity and resilience. *MIT Sloan Management Review*, **46** (4), 61–65.

Ressler, S. (2006). Social network analysis as an approach to combat terrorism: Past, present, and future research. *Homeland Security Affairs*, **2**, 1–10.

Rich, B.L., LePine, J.A. and Crawford, E.R. (2010). Job engagement: Antecedents and effects on job performance. *Academy of Management Journal*, **53**, 617–635.

Rigby, D.K., Sutherland, J. and Takeuchi, H. (2016). Embracing agile. *Harvard Business Review*, May, 41–50.

Rigby, R. (2007). Pet-friendly offices take the lead by letting the dogs in. *Financial Times*, 28 August, 20.

Riolli, L. and Savicki, V. (2003). Information system organizational resilience. *Omega*, **31**, 227–233.

Robertson, B.J. (2015). *Holacracy: The New Management System for a Rapidly Changing World*. New York: Macmillan.

Rodriguez, C. (2016). The night Linsanity died at the hands of the Miami Heat: Today marks the fourth anniversary of the Heat's smothering defense that shut down Jeremy Lin at the height of Linsanity. S*BNation*, 23 February, https://www.hothothoops.com/2016/2/23/11100332/night-linsanity-died-hands-miami-heat-jeremy-lin-wade-lebron-knicks.

Rogers, K.M. and Ashford, B.E. (2017). Respect in organizations: Feeling valued as 'We' and 'Me'. *Journal of Management*, **43** (5), 1578–1608.

Romero, S. (2013). After years in solitary, an austere life as Uruguay's President. *New York Times*, 5 January, A1.

Rorlich, A.A. (2017). *Volga Tatars: A Profile in National Resilience*. Stanford, CA: Hoover Press.

Rosenberg, M.B. (2003). *Nonviolent Communication: A Language of Life*, 2nd edn. Encinitas, CA: Puddle Dancer.

Rothschild, J. (2008). Freedom of speech denied, dignity assaulted: What the whistleblowers experience in the US. *Current Sociology*, **56** (6), 884–903.

Rottinghaus, B. and Vaughn, J. (2015). New ranking of US presidents puts Lincoln at No. 1, Obama at 18; Kennedy judged most overrated. *Washington Post*, 16 February, https://www.washingtonpost.com/news/monkey-cage/wp/2015/02/16/new-ranking-of-u-s-presidents-puts-lincoln-1-obama-18-kennedy-judged-most-over-rated/.

Roux-Dufort, C. (2007). Is crisis management (only) a management of exceptions? *Journal of Contingencies and Crisis Management*, **15**, 105–114.

Sable, P. (1995). Pets, attachment and well-being across the life cycle. *Social Work*, **40** (3), 334–341.

Saïd Business School and Heidrick & Struggles (2015). *The CEO Report: Embracing the Paradoxes of Leadership and the Power of Doubt*. London: Saïd Business School and Heidrick & Struggles.

Salahpour, S. (2018). FC Barcelona: Andre Gomes opens up on personal problems. *Everything Barça*, 12 March, https://everythingbarca.com/2018/03/12/andre-gomes-opens-personal-problems/ (accessed 29 March 2018).

Salomon, A. (2014). Suicide, a crime of loneliness. *New Yorker*, 14 August, https://www.newyorker.com/culture/cultural-comment/suicide-crime-lone liness.

Sanchez, R., Parkin, J.C., Chen, J.Y. and Gray, P.B. (2009). Oxytocin, vasopressin, and human social behavior. *Frontiers in Psychology*, **30** (4), 548–557.

Sandberg, S. (2017). How to build resilient kids, even after a loss. *New York Times*, 24 April, A23.

Sandberg, S. and Grant, A. (2017). *Option B: Facing Adversity, Building Resilience, and Finding Joy*. New York: Knopf.

Sanner, B. and Bunderson, J.S. (2018). The truth about hierarchy. *MIT Sloan Management Review*, **59** (2), 49–52.

Schein, E.H. (2009). *Helping: How to Offer, Give and Receive Help*. San Francisco, CA: Berett-Koehler.

Schoemaker, P.J. and Tetlock, P.E. (2012). Taboo scenarios. *California Management Review*, **54** (2), 5–24.

Schoemaker, P.J.H., Krupp, S. and Howland, S. (2013). Strategic leadership: The essential skills. *Harvard Business Review*, **91**, 131–134.

Schreffler, R. (2012). Quake changes little in Toyota's supply-chain strategy. *WardsAuto*, 16 May, http://wardsauto.com/supply-chain/quake-changes-little-toyota-s-supply-chain-strategy-0.

Schwaber, K. and Beedle, M. (2001). *Agile Software Development with Scrum*. Upper Saddle River, NJ: Prentice Hall.

Sciolino, E. (1992). Female POW is abused, kindling debate. *New York Times*, 29 June, A1.

Seligman, M.E. (2011a). Building resilience. *Harvard Business Review*, **89** (4), 100–106.

Seligman, M. (2011b). *Flourish: A Visionary New Understanding of Happiness and Well-Being*. New York: Free Press.

Sharma, S. and Sharma, S.K. (2016). Team resilience: scale development and validation. *Vision*, **20** (1), 37–53.

Sibley, S., Sauers, L. and Daltry, R. (2018). Humanity and resilience project: The development of a new outreach program for counseling centers at colleges and universities. *Journal of College Student Psychotherapy*. doi.org/10.1080/87568225.2018.1436410.

Siggelkow, N. (2007). Persuasion with case studies. *Academy of Management Review*, **50** (1), 20–24.

Simpson, A., Cunha, M.P. and Clegg, S.R. (2015). Hybridity,

sociomateriality and compassion: What happens when a river floods and a city's organizations respond? *Scandinavian Journal of Management*, **31** (3), 375–386.

Sinek, S. (2011). *Start with Why: How Great Leaders Inspire Everyone to Take Action*. London: Penguin.

Smith, B.W., Dalen, J., Wiggins, K., Tooley, E., Christopher, P. and Bernard, J. (2008). The brief resilience scale: Assessing the ability to bounce back. *International Journal of Behavioral Medicine*, **15**, 194–200.

Smith, K. (2013). *Environmental Hazards: Assessing Risk and Reducing Disaster*, 6th edn. New York: Routledge.

Smith, W.K. and Lewis, M.W. (2011). Toward a theory of paradox: A dynamic equilibrium model of organizing. *Academy of Management Review*, **36**, 381–403.

Smith, W.K., Lewis, M. and Tushman, M.L. (2016). 'Both/and' leadership. *Harvard Business Review*, **94**, 63–70.

Smith, W.K. and Tracey, P. (2016). Institutional complexity and paradox theory: Complementarities of competing demands. *Strategic Organization*, **14** (4), 455–466.

Somers, S. (2009). Measuring resilience potential: An adaptive strategy for organizing crisis potential. *Journal of Contingencies and Crisis Management*, **17**, 12–23.

Sommer, S.A., Howell, J.M. and Hadley, C.N. (2016). Keeping positive and building strength: The role of affect and team leadership in developing resilience during an organizational crisis. *Group and Organization Management*, **41** (2), 172–202.

Sonnentag, S., Niessen, C. and Neff, A. (2012). Recovery: Nonwork experiences that promote positive states. In Cameron, K.S. and Spreitzer, G.M. (eds), *The Oxford Handbook of Positive Organizational Scholarship* (pp. 867–881). Oxford: Oxford University Press.

Southwick, F.S., Martini, B.L., Charney, D.S. and Soutwick, S.M. (2017). Leadership and resilience. In Marques, J. and Dhiman, S. (eds), *Leadership Today: Practices for Personal and Professional Performance* (pp. 315–334). Berlin: Springer.

Spreitzer, G. (2007). Giving peace a chance: Organizational leadership, empowerment, and peace. *Journal of Organizational Behavior*, **28**, 1077–1095.

Spreitzer, G. and Porath, C. (2012). Creating sustainable performance. *Harvard Business Review*, **90**, 93–99.

Spreitzer, G., Sutcliffe, K., Dutton, J., Sonenshein, S. and Grant, A. (2005). A socially embedded model of thriving at work. *Organization Science*, **16**, 537–549.

Starbuck, W.H. and Farjoun, M. (eds) (2005). *Organization at the Limit*. Malden, MA: Blackwell.

Starbuck, W.H. and Milliken, F.J. (1988). Challenger: Fine-tuning the odds until something breaks. *Journal of Management Studies*, **25**, 319–340.

Staw, B.M., Sandelands, L. and Dutton, J.E. (1981). Threat-rigidity effects in organizational behavior: A multi-level analysis. *Administrative Science Quarterly*, **26**, 501–524.

Stephens, J.P., Heaphy, E.D., Carmeli, A., Spreitzer, G.M. and Dutton, J.E. (2013). Relationship quality and virtuousness: Emotional carrying capacity as a source of individual and team resilience. *Journal of Applied Behavioral Science*, **49** (1), 13–41.

Stephens, J.P., Heaphy, E. and Dutton, J.E. (2012). High quality connections. In Cameron, K.S. and Spreitzer, G.M. (eds), *The Oxford Handbook of Positive Organizational Scholarship* (pp. 385–399). Oxford: Oxford University Press.

Stevenson, J.R., Chang-Richards, Y., Conradson, D., Wilkinson, S., Vargo, J., Seville, E. and Brunsdon, D. (2014). Organizational networks and recovery following the Canterbury earthquakes. *Earthquake Spectra*, **30** (1), 555–575.

Stone, M. (2016). Meet the adorable pets of tech's most influential executives. *Business Insider*, 22 June, http://www.businessinsider.com/adorable-pets-of-tech-executives-2014-6.

Story, J.S.P., Youssef, C.M., Luthans, F., Barbuto, J. and Bovaird, J. (2013). Contagion effect of global leaders' positive psychological capital on followers: Does distance and quality of the relationship matter? *International Journal of Human Resource Management*, **24**, 2534–2553.

Sull, D. (2005). Strategy as active waiting. *Harvard Business Review*, **83**, 120–129.

Sull, D. and Eisenhardt, K.M. (2012). Simple rules for a complex world. *Harvard Business Review*, **90**, 68–74.

Sun, P.Y. and Anderson, M.H. (2010). An examination of the relationship between absorptive capacity and organizational learning, and a proposed integration. *International Journal of Management Reviews*, **12**, 130–150.

Sutcliffe, K.M. and Vogus, T.J. (2003). Organizing for resilience. In Cameron, K.S., Dutton, J.E. and Quinn, R.E. (eds), *Positive Organizational Scholarship: Foundations of a New Discipline* (pp. 94–110). San Francisco, CA: Berrett-Koehler.

Sutcliffe, K.M. and Vogus, T.J. (2008). The pragmatics of resilience. In Hansen, H. and Barry, D. (eds), *Handbook of New Approaches in Management and Organization* (pp. 498–500). Thousand Oaks, CA: SAGE.

Sutton, R.I. (2010). The boss as human shield. *Harvard Business Review*, **88** (9), 106–128.

Tax, S.S. and Brown, S.W. (1998). Recovering and learning from service failure. *Sloan Management Review*, **40**, 75–88.

Taylor, B. (2017). How Coca-Cola, Netflix, and Amazon learn from failure. *Harvard Business Review*, Digital Articles, 11 October, pp. 2–4. https://hbr.org/2017/11/how-coca-cola-netflix-and-amazon-learn-from-failure.

Tedeschi, R.G. and Calhoun, L.G. (2004). Posttraumatic growth: Conceptual foundations and empirical evidence. *Psychological Inquiry*, **15**, 1–18.

Thompson, M., II (2011). Golden State Warriors notebook: Stephen Curry misses practice with bad ankle. *Mercury News*, 27 December, updated 13 August 2016, https://www.mercurynews.com/2011/12/27/golden-state-warriors-notebook-stephen-curry-misses-practice-with-bad-ankle/ (accessed 13 July 2018).

Thomson, J. (2017). Risk is inevitable. Resilience is everything. *Forbes*, 7 June, https://www.forbes.com/sites/jeffthomson/2017/06/07/risk-is-inevitable-resilience-is-everything/#3b0a70e1480b.

Thornton, P.H. and Ocasio, W. (1999). Institutional logics and the historical contingency of power in organizations: Executive succession in the higher education publishing industry, 1958–1990. *American Journal of Sociology*, **105** (3), 801–843.

Tillement, S., Cholez, C. and Reverdy, T. (2009). Assessing organizational resilience: an interactionist approach. *M@n@gement*, **12**, 230–264.

Tops, M., Buisman-Pijlman, F.T. and Carter, C.S. (2014). Oxytocin and attachment facilitate a shift from seeking novelty to recognizing and preferring familiarity. In Kent, M., Davis, M.C. and Reich, J.W. (eds), *The Resilience Handbook: Approaches to Stress and Trauma* (pp. 115–130). New York, USA and London, UK: Routledge.

Tranfield, D., Denyer, D. and Smart, P. (2003). Towards a methodology for developing evidence-informed management knowledge by means of systematic review. *British Journal of Management*, **14**, 207–222.

Tsoukas, H. (2005). *Complex Knowledge*. Oxford: Oxford University Press.

Tsoukas, H. and Chia, R. (2002). On organizational becoming: Rethinking organizational change. *Organization Science*, **13** (5), 567–582.

Tsoukas, H. and Vladimirou, E. (2001). What is organizational knowledge? *Journal of Management Studies*, **38**, 973–993.

Tugade, M.M. and Fredrickson, B.L. (2004). Resilient individuals use positive emotions to bounce back from negative emotional experiences. *Journal of Personality and Social Psychology*, **86**, 320–333.

Tugade, M.M. and Fredrickson, B.L. (2007). Regulation of positive emotions: Emotion regulation strategies that promote resilience. *Journal of Happiness Studies*, **8**, 311–333.

Tugade, M.M., Fredrickson, B.L. and Feldman Barrett, L. (2004). Psychological resilience and positive emotional granularity: Examining the benefits of positive emotions on coping and health. *Journal of Personality*, **72**, 1161–1190.

Turner, M.E. and Pratkanis, A.R. (1997). Mitigating groupthink by stimulating constructive conflict. In De Dreu, C.K.W. and Van de Vliert, E. (eds), *Using Conflict in Organizations* (pp. 53–71). London: SAGE.

Turner, N., Swart, J. and Maylor, H. (2013). Mechanisms for managing ambidexterity: A review and research agenda. *International Journal of Management Reviews*, **15**, 317–332.

Uhl-Bien, M. (2006). Relational leadership theory: Exploring the social processes of leadership and organizing. *Leadership Quarterly*, **17** (6), 654–676.

UN (2015). Global Assessment Report on Disaster Risk Reduction 2015 – Making development sustainable: The future of disaster risk management. Geneva: United Nations, http://www.preventionweb.net/english/hyogo/gar/2015/en/gar-pdf/GAR2015_EN.pdf.

UNISDR (2015). Sendai Framework for Disaster Risk Reduction 2015–2030. Geneva: UNISDR, http://www.preventionweb.net/files/43291_sendaiframeworkfordrren.pdf.

Useem, M., Jordan, R. and Koljatic, M. (2011). How to lead during a crisis: Lessons from the rescue of the Chilean miners. *MIT Sloan Management Review*, **53** (1), 49–55.

Välikangas, L. (2010). *Resilient Organization, How Adaptive Cultures Thrive Even When Strategy Fails*. New York: McGraw-Hill.

Välikangas, L. and Romme, A.G.L. (2013). How to design for strategic resilience: A case study in retailing. *Journal of Organization Design*, **2**, 44–53.

Van Der Vegt, G.S., Essens, P., Wahlström, M. and George, G. (2015). Managing risk and resilience. *Academy of Management Journal*, **58**, 971–980.

van Dierendonck, D. and Patterson, K. (2015). Compassionate love as a cornerstone of servant leadership: An integration of previous theorizing and research. *Journal of Business Ethics*, **128**, 119–131.

Van Hove, A.J., Herian, M.N., Harms, P.D. and Luthans, F. (2015). Resilience and growth in long-duration isolated, confined and extreme (ICE) missions. NASA/TM-2015-218566. Johnson Space Center, Houston, TX: National Aeronautics and Space Administration.

Vaughan, D. (1996). *The Challenger Launch Decision: Risky Technology, Culture and Deviance at NASA*. Chicago, IL: University of Chicago Press.

Vera, D. and Crossan, M. (2004). Theatrical improvisation: Lessons for organizations. *Organization Studies*, **25**, 727–749.

Verleysen, B., Lambrechts, F. and van Acker, F. (2015). Building psychological capital with appreciative inquiry: Investigating the mediating role of basic psychological need satisfaction. *Journal of Applied Behavioral Science*, **51** (1), 10–35.

Vince, R. and Broussine, M. (1996). Paradox, defense and attachment: Accessing and working with emotions and relations underlying organizational change. *Organization Studies*, **17**, 1–21.

Vogus, T.J. and Sutcliffe, K.M. (2007). Organizational resilience: Towards a theory and a research agenda. *ISIC. IEEE International Conference on Systems, Man and Cybernetics*, Montreal, October, 3418–3422.

Vogus, T.J. and Sutcliffe, K.M. (2012). Organizational mindfulness and mindful organizing: A reconciliation and path forward. *Academy of Management Learning and Education*, **11**, 722–735.

von Begen, C.W. and Bressler, M.S. (2015). Employees' best friends and other animals in the workplaces. *Employee Relations Law Journal*, **41** (1), 4–34.

Wagnild, G.M. (2009a). A review of the resilience scale. *Journal of Nursing Measurement*, **17**, 105–113.

Wagnild, G.M. (2009b). *The Resilience Scale User's Guide for the US English Version of the Resilience Scale and the 14-Item Resilience Scale (RS-14)*. Montana: Resilience Center.

Wagnild, G.M. and Young, H.M. (1993). Development and psychometric evaluation of the resilience scale. *Journal of Nursing Measurement*, **1** (2), 165–178.

Waite, P.J. and Richardson, G.E. (2004). Determining the efficacy of resiliency training in the work site. *Journal of Allied Health*, **33**, 178–183.

Walker, J. and Cooper, M. (2011). Genealogies of resilience: From systems ecology to the political economy of crisis adaptation. *Security Dialogue*, **42**, 143–160.

Walumbwa, F.O., Luthans, F., Avey, J.B. and Oke, A. (2011). Authentically leading groups: The mediating role of collective psychological capital and trust. *Journal of Organizational Behavior*, **32**, 4–24.

Ward, M.J., Ferrand, Y.B., Laker, L.F., Froehle, C.M., Vogus, T.J., Dittus, R.S., Kripalani, S. and Pines, J.M. (2015). The nature and necessity of operational flexibility in the emergency department. *Annals of Emergency Medicine*, **65**, 156–161.

Watson, S. (2005). Attachment theory and social work. In Kieran, O., Munford, R., O'Donoghue, K. and Nash, M. (eds), *Social Work Theories in Action* (pp. 208–222). London: Jessica Kingsley Publishers.

Waugh, C.E., Fredrickson, B.L. and Taylor, S.F. (2008). Adapting to life's slings and arrows: Individual differences in resilience when recovering from an anticipated threat. *Journal of Research in Personality*, **42**, 1031–1046.

Waugh, C.E., Thompson, R.J. and Gotlib, I.H. (2011). Flexible emotional responsiveness in trait resilience. *Emotion*, **11**, 1059–1067.

WEF – World Economic Forum (2015). *Global Risks 2015*, 10th edn. Geneva: World Economic Forum. http://www3.weforum.org/docs/WEF_Global_Risks_2015_Report15.pdf.

Weick, K.E. (1979). *The Social Psychology of Organizing*, 2nd edn. Reading, MA: Addison Wesley.

Weick, K. (1988). Enacted sensemaking in crisis situations. *Journal of Management Studies*, **25**, 305–317.

Weick, K.E. (1993). The collapse of sensemaking in organizations: The Mann Gulch disaster. *Administrative Science Quarterly*, **38** (4), 628–652.

Weick, K.E. (1998). Introductory essay: Improvisation as a mindset for organizational analysis. *Organization Science*, **9** (5), 543–555.

Weick, K.E. (1995). Creativity and the aesthetics of imperfection. In Ford, C.M. and Gioia, D.A. (eds), *Creative Action in Organizations: Ivory Towers and Real World Voices* (pp. 187–192). Thousand Oaks, CA: SAGE.

Weick, K.E. and Sutcliffe, K.M. (2001 [2007]). *Managing the Unexpected: Resilient Performance in an Age of Uncertainty*. San Francisco, CA: Jossey Bass.

West, B.J., Patera, J.L. and Carsten, M.K. (2009). Team level positivity: Investigating positive psychological capacities and team level outcomes. *Journal of Organizational Behavior*, **30**, 249–267.

White, J. (2014). *A Matter of Life and Death: A History of Football in 100 Quotations*. London: Head of Zeus.

Whiteman, G. and Cooper, W.H. (2011). Ecological sensemaking. *Academy of Management Journal*, **54**, 889–911.

Whiteman, G. and Yumashev, D. (2018). Poles apart: The Arctic and management studies. *Journal of Management Studies*, **55** (5), 873–879.

Whitman, Z.R., Kachali, H., Roger, D., Vargo, J. and Seville, E. (2013). Short-form version of the Benchmark Resilience Tool (BRT-53). *Measuring Business Excellence*, **17** (3), 3–14.

Wildavsky, A. (1988). *Searching for Safety*. New Brunswick, CT: Transaction Books.

Wilson, G.A. (2018). 'Constructive tensions' in resilience research: Critical reflections from a human geography perspective. *Geographical Journal*, **184** (1), 89–99.

Williams, T.A., Gruber, D.A., Sutcliffe, K.M., Shepherd, D.A. and Zhao, E.Y. (2017). Organizational response to adversity: Fusing crisis management and resilience research streams. *Academy of Management Annals*, **11** (2), 733–769.

Williams, T.A. and Shepherd, D.A. (2016). Building resilience or providing sustenance: Different paths of emergent ventures in the aftermath of the Haiti earthquake. *Academy of Management Journal*, **59** (6), 2069–2102.

Winston, A. (2014). Resilience in a hotter world. *Harvard Business Review*, **92**, 56–64.

Wrzesniewski, A. and Dutton, J.E. (2001). Crafting a job: Revisioning employees as active crafters of their work. *Academy of Management Review*, **22**, 179–201.

Xavier, W.G., Bandeira-de-Mello, R. and Marcon, R. (2014). Institutional environment and business groups' resilience in Brazil. *Journal of Business Research*, **67**, 900–907.

Yam, K. (2015). 'World's poorest President' stops his car to give hitchhiker a ride. *Huffington Post*, 29 January, https://www.huffingtonpost.com/2015/01/29/jose-mujica-hitchhiker_n_6573532.html.

Yanow, D. and Tsoukas, H. (2009). What is reflection-in-action? A phenomenological account. *Journal of Management Studies*, **46**, 1339–1364.

Yarborough, B.J.H., Owen-Smith, A.A., Stumbo, S.P., Yarborough, M.T., Perrin, N.A. and Green, C.A. (2017). An observational study of service dogs for veterans with posttraumatic stress disorder. *Psychiatric Services*, **68** (7), 730–734.

Yukl, G. (2012). Effective leadership behavior: What we know and what questions need more attention. *Academy of Management Perspectives*, **26**, 66–85.

Zahra, S.A. and George, J.M. (2002). Absorptive capacity: a review, reconceptualization, and extension. *Academy of Management Review*, **27**, 185–203.

Zanko, M. and Dawson, P. (2012). Occupational health and safety management in organizations: A review. *International Journal of Management Reviews*, **14**, 328–344.

Zhang, R. and Liu, W. (2012). Organizational resilience perspective: Facilitating organizational adaptation analysis. *International Proceedings of Economics Development and Research*, **28**, 55–59.

Zolli, A. and Healy, A.M. (2012). *Resilience: Why Things Bounce Back*. London: Headline.

Index

Printed and bound by CPI Group (UK) Ltd, Croydon, CR0 4YY

23/04/2025

14660981-0002